You Can't Come to My Birthday Party!

Related Resources From High/Scope® Press

Books

Educating Young Children: Active Learning Practices for Preschool and Child Care Programs, Second Edition

A Study Guide to Educating Young Children: Exercises for Adult Learners, Second Edition

Supporting Young Learners: Ideas for Preschool and Day Care Providers

Supporting Young Learners 2: Ideas for Child Care Providers and Teachers

Supporting Young Learners 3: Ideas for Child Care Providers and Teachers

Tender Care and Early Learning: Supporting Infants and Toddlers in Child Care Settings

Other Resources

Steps in Resolving Conflicts (poster)

Supporting Children in Resolving Conflicts (video)

Initiative and Social Relations (from *High/Scope Preschool Key Experiences* video series)

Adult-Child Interactions: Forming Partnerships With Children (video)

Extensions—Newsletter of the High/Scope Curriculum

Available from

High/Scope® Press
A division of the High/Scope Educational Research Foundation
600 N. River Street, Ypsilanti, MI 48198-2898

You Can't Come to My Birthday Party!

Conflict Resolution With Young Children

Betsy Evans

HIGH/SCOPE® PRESS

Ypsilanti, Michigan

Published by

HIGH/SCOPE® PRESS
A division of the HIGH/SCOPE EDUCATIONAL RESEARCH FOUNDATION
600 NORTH RIVER STREET
YPSILANTI, MICHIGAN 48198-2898
734/485-2000, FAX 734/485-0704
press@highscope.org

Editor: Nancy Brickman

Cover design, text design: Judy Seling of Seling Design

Photography:

Patricia Evans—front cover (left), back cover, 6, 7, 9, 12, 13, 15, 22 (center), 25–27, 29–31, 37, 44, 45, 51, 54, 55, 60, 69, 70, 77, 87, 96, 99, 108, 122, 129, 138, 139, 143, 154, 159, 166, 167, 187, 189, 191, 192, 199, 203, 209, 211, 212, 224, 233, 237, 243–246, 250, 251, 264, 265, 282, 287, 289, 292, 296, 306, 309, 317 (top left & right), 320, 325, 329, 330–33, 336, 337, 339 (top), 340, 345, 354, 358, 361, 378, 411

Gregory Fox Photography—front cover (center & right), 20, 21, 22 (left & right), 47, 72, 75, 78, 91–93, 97, 98, 111, 119, 121, 142, 151, 152, 160, 170, 196, 205, 241, 252, 253, 258, 270, 281, 286, 288, 291, 297, 299 (bottom), 301, 310, 317 (bottom left & right), 322, 323, 326, 327, 335, 362

The Recorder—Paul Franz, 341 (top), 342, 386; Peter MacDonald, 339, 341 (bottom); 379

Betsy Evans—24, 73, 88, 89, 130, 134, 242, 299 (top), 300

Rachael Underwood—62

Library of Congress Cataloging-in-Publication Data

Evans, Betsy.
    You can't come to my birthday party!: conflict resolution with young children/Betsy Evans.
        p. cm.
    Includes bibliographical references and index.
    ISBN 1-57379-159-8
    1. Interpersonal conflict in children. 2 Interpersonal relations in children.
  3. Adjustment (Psychology) in children. 4. Child rearing. I. Title.
  BF723.I645 E93 2001
  649'.1--dc21

                                              2001039867

Printed in the United States of America

10 9 8 7 6 5 4 3

Contents

3—Getting to Solutions 91

4—When Adults or Children Feel Upset: Responding to Strong Emotions 121

5—Learning to Problem-Solve: How Change Happens, One Child at a Time 191

Chapter 6—Small-Group Problem Solving 243

Chapter 8—Mediation in Elementary Schools 339

Afterword

Preface

The problem-solving approach to young children's conflicts presented in this book builds on the work of many others in the fields of early childhood education and conflict mediation. This approach integrates conflict mediation strategies from various sources with the child development and teaching framework of the High/Scope Preschool Curriculum, an approach I have used since 1989 in various teaching and supervisory roles at the Giving Tree School in Gill, Massachusetts, and as a field consultant and teacher-trainer for High/Scope Educational Research Foundation.

During the 1980's, a variety of responses to children's conflict situations, including both punishment and behavior modification techniques, continued to be a source of debate in the educational field. In the late 1980's and early 1990's, High/Scope staff began the development of conflict-related teaching strategies based on the principle of "active learning."* As a part of High/Scope's development effort, teacher/consultants Michelle Graves and Ruth Strubank (1988/1991) described a "child management" approach (p. 35) that emphasized prevention of conflicts as well as techniques for "on-the-spot management" (p. 39).

The interest of High/Scope's curriculum developers in preventing classroom conflicts was one facet of a broader effort to define the adult/child interaction strategies that support young children's learning. In this vein, Amy Powell (1990/1991) explored the importance of being responsive to children's needs and feelings, using research on the factors of intrinsic motivation as a rationale for responsive teaching strategies.

Inspired by the compelling and heartfelt expressions I heard from children during disputes, I began in 1989 to take a more in-depth look at conflicts in the classroom. I developed new teaching strategies as I worked with my own preschool stu-

---

*For more information on active learning and other central elements of the High/Scope approach to preschool education, see the High/Scope preschool manual *Educating Young Children: Active Learning Practices for Preschool and Child Care Providers,* Second Edition (Hohmann & Weikart, 2002).

dents at the Giving Tree School, adapting from mediation practices used elsewhere with older children and adults.

In developing strategies to involve preschoolers in conflict resolution, I drew on many resources: the work of award-winning musician and author Sarah Pirtle (1998a, 1998b) and the publications of Diane Levin (1996), Adele Faber and Elaine Mazlish (1999), and Daniel Gartrell (1994). My friendship and collaborative training efforts with Rachael Underwood, a High/Scope field consultant, trained mediator, and former preschool teacher, was another important resource. I also drew on mediation strategies I had learned in a lengthy training with The Mediation & Training Collaborative of Greenfield, Massachusetts; these strategies are widely used by adults for settling legal, family, and neighborhood disputes, as well as being taught in many public elementary and high schools.

Learning from all these resources and integrating what I learned with High/Scope's educational model, I eventually developed a problem-solving approach to conflict that includes six steps adults can use to help children resolve disputes. This sequence of mediation steps is designed to meet the specific needs and abilities of very young children. The word *problem solving* refers to the broad intention behind this approach: to support, in various ways, children's emerging skills in finding solutions to their disputes. The words *conflict mediation* refer to the actual dialogue, facilitated by an adult, in which children discuss and resolve a dispute.

As I continued to refine this teaching approach (Evans, 1992/1996a, 1992/1996b, 1995/1996a, 1995/1996b, 1996/1996a, 1996/1996b), I incorporated strategies for encouraging rather than praising children based on the work of High/Scope consultant Mark Tompkins (1991/1996) and author, lecturer, and former teacher Alfie Kohn (1993). Using these strategies, teachers focus on the process rather than product of children's efforts and give descriptive, nonjudgmental feedback rather than evaluation, rewards, or punishment. Beginning in 1994, I began to work collaboratively with Rachael Underwood. She assisted me in further developing training materials and strategies related to conflict resolution. Her contribution, in particular, to my understanding of emotion and its importance in the conflict resolution process (and in other areas of life as well) has been pivotal to the evolution of this material.

The development of the problem-solving approach has also been influenced by research on the drawbacks of behavior modification approaches (Kohn, 1993; Kamii, 1984), as well as by research on the benefits of a mediation approach with children (see, for example, Slaby, Roedell, Arezzo, & Hendrix, 1995).

The inspiration for this book was my wish that other teachers and parents could really "hear" what children think and feel as they resolve disputes. The children's words in the conflict stories presented here are actual transcriptions from classroom and family experiences. I hope these young voices will be heard as a resounding call for change, a need some children themselves are able to articulate. One morning I had a conversation with my 4-year-old neighbor, David Ramlow Sachs, about my work for change, and I got an enthusiastic endorsement. As I walked with David to school, I told him I would be taking a trip soon to talk to teachers about children's conflicts. I described how I especially wanted the teachers to know how capable children were at resolving their problems in the way I'd seen him do only the day before. "Yeah!" he said excitedly, "You tell them that kids can think of their own ideas *themselves!*"

This book is my effort to do just that. The conflict mediation experiences presented here were tape-recorded, a technique inspired by the work of Vivian Gussin Paley (1986; Paley & Jackson, 1987), who tape-recorded conversations in her Chicago preschool classroom. This book's conflict interactions were recorded at the Giving Tree School and other classrooms in rural Massachusetts; at a Head Start program in Harlem, New York City; and at the High/Scope Demonstration Preschool in Ypsilanti, Michigan. Rachael Underwood also contributed tape recordings made in classrooms in urban areas of Great Britain. The majority of children in these recorded incidents were from low- to middle-income families living in rural or inner-city areas. They were from diverse linguistic, economic, and cultural backgrounds and their ages ranged from 1½ to 12 years at the time the recordings were made. In the preschool classroom stories, all the adult mediators had received training in the problem-solving approach and mediation steps described in this book and were at different stages of implementation of these skills. The teachers in the elementary schools described in Chapter 8 were trained in a mediation approach typically used at the elementary level.

When possible, the tape-recorded incidents were transcribed verbatim to illustrate how the mediation steps work in different settings and with teachers and children of varying individual needs. Additions and changes were made to these transcriptions only where words were confusing, not audible, or when the recording was started after the mediation began. A few incidents were described from memory, as is indicated in the introductions to these stories. In all stories, every effort was made to be as true to the incident as possible. Sometimes, for the sake of brevity, there is a summary of what occurred, but for the most part, there is a full transcription of the interactions exactly as they happened.

The names of children have been changed in all the transcriptions, except when permission was given for use of real names or when an incident is also shown in High/Scope training videos. In the latter case, the actual child names are used to avoid confusion for those using both resources.

The stories, insights, and strategies described in this book truly represent a unique collaboration among educators, parents, and children. It is my great honor and good fortune to be their spokesperson.

I am very grateful to my fellow preschool and elementary educators and parents who shared their insights, assistance, and stories: Kerrie Andrew, Martha Aponte, Rabb Bannister, Marilyn Barnwell, Joan Deely, Joyce Dye, Ann Epstein, Cheryl Fox, Jan Frazier, Merrilee Kane, Sue Kramer, Chantal LaFortune, Michelle Graves, Mary Hohmann, Sue O'Reilly-McRae, Beth Marshall, Sarah Pirtle, Lisa Ramlow, Cathy Rowen, Rose Sheehan, Rick Stone, Eileen Storer, Ruth Strubank, José Velilla, David Weikart, Jan Yourist, and John Zurbrigg. Thanks also to Pattie McDonald for her careful manuscript preparation and coding. Acknowledgments are also due to the elementary school staff and students of western Massachusetts (who have chosen to remain anonymous for reasons of confidentiality) and the Colorado School Mediation Project for the essential material they contributed for Chapter 8.

I also want to thank my sister, Patricia Evans, for the sensitive insights contributed by her photographs, which so vividly extend and enrich the material.

Two readers, Rachael Underwood and Suzanne Barkin, gave me honest, humorous, loving, and very detailed feedback that was essential throughout the long creation of the book. Nancy Brickman, my editor, provided me with many patient hours of professional support, helping with content and organization, using her unique ability to envision the forest for the trees.

To my husband, Jeff, who expressed unwavering confidence in this lengthy project and provided a daily model of pursuing a vision with determination, I am forever grateful. If finding one's soul mate is a matter of chance, then I can't believe my luck. I also thank my sons, who inspire me by example: Tryfan with his scholarly energy and deep concern for family and friends, Devon with his graceful endurance and desire to give, and Sorrel with his humorous, bold, and optimistic view of the world. A special thanks as well to my parents, who supported me in so many ways. My family, immediate and extended, gave me the love, understanding, and practice I needed to complete this book.

You Can't
Come to My
Birthday
Party!

Introduction

Young children in the preschool years provide many challenges to the educators and parents who support their explorations and developing understanding of the world. Working with these young learners requires energy, patience, creativity, insight, and a wide array of skills. As a new parent and teacher almost 30 years ago, I found that some of these skills came naturally, some I had learned in college, and some escaped me completely. I thoroughly enjoyed spending time with young children, except for those intense and frustrating moments when squabbling and fighting destroyed the fun. The same arguments and accusations surfaced over and over—"That's mine!" "I had it first!" "He's being mean to me!" "She can't play with us!" I was baffled by the repetitiveness of children's squabbles and by my own intense reactions to them. During and after these conflicts, I questioned both my skills with children and, on the really challenging days, even the decision I had made to become a teacher.

The difficulties and dilemmas generated in these conflict moments ran deep. As I look back now on my years working with young children, I see that a change eventually occurred in my own attitude about their conflicts, and that this change came about as a direct result of my efforts to understand and use a problem-solving approach during these episodes. As I explored and learned how to apply the strategies of conflict mediation with young children, I discovered not only that dealing with conflict could be a satisfying and enjoyable part of teaching but also that children, when given support, were enormously capable problem solvers. The moments that I had once dreaded as a teacher and a parent gradually became opportunities for the children to learn new skills and for me to deepen and enrich my perceptions of children. Conflicts became occasions for hope; the children and I were learning together that diverse points of view need not lead to unresolved frustration and anger. Instead, we were discovering that conflicts and disputes can actually be

NAEYC Accreditation Criteria Reflect Problem-Solving Approach

Many professional standards for early childhood educators (such as these excerpts from NAEYC's 1998 *Accreditation Criteria and Procedures*) now endorse problem-solving rather than punitive approaches.

- "Teachers use children's mistakes as learning opportunities, describing the situation and encouraging children's evaluation of the problem rather than imposing the solution" (from A-6a, p. 19).

- "Teachers abstain from corporal punishment or humiliating or frightening discipline techniques" (from A-6b, p. 19).

- "Teachers help children deal with anger, sadness, and frustration by comforting, identifying, and reflecting feelings, and helping children use various strategies to express emotions and solve social problems. Children are encouraged to verbalize feelings and ideas. Teachers intervene quickly when children's responses to each other become aggressive, unacceptable, or harmful, discuss the inappropriateness of such responses, and help children develop more positive strategies" (from A-8, p. 20).

a starting point for honest exchanges that lead to stronger and more gratifying relationships.

I am now enormously grateful that my career survived my misgivings and that I have seen the acceptance of conflict mediation by the education community. (For example, the National Association for the Education of Young Children [NAEYC] advocates the use of problem-solving rather than punitive approaches in its 1998 criteria for program accreditation.) During the ten years that I have used conflict mediation strategies in working with young children, I have felt enormous respect and admiration for the inspired, thoughtful ways that they express their needs and wants while negotiating solutions that work for everyone. As I approach a conflict now, I find myself looking forward to children's often surprising and original solutions.

I wrote this book to share this enthusiasm and to help teachers and parents bring this positive, constructive approach to the young people in their care. While there is a large body of research and writing describing the strategies and rationale for engaging children in mediation approaches to conflict, few of these resources provide in-depth examples specific to the needs of adults working with toddlers, preschoolers, and school-aged children. As an early childhood trainer, I've learned that teachers are sometimes hesitant to try mediation because they find it difficult to envision how the process works. Moreover, those teachers who have already begun to try this new approach often want further guidance and support in using its steps and strategies. This book is designed to answer these needs.

To help educators and parents develop a more concrete understanding of the problem-solving approach to conflict and the steps in mediation, this book presents and discusses true stories of children resolving disputes with the support of adult mediators. These stories provide an opportunity for educators and parents to "see" the problem-solving approach in action, to "hear" how the children respond when supported during conflicts, and to understand the purpose of each of the approach's strategies and steps. Getting beneath the surface of each conflict episode in this way clarifies how the mediation steps work, while illuminating many of the subtleties of individual child and adult reactions.

Most of the children in these stories are of preschool age (2 to 6 years) but the general approach modeled can be adapted for children of any age. Chapter 8 provides stories illustrating conflict mediation with school-aged children; other chapters include a few stories showing the beginnings of this process with toddlers as young as 1½ years.

The stories told here depict children and adults at tense and emotional crossroads. The choices they make during these critical moments may result in further harm or an opportunity for strengthening communication. These stories verify what research describes in its findings and statistics; children as young as 18 months have emerging problem-solving skills. As a result of, not despite, their still-developing cognitive and social abilities, children are capable of quick, honest expressions of feeling and simple, creative solutions to problems. Among these potential abilities are the skills of constructive conflict resolution and consequently the tools for violence prevention and effective communication. As children resolve disputes with the support of adult mediators, they are actively learning a communication process that will be useful to them throughout their lives. This process can transform conflicts from angry, potentially violent exchanges to fruitful dialogues that nurture children's respect for and understanding of others.

Experiences with conflict mediation help children develop as caring, cooperative individuals.

Because of the recent explosion of angry feelings and violent actions among children and young adults, our schools and communities are crying out for help. These incidents force us to admit that our traditional ways of dealing with conflict—punishing children, or dictating solutions to their disputes—have not worked. While these adult-directed responses may inhibit conflict for brief periods, they do not reduce disputes and violence over the long term because they do not build constructive, long-term, life skills for children.

Often when educators discuss the need for conflict mediation in our schools, violence prevention is the primary focus. However, it is imperative that we ask more of our educational practice than prevention of violence. While many of our children are not at risk for violent behaviors, the majority *are* at risk for not reaching their full potentials as caring friends, loving spouses, supportive parents, and cooperative work colleagues. It is important for us to see the current interest in conflict mediation as an opportunity not only to prevent the spread of violent behaviors among our children and youth but also to support their growth as productive and independent members of society. It is this potential of young children to develop as creative problem solvers and sensitive, caring people that now requires our serious attention. It is my profound belief that conflict mediation for educators, parents, and children is the bridge to this possibility, and I sincerely hope that this book will help with the journey.

 # Overview of the Problem-Solving Approach

Screams come from a corner of the preschool classroom. Two children are hitting each other and yelling. The construction toys they were using are scattered across the floor. Having just dealt with a fight between the same children moments before, the adult groans with frustration. Now, instead of two, three people are upset....

Making sense out of emotional moments like these can present enormous challenges for those of us who work with and care for young children. To respond to children's conflicts without merely adding to the number of upset people, teachers and parents need a clear method. This book describes such a method—the **problem-solving approach to conflict.** As a preschool teacher and as an early childhood trainer, I have worked with many teachers and parents as they learned to use this approach. The triumphs and challenges they and I have experienced as we learned are described in the real stories told throughout this book.

The problem-solving approach includes six **mediation steps** for working with young

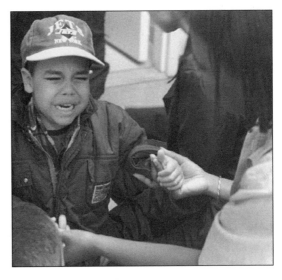

The six mediation steps can help adults respond constructively to children during emotionally charged conflict situations.

Terms to Understand

▲ **Problem-solving approach.** A broad approach used by teachers or parents to help young children learn to resolve differences. This approach is based on child development theory and research, strategies from the field of dispute resolution, and the practical experiences of teachers. Included in this approach are **six mediation steps,** a **small-group problem-solving process,** and **prevention strategies** to reduce the level of conflict in a classroom.

▲ **Conflict mediation.** A dialogue in which children discuss and resolve a dispute with the help of an adult or child mediator. In this process, the mediator uses six steps (called **problem-solving steps** or **mediation steps**) to encourage children to discuss what happened and reach an

agreement about how to solve their problem. Eventually, children internalize these steps and learn to resolve problems independently.

▲ **Small-group problem solving.** A group discussion, guided by an adult, in which children talk over chronic problems that affect the security and comfort of the group, such as running in the classroom and playground safety issues. While conflict mediation is used to resolve disputes in the heat of the moment, small-group problem solving is usually a planned event, held to discuss recurring problems.

▲ **Adult-child interaction strategies.** Techniques for using speech or body language to communicate with children and encourage learning.

children during emotionally charged conflict situations. Teachers or parents use the six steps to act as facilitators in children's conflicts; through these experiences with mediation, children eventually learn to resolve conflicts independently. Chapters 1 through 4 explain the rationale for the problem-solving approach and introduce and then explore in depth each of the six steps in mediation. Chapter 5 describes the growth of two young problem solvers during their preschool years. The problem-solving approach also includes a **small-group discussion** process, discussed in Chapter 6, that adults can use, at non-conflict times, to encourage children to talk over chronic problems. **Prevention strategies** for reducing the frequency of classroom conflicts are discussed in Chapter 7. Chapter 8 details the strategies of peer mediation in elementary schools and describes a school-wide mediation structure and group-discussion curriculum.

The problem-solving approach is a set of practical tools that can help us deal with some of the most challenging issues we face as teachers and parents. These tools include strategies for dealing with strong feelings (both our own and those of the children) as well as for supporting the children in thinking through and choosing solutions. The approach is based on several basic adult-child interaction strategies: listening actively, acknowledging feelings and ideas, and encouraging decision-making. Used to support children at moments of heightened emotion and need, these strategies are the core of exchanges that can help children learn to respect and understand differences.

Though most of us do not savor the possibility of conflict, conflict situations contain rich possibilities for learning. If we can approach children's disputes with more than the sole purpose of stopping hurtful behavior, and if we are also prepared to support their emerging skills, these conflict occasions can become enriching learning opportunities that are productive and satisfying for everyone involved.

The problem-solving approach is a set of practical tools that can help us deal with some of the most challenging issues we face as teachers and parents.

Traditional Approaches to Conflict

To understand and use this positive approach to conflict, we need to be aware of the alternatives to it. Traditionally, adults in our culture have reacted to children's conflicts with responses that fall into two broad categories: the **authoritarian** approach and the **avoidance** approach. Adults who solve children's problems by directing the child or children to behave differently are using the *authoritarian* approach. In carrying out this approach, they may use any of the following strategies: threatening punishment or actually punishing children, either physically or verbally; blaming children or making accusations; and expressing their own strong feelings while leaving children's feelings unresolved and unheard and their needs unmet. Students of mediation often refer to this as the "shark," "bull," or "lion" approach.

In the second traditional approach, the *avoidance* approach, adults try to avoid conflict. Students of mediation often refer to this pattern as the "ostrich," "turtle," or "mouse" approach. Many adults find conflicts unpleasant and upsetting, so it is understandable that they would want them to end quickly. To reduce their discomfort, they may avoid involvement completely, or they may try to "fix" the problem by taking care of it themselves or telling the children how to fix it: "Pat, you use the toy first for five minutes. Devin, then it will be your turn for five minutes. I will time you." Adults who impose such solutions on children often do so with the best of intentions (wanting children to learn to "be nice," for example). Looking back on my pre-mediation days, I think this approach was my most frequent reaction to conflict. I may have imposed my solution in a tone of pleasant suggestion or with subtle guilt and blaming, but regardless of my demeanor, the children lost an opportunity to learn to solve problems independently. And, like many adults who use this "fix-it" approach, I often felt exhausted, resentful, and inadequate at the end of a long day of taking over in every crisis. Those who try to avoid or ignore conflict often wonder why children can't just learn to "behave."

As children, most of us experienced either the "shark" or the "ostrich" approach, or possibly a combination of these approaches. Lacking an alternative, we tend to repeat these approaches in our own interactions with children. We often justify this by stating two beliefs: (1) "This is how conflicts were handled for me and I turned out okay, right?" and/or (2) "Children don't know how to resolve their own conflicts anyway." These beliefs can leave us stuck in a pattern of responding to conflict that does not help children gain new skills. If Johnny hits to get a truck and the adult tries to fix the problem by giving him a second truck and telling him to "be nice," Johnny still hasn't learned *how* to be nice.

In a similar way, when adults resort to punishment instead of using the fix-it approach, children rarely have a chance to learn new skills. Moreover, those who are having behavior difficulties repeatedly experience a punitive system. Rather than strengthen the child by offering an alternative strategy, this system must itself be strengthened by the substitution of bigger and stronger punitive systems as children grow older. Preschool "time-outs" are replaced by elementary school visits to the principal's office, these visits are replaced by high school detention or suspension, and these sanctions are later replaced by trips to the juvenile court and possibly prison. In such an approach, children are told how *not* to behave but are never helped to learn new communication and cooperation skills for solving their problems the next time. Yet research tells us (see right) that when children are helped to learn negotiation and mediation skills, these skills generalize to other situations.

> "When students are taught negotiation and mediation skills, studies show that they use these skills at school as well as at home, where the majority of conflicts take place."
>
> —*David W. Johnson, Roger Johnson, Bruce Dudley, Marty Ward, and Douglas Magnuson (1995, p. 841)*

Why Conflict Mediation Works: Premises to Consider

The effects of these traditional approaches to children's conflicts are profound and long-lasting. To find an alternative, we have to reconsider our basic assumptions about how children develop and learn. Following are six premises that make a convincing case for trying conflict mediation as we work with children. (Note: these six *premises* are not to be confused with the six *mediation steps* presented later in this chapter.)

The first premise is that **we learn, really learn, when the motivation to learn comes from within.** Research tells us that we are likely to be *intrinsically motivated* to achieve new skills when at least one of several factors is part of the learning experience: we are having *fun;* we are doing something that satisfies our personal *needs* or *interests;* we are making *choices* (or otherwise have some *control* over the activity), and we have opportunities to experience *success* (Powell, 1990/1991). When these factors are in place, children and adults are likely to want to learn new skills. Using these factors to look at what happens in children's conflicts, we can see that children who are involved in a dispute are already highly motivated to learn, be-

In order for long-term learning to occur, we need to provide the conditions that will help children want to learn: opportunities to have fun, to learn something new that interests them, and/or to make choices that will help them fulfill a need or wish.

cause of their intense personal interest in the outcome. When we engage them in problem solving, a process that provides them with many choices and often leads to a successful solution, we are tapping into and building on their intrinsic motivation—we are encouraging their readiness to express feelings and thoughts in new ways. In the opposite of this approach, one based on *extrinsic motivation,* we assume that children will learn a desirable new behavior because a reward is promised or because they fear being punished. The learning that occurs under these extrinsic pressures is short-term, however; when fear or the anticipation of reward are no longer present, children's desire to engage in the new behavior is gone as well (Kohn, 1993). In order for long-term learning to occur, we need to provide the conditions that will help children *want* to learn: opportunities to enjoy a task, to work to learn something new that interests them, and/or to make choices that will help them fulfill a need or a wish.

The second premise is that **children don't misbehave, they make mistakes.** Daniel Gartrell (1995, p. 27) explains this view: "Traditionally, misbehavior implies willful wrongdoing for which a child must be disciplined (punished)." On the other hand, when we see children's immature actions as mistakes rather than "bad behaviors," we can respond more constructively, Gartrell says. Most of us would agree that when a child puts shoes on the wrong feet, this is not "being bad," it is a mistake. Likewise, when a child says *yesterday* but means *tomorrow,* it is a mistake, and when a child runs, trips, and falls down, it is a misstep. By the same token, when a child sees adults (or television characters) solve problems with vio-

lence and then kicks another child in order to get a toy, this, too, must be seen not as "badness" but as a mistake. If we want to help children develop new and lasting social skills, then we must respond to their social mistakes with kindness and understanding, just as we do when they make other kinds of mistakes.

Mistakes lead to opportunities: to explore feelings, to hear different points of view, and to discuss ideas for solutions.

What Are Natural, Punitive, and Logical Consequences?

▲ **Natural consequences** are events that occur as the natural result of an action. Example: A child runs through the classroom and collides with another child, causing that child to fall into a block tower and knock it over. The collision and toppling are natural consequences of the child's choice to run through the classroom.

▲ **Punitive consequences** are imposed by adults to punish children for "bad" behavior. A punitive consequence is an unpleasant experience that is intended to discourage the child from repeating the "bad" behavior. The consequence is usually not directly related to the child's "bad" actions or the situation that led to them. Example: The adult sends a child to the time-out chair for hitting another child.

▲ **Logical consequences** are activities initiated by the adult in response to a child's mistaken actions. The activities are closely tied to the child's actions and are intended to resolve the situation, not to punish the child. Examples: A child who has spilled paint may be given a sponge to wipe it up; two children who are fighting may be expected to enter a problem-solving discussion.

The third premise is that **children *can* learn from mistakes, but only if our response includes a willingness to regard the mistake as a solvable problem.** The conflicts that result from social mistakes provide dynamic learning opportunities; children are likely to be highly motivated to learn because of strong personal interest in the outcome. Consequently they are often willing to attempt a new task or skill (such as describing the details of a problem or using timers to share) in order to get what is wanted. Mistakes thus lead to opportunities: to explore feelings, to hear differing points of view, and to discuss ideas for solutions. The result is an experience in cooperative teamwork, in which children are engaged in carefully analyzing a problem, evaluating possible solutions, and choosing the solution that works for everyone.

The fourth premise, that **problem solving is a *logical consequence* for children who have made a social mistake,** follows naturally from the previous premise. If Jessica has grabbed a toy from another child, it is important to say to Jessica, "I can see you're feeling upset. Kicking and grabbing need to stop." If we then want to help Jessica know what to do differently the next time, we must do more than this—we must follow our response with "Let's talk about the problem and think of what you could do if you want a turn." It does *not* make sense to grab the toy from Jessica (the very behavior that we are trying to discourage!) and place her in a corner to "think about it." She can learn nothing there about what to do the next time she wants a toy that someone else has. It is critical for us to support children in learning new skills when they most need the new skill.

When a conflict mediation begins, as in this elementary classroom, other children often gather around, eager to listen or perhaps help with the solution.

The fifth premise is that **problem solving can be, for both adults and children, surprisingly fun as well as enlightening.** Conflicts can help people connect with one another. Those involved in a conflict, as well as children looking on, often enjoy working together to find a solution that works for everyone. When a conflict mediation begins, other children of-

Premises Behind Problem Solving

1. We learn, really learn, when the motivation to learn comes from within.

2. Children don't misbehave, they make mistakes.

3. Children can learn from mistakes, but only if our response includes a willingness to regard the mistake as a solvable problem.

4. Problem solving is a logical consequence for children who have made a social mistake.

5. Problem solving can be, for both adults and children, fun and interesting.

6. Children are capable of solving problems.

ten gather around, eager to listen or perhaps help with the solution. Once adults are confident of their problem-solving skills, they often find great joy in children's surprisingly earnest responses. In my mediations with children, I now truly look forward to hearing the solution children have decided on. It is frequently different from what I would have expected, and is often much more creative!

As for the sixth premise, it is simply this: **children are capable of solving problems.** Children can say what they feel, want, and need, and they can come up with solutions that work. The bonus for those of us who invest time in supporting them is seeing that children learn a great deal about themselves and others as they problem-solve AND enjoy the challenge of finding solutions. These positive outcomes continue to build, and consequently children do more and more problem-solving without our help. In time, they become more capable of expressing strong feelings constructively and responding respectfully to differences.

The premises in action

The following true story of a child conflict in my own preschool classroom illustrates these six premises.

Carly and Sam both want the last block

Premise 1: Carly is interested in putting away a block, creating high motivation for following through on problem solving when Sam wants to put away the same block.

▶ Carly, a tall 4-year-old, and Sam, a small 3-year-old, were in the Block Area putting away the hollow blocks at cleanup time. Simultaneously they reached for the last block, a large rectangular one.

"I got it," Sam told Carly quietly.

"No, I do!" Carly answered loudly, yanking the block from Sam's hands.

Premise 2: Carly makes a social mistake and yanks the block from Sam.

▶ Sam fell backward to the floor, landing in a sitting position with a soft thud. His mouth opened with surprise, and his chin quivered as he began to cry. Without looking at him, Carly walked toward the stack of blocks.

Hearing Carly's loud response, I approached them quickly. Before Carly could get to the block stack, I called out to her gently, "Please wait, Carly. Sam is upset. Come on back with the block and let's figure this out." Carly turned, looked at us both, and came back.

◀ **Premise 3:** Carly and Sam's conflict is regarded as a solvable problem by the adult, who engages them in a discussion of what to do.

I knelt by Sam and softly rubbed his back. "You're feeling really sad, Sam."

"She...she took the block," he sobbed.

"I want to put away this one!" Carly told me with determination, holding the block tightly.

"Carly, I see that you really want to put that one away. But I'd like you to put the block down until we can figure this out." Carly came closer to us and laid the block down. "What seems to be the problem?" I asked Carly.

◀ **Premise 4:** The problem solving discussion is a logical (rather than punitive) consequence that helps them to know what to do if they encounter a similar situation another day.

"I want to do this one." She told me again.

"So you really want to put that one away. And Sam, you do, too?" (He had stopped crying.) He nodded. "What can we do to solve this?" I asked them both.

Carly repeated, "I want to do this one."

Quietly Sam suggested, " How 'bout we can together?"

"No!" Carly responded loudly, "I wan...want to do it myself!"

"So you don't want to do it together, Carly. Can you think of some other way to solve this?" I asked.

I noticed that a small group was gathering. Three children who had been cleaning up nearby had come over to listen to our discussion. As I observed the intense concentration on the children's faces, I realized what a fascinating moment this was for them. They had been drawn into the challenge of problem solving; I knew they had experienced the satisfaction of coming up with "win-win" solutions on previous occasions, and they were eager to see, and perhaps participate in, the outcome. Surrounded by this tiny ring of faces, I felt caught up in the most exquisite kind of learning moment, one that involves a collective of creative minds concentrated on a single problem.

◀ **Premise 5:** Other children become interested in the discussion and contribute ideas. The adult facilitates the discussion, without imposing solutions, and enjoys watching the children try to come up with an idea that will work for both Carly and Sam.

"He can put that one away," Carly suggested as she pointed to a small block that was partially hidden by a shelf.

"I wanna do the big one," Sam told us calmly. He was sitting up confidently now.

"So you want to put away one that size, Sam?" I asked. He nodded.

Roberto, one of the children who had joined us, offered, "How 'bout if Carly puts it away, then back down, then Sam does."

Both children shook their heads no.

Then Juanita, another child who had been listening intently, excitedly suggested, "Hey, what if they take down one **like** that…then they both have a big one!"

Premise 6: Carly and Sam agree on a solution that has been suggested by another child. Both of them are pleased with the outcome, and so is the adult!

Sam and Carly looked at each other, and their faces melted into smiles. Carly turned quickly and got down another large rectangular block. She carried it over to Sam and handed it to him.

"So Sam, you're going to put that one away?" I asked.

"Yeah!" he said enthusiastically as he stood up, awkwardly holding the block. (I noticed then that the block was only about a foot shorter than Sam.) Carly picked up the original, contested block and placed it on the stack. I smiled broadly as she turned and looked at me. She smiled too as she turned and waited for Sam. We all watched as Sam took his block to the stack, which was now as high as his shoulders. He slowly lifted the block toward the top but it slipped from one hand and one end slid to the floor. As he held the other end, he looked up at Carly and quietly asked, "Carly, could you help me?"

Without hesitation, she stepped forward and picked up one end of the block. In one perfect moment, before a small audience of interested young problem-solvers, they lifted it together to the top of the stack. "There!" Sam exclaimed loudly, brushing his bangs from his eyes and glancing happily at Carly. He stood back admiring the stack.

Very excited myself, I told them, "You did it! Juanita, you gave them an idea that worked!" She looked at me, smiling shyly. "And Sam and Carly, you solved this problem together!"

They nodded, giggling with relief. Responding to the feelings on their faces, I said, "You're really happy about that, aren't you!"

They nodded together.

"Let's go to recall," I told everyone. (Recall time is the next event in our daily routine.) Together Sam, Carly, and the little band that had gathered to watch them walked away with a new confidence that their problems were not only solvable but also that they had the ability to solve them.

I realized as they walked away that Sam was probably happiest about having accomplished something with Carly. When it came time for him to put up his block, he had not become frustrated when he had difficulty putting it away himself. Instead he had seemed pleased to have a reason to ask Carly for help. I remembered that his first idea for solving the problem had been for him and Carly to do it together, and in the end he had gotten what he wanted most: a cooperative moment with a new friend.

◆

Child Development: Its Impact on Problem Solving With Young Children

The last part of this chapter introduces the six-step mediation process illustrated in the story of Sam and Carly. Before taking a closer look at each of the problem-solving steps, however, it is important to consider the developmental characteristics unique to young children. To understand how to support preschoolers in expressing themselves as fully as possible, we need to consider how children in this age group typically experience the world and how their thinking and emotions differ from those of the typical adult. This perspective can help us understand the child's point of view and the special strengths (as well as limitations) that they bring to conflict interactions.

Some of the important characteristics of preschool-aged children are described next, based on the High/Scope child development framework described by Mary Hohmann and David Weikart (2002). Throughout this discussion, the Carly and Sam incident is used to illustrate how each of these characteristics affects problem solving.

Egocentrism

Young children are **egocentric;** they view the world from the standpoint of their own feelings and needs. Initially Carly and Sam saw their dilemma only from their own points of view. This is understandable, since at this stage of development children have very little awareness of the viewpoints of others. Conflicts present a special opportunity for children to hear feelings and thoughts that are different from their own. Though children cannot usually be directly taught to be less egocentric, they can learn how to satisfy their own wants and needs while beginning to accommodate to the requests of others.

Concrete thinking

Young children are *concrete thinkers*—they base their understanding of the world on obvious physical characteristics. (Piaget called this stage "preoperational.") While children usually must

Because they think concretely, these children need to be able to look at the boards as they resolve a conflict about how to build with them.

temporarily halt their activities in order to problem-solve, perhaps even letting the adult hold a material in question, it is also important that the material stay in plain view. Because children think concretely, they need to see the disputed object in order to envision solutions.

As Carly, Sam, and the other children discussed solutions, they looked frequently at the disputed block and the stack of blocks. During this phase of a mediation, children will often suggest general solutions they've heard from adults, such as "share" or "take turns." However, such vague solutions usually do not provide enough concrete detail to be implemented successfully by young children. If we probe further with questions like "What will that look like?" or "What will you do?" this often encourages children to describe their solution in terms of specific actions or details. For Carly and Sam, it was the shape and size of the block that inspired the final solution.

Limited verbal skills

Language skills are still limited for many young children, so it can be *very* challenging for them to find the words that clearly articulate their feelings and needs during a conflict. Once problem solving is under way, they may also encounter new words, such as "problem," "solve," or "solution." In addition, the emotional tension of most conflicts can add to children's difficulties in using language. As a result, when we ask them to explain what happened or to suggest solutions, we need to give them lots of time to respond. Once they have responded, restating the problem in clear, simple language is usually a help-

For toddlers and young children with language delays, the adult must provide a lot of the language needed to discuss feelings and problems.

ful strategy. In addition, it is sometimes necessary to reframe children's hurtful words into more appropriate feeling words (see pp. 70–72).

For toddlers and young children with language delays, the adult must provide a lot of the language needed for problem solving. We can do this by asking questions that a young child can answer with a yes, a no, or a nod of the head, for example, "You're both feeling sad [pause]," "You both want some play dough, is that right? Shall I give some to each of you? There, does that solve it?" (For more on mediation with toddlers, see Chapter 7, p. 293.)

Physical expressiveness

Young children express most of what they feel with their bodies. Until their verbal skills are established, children will show frustration or anger by hitting or grabbing, as Carly did. Like adults learning a foreign language, children need time and practice to learn to express themselves in words. Even after children have begun to learn about problem solving, fatigue, hunger, or other stresses may cause them to regress to less mature responses such as hitting or grabbing. It is important for us to discourage, but not punish, these physical responses, focusing instead on encouraging problem-solving skills that will eventually replace them.

Young children express most of what they feel with their bodies. Until their verbal skills are established, most children will show frustration or anger by hitting, grabbing, screaming, or crying.

Striving for independence

Doing things without adult help is also of great interest to young children. Their developing independence is central to their growth, often providing strong motivation to learn new skills. As children are developing confidence in their skills, they may declare, as Carly did, "I want to do it myself!" Young children's interest in independent action, combined with their egocentrism, can sometimes be a recipe for exasperating conflicts. However, if we share control with children, giving them plenty of room to exercise their emerging skills, this struggle can result in important new learning.

"One-thing-at-a-time" thinking

Children can focus on only one or two attributes or ideas at a time. As a result, conflicts for them can be confusing, muddled experiences in which they feel overwhelmed by the rush of emotions and demands. By noticing children's feelings and restating the essential details of a problem, adults can help children find a way out of this confusion. When children feel that their wants and needs have been completely understood, it becomes easier for them to move forward and consider solutions. Sometimes during conflicts there will be a lot of information to discuss, or possibly interruptions. At these times, children's tendency to focus on one thing at a time may cause them to become distracted by other things going on, or they may simply forget about an important factor of the conflict. Adults can insure the completion of the problem solving by restating one or two details of the problem, refocusing the discussion on possible solutions.

Developing capacity for empathy

The ability to empathize (understand how another feels) begins to appear at the end of the second year of life (Greenspan, 1997) and develops over the early childhood years. Even though children have been found to be aware of the emotions of others at a very early age, they are still egocentric, and consequently their own strong needs and wants can sometimes

Really listening, with full attention, to all of children's feelings—happy and sad—helps children understand that feelings are important.

overwhelm their developing capacity to react sensitively. As a result, they need our support to notice and respond to the feelings of others.

When adults acknowledge—notice and name—children's feelings, they support children's self-awareness, and by extension, their awareness of the feelings and needs of others. With my help as the mediating adult, Carly and Sam listened to each other's feelings and ideas. The little group of children who crowded around to listen as Carly and Sam talked over their problem were drawn in by their developing empathy for and responsiveness to their schoolmates. Because these children were not directly (or egocentrically) involved, it was easier for them to see both points of view and come up with a solution that worked for both children; it was easier for them to be empathic.

The Mediation Steps: An Introduction

Now that we have a clearer picture of how the young child feels and thinks, we can look closely at the mediation steps. Note how the steps enable teachers and parents to support children *as they are,* accepting what they can do at their developmental levels while encouraging the development of new skills. Throughout the steps, the adult's role is to act as a *neutral facilitator.* The following section describes each of the steps and illustrates their functions.

Six Steps in Conflict Mediation

1. Approach calmly, stopping any hurtful actions.
2. Acknowledge children's feelings.
3. Gather information.
4. Restate the problem.
5. Ask for ideas for solutions and choose one together.
6. Be prepared to give follow-up support.

Steps 1 and 2: Supporting feelings

The first two steps in problem solving encourage children to express their strong feelings, giving them the time and acceptance they need to make their feelings known.

Step 1: Approach calmly, stopping any hurtful actions. In the first step, adults, as calmly as possible, go to the children who are having a problem, stopping any hurtful actions or words. When children are hurting one another or yelling, there is an immediate need to respond, and staying calm can be a challenging task. When I am moving toward children in conflict, I calm myself by thinking "This is an important learning moment. As hard as this looks, what I want is to support children to learn new skills." This kind of inner conversation helps to bolster confidence. (It can be an especially useful strategy for adults who are just learning the skills of problem solving.)

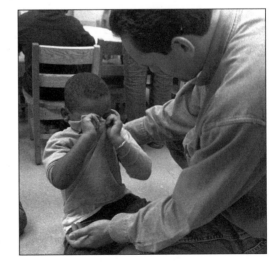

Step 1: *Seeing that a child is crying, José approaches calmly. (See the following pages for the rest of this sequence.)*

As we approach children, it's also important for us to notice our *body language.* Children give more attention to adult body language than to words, so it is necessary to show our trust and respect for children by getting down on their level, using a calm voice, and, when appropriate, touching the children gently. Adults need to consider children's personal responses and the cultural context when offering physical or eye contact. Gentle body language helps to calm children's emotions and communicates confidence that the children can work out the problem. If we approach a conflict with intensity, using a loud voice, grabbing children, and speaking down to them from above, the children's feelings may escalate or children may withdraw in fear, refusing to show or tell us their feelings or needs.

Step 2: Acknowledge children's feelings. In this second essential step, we communicate our concern for what children are feeling by making simple statements: "Abby and Colin, you are feeling very sad." "Bobby, you are feeling really frustrated." Responding to children in this way allows them to fully express their feelings, making it possible for them to move on to thoughtful solutions. Without this step, the mediation may fail completely.

These acknowledging comments about children's feelings communicate to them that their feelings are okay and that it is safe to express them. It may be enough to simply say "You're feeling really upset [mad/sad/frustrated] about this." If a child is very emotional, however, we may need to spend more time on this step, acknowledging the child's feelings over and over until they have subsided. Sometimes children will need adult guidance in reframing feelings they have expressed hurtfully (see pp. 70–72); this is part of the learning process as well.

Step 2: *As José acknowledges the child's feelings, the child cries openly, fully expressing his sadness and frustration. A girl who is also involved joins them.*

For example, if a child says "I hate you!" we can reframe this by saying "You're feeling *very* angry about this." When children's feelings have been supported, they are able to empty them out completely. This makes it possible for them to consider solutions without strong feelings getting in the way.

Steps 3, 4, 5, and 6: Supporting children's solutions

In the last four steps in mediation, children take the initiative in finding a solution. These steps are the "thinking" part of problem solving.

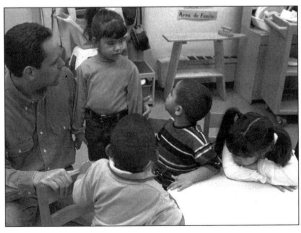

Step 3: After they walk together to where others who are involved are sitting, José gathers information from everyone. (The conflict is about how four children will play together.) They talk to José and to each other about what happened. José listens to what the others have to say, while reassuring one of the children with a gentle hug.

"The emotional brain...[is] an integral part of the circuitry that activates and directs messages to the cortex, and the crux of the attention system. It can either facilitate learning or, quite literally, shut down the thinking systems...."

—*Jane Healy (1994, p. 214)*

Step 3: Gather information. In this step the children tell what they think has happened or what they want. This step can best be carried out once children's feelings have calmed. Recent brain research helps us understand that strong emotions cause the emotional part of the brain to take over, "flooding" the areas of the brain responsible for reasoning (Healy, 1994). This "flooding" reaction is something that most of us have experienced during upsetting or enraging moments. It is helpful when scientific research confirms that this response is inherently human; we might otherwise be tempted to think of this temporary loss of rational thought as a personal weakness, causing us to label children as "hysterical" or "too emotional." This knowledge of how the brain handles sudden emotion is important to keep in mind when we are preparing to ask children for ideas on solving a problem. Children can't consider possible solutions when their brains are still "flooded"; therefore, we need to observe sensitively for signs that children's feelings are subsiding and the ability to reason has returned. It is usually easy to tell when children are satisfied that their feelings have been heard. Their young, expressive bodies communicate this quite clearly: loud voices become quieter, crying begins to subside, regular breathing returns, tense hands and limbs relax, and facial expressions soften. Once children's emotions have calmed, it is easier for us to gather unmuddled, rational information and for children to thoughtfully consider solutions.

Asking "What's the problem?" and then pausing to listen are useful strategies for gathering information once children have calmed. We need to listen carefully for the details children share about their problems, since the beginnings of solutions are often embedded in these accounts. Pausing to consider what children have said is important for two reasons: it helps us to listen actively, and it gives children the response time they need to find words for their concerns. (It can take children a few seconds to respond.) It is helpful to keep in mind that as children haltingly describe the details of a problem, they are clarifying those details for themselves as well as others. As we wait for children to respond, a simple "hmmm" can help us avoid jumping in and can reassure children that we are still there, listening and supporting them.

The type of question we ask during this phase of the problem solving is also important. Simple "what" questions gather information most effectively: for example, "What happened?" "What were you upset about?" "What is the problem?" "What do you need?" "What do you want to tell him?" These kinds of questions elicit concrete facts and details. By contrast, "why" questions are very difficult for children. They are abstract and often seem to assign blame, which will not help to solve the problem. A more effective approach is to support children in taking responsibility for what has happened as they describe the problem and look for a solution. By focusing on physical facts and clear details as we gather information, we are helping young, concrete thinkers lay the foundation for successful solutions.

Step 4: Restate the problem. This step helps to clarify details. Often, at the beginning of problem solving there is so much emotion that some information may not be heard. At this point it is very useful for us to repeat information children have shared, in a neutral, calm way, so the children can focus on the one or two most relevant details. To restate the problem we make a simple summary of the pertinent information: "So the problem is that you both want this red truck" or

Step 4: *José restates what he has heard.*

Step 5: José asks the children what can be done to solve the problem. At left one child describes his idea of a solution while the others listen. Below, another child gives her idea for a solution.

"So the problem is, you both want to be first." Note that the phrase "So the problem is…" is a very effective way to begin this summary.

Step 5: Ask for ideas for solutions and choose one together. In this step, the mediating adult simply asks the children a question like "What can we do to solve this problem?" This can be the fun, creative part of problem solving; children's solutions are often delightfully original and inventive! As children tell us their ideas, we encourage all the parties in the dispute to consider whether the proposed solution will work for them. We can facilitate a firm agreement by checking in with each child individually: "So the solution is…Is that okay with you?" This lets children know they are in control of the outcome. As children suggest and weigh ideas for a solution, they are gaining experience in problem solving and cause-and-effect thinking. This step ensures that the agreed-upon solution meets everyone's needs.

Step 6: Be prepared to give follow-up support. This step helps children make a transition from conflict back to play. Two strategies may be used. First, we can make a statement of encouragement to help children realize that they have solved the problem: for example, saying with enthusiasm "You solved this problem!" Statements like this are important because, when an

Step 6: At left, they all agree on a solution, and José gives follow-up support by pointing out what they've decided. A few minutes later he checks in with one of the boys to see how he's doing, below left and right. The child's sad feelings are now resolved, and they share a happy moment. ◆

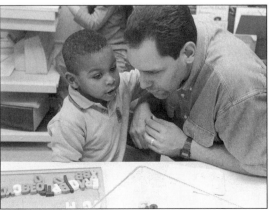

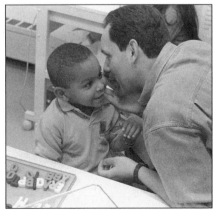

adult is present, children sometimes aren't aware of the role they played in developing the solution. These simple statements give children confidence that *they* are problem-solvers.

Another strategy is to be observant of the children, perhaps from some distance, for a short time following the conflict. Most of the time the child-chosen solution works; sometimes it is useful for us to stay in the area briefly with very young or potentially hurtful children, while avoiding "hovering" too closely. If there is any sign that either child has not resolved all the emotions of the conflict or that the solution is not working, it is critical for us to be ready to give follow-up support. Looking for body language cues can help. During the mediation with Jerome and Bobby that follows, I noticed the changes in Bobby's body language as the two children implemented the solution they had agreed upon. As I watched, Bobby's body became completely relaxed, the emotion left his voice, he nodded his head in agreement, and he became completely absorbed in Jerome's efforts. I felt quite confident that the problem had been resolved.

The steps in action

Following is the story of Jerome and Bobby, which provides a clear illustration of the six steps. The steps are noted in the text as they occur.

Jerome and Bobby: "It's my turn!"

1. Approach calmly, stopping any hurtful actions.

▶ During work time I heard Bobby's voice rising with both sadness and frustration. I went over and sat between him and Jerome, who were both 4 years old. Jerome was working at the computer, sitting very straight, his eyes riveted to the screen. Bobby was sitting next to him, his shoulders slumped and head hanging down. As he looked up at me, he was frowning; his eyebrows almost touched. I gently laid a hand on each of the boys' shoulders.

Bobby, who seemed close to tears, told me, "Jerome won't tell me when he's done...and it's my turn."

2. Acknowledge children's feelings.

▶ As Bobby talked, I gently rubbed his back and said, "You're feeling pretty upset." Bobby nodded.

"Jerome, Bobby is feeling upset," I said. Jerome didn't respond.

"Bobby, do you want to tell him what you're upset about?"

"He already knows!" Bobby told me in a voice that was shifting from sadness to frustration.

"It sounds like you tried to tell him what you were upset about and you're frustrated that he isn't answering you," I said.

Bobby nodded, straightening his body from its slumped position. He took a deep breath and his face relaxed.

"What is the problem, Jerome?" I asked. Jerome stiffened his back even more. He lifted his chin as he said in a very tight, high voice, "Yeah, but I want to spend my whole time on the 'puter."

◀ 3. Gather information.

"You're feeling really strongly about that," I told him. He nodded.

"Hmmm," I said as I paused for a few seconds, thinking about what I knew already about Jerome. Jerome was new to our program and had been struggling socially. He frequently asked children if they liked him, and appeared to feel anxious about his abilities. The adults had referred children to him for help with this computer game, Word Search. He had realized that he was skilled at it and was spending more time on it.

"So the problem is, you really want to spend a lot of time here, Jerome." I put my hand gently on his back, which had begun to relax. Jerome nodded. "And Bobby, you heard that Jerome's wanting to be here a long time and you want him to tell you when he's finished." I touched Bobby's shoulder and he nodded. "Jerome, Bobby heard that you're wanting to be here a long time. He just wants you to come and tell him when you're finished."

◀ 4. Restate the problem.

"I'm gonna do all the levels, "Jerome informed us both proudly.

"Wow, all the levels," I repeated, pausing to appreciate the size of his chosen task. "So what do you think we can do to solve this problem, Bobby and Jerome?"

◀ 5. Ask for ideas for solutions and choose one together.

"When I'm done, I'll come tell him," Jerome tells us as he concentrates on the screen.

"Bobby, is that okay with you…? He'll come and find you? It's going to be a pretty long time. He wants to do all the levels."

"All the levels that would go up to 12," Bobby calculated, the upset feelings now gone from his voice.

"It will take a long time, won't it?" I re-emphasized. Bobby nodded.

Jerome added thoughtfully and with confidence, "Every day, it will take a long time."

Bobby was not responding to the issue of length of time; he was watching the game with interest. It seemed to me that they had reached an agreement, but I decided to go over the solution again with Bobby. "Bobby, he did say he would come and find you. Is that okay?" Bobby nodded as he watched the screen. "I think he was worried that it would take such a long time, and he wanted to make sure you knew that."

6. Be prepared to give follow-up support. ▶

"You solved this problem, Bobby and Jerome! You found a solution," I said. "So, Bobby, are you going to make another plan now, or are you going to watch?"

Very absorbed now in the computer game, Bobby said, without looking at me, "I'm going to watch." I stayed nearby as Jerome succeeded at one level and moved up another level. Bobby cheered him on: "Level 3, Jerome, you did it!" Jerome smiled as he glanced over at Bobby, his back relaxing. Bobby watched for another 15 minutes, giving tips as Jerome proceeded through the levels.

At level 7 Jerome stopped and told Bobby. "That's all. Your turn, Bobby." Bobby switched places with Jerome, who stayed to watch. They stayed at the Computer Area until cleanup, continuing to work cooperatively as Bobby did levels 1 and 2.

This story illustrates how children's solutions reflect their own level of maturity; some solutions are quite egocentric, while some are more responsive to the interests of others. This sometimes results in arrangements that adults might not consider ideal or "fair." In Jerome's case, time spent at the computer was apparently providing the boost that his self-esteem needed. Once Bobby had been heard and his emotions had been accepted and understood, he became interested in Jerome's play and was willing to wait. He did wait a long time, but the fact that he and Jerome chose the outcome together was more important than exact fairness. Bobby and Jerome had exchanged feelings and ideas. As a result, Bobby offered enthusiastic support as Jerome proceeded towards his goal, providing the beginning of a new friendship. Over the next two months, Bobby and Jerome became good friends, sharing interest in the "'puter" as well as other activities. It can sometimes be difficult to keep in mind that the goal of the problem-solving process is to find a solution that results in *agreement* from the children involved, even though the solution may not necessarily result in *equality* for the children. Accepting children's agreements empowers them as problem-solvers.

◆

Punishment or Problem Solving: What Each Teaches

The previous stories, of Carly and Sam and of Bobby and Jerome, offer clear examples of what children can learn through the problem-solving approach. Teachers and parents who are considering adopting this mediation approach in their own work with children may find it helpful to look now at the differences between this approach and traditional, punitive approaches to conflict and to consider what children learn from each.

As we make decisions about how to respond to conflicts, having a consistent intention is a critical consideration. If we are convinced that we want to support children's *intrinsic motivation* to learn, then we must try to carry out this intention in all our interactions with children, including those that occur during conflicts. Another important consideration is the way we choose to approach children's social mistakes. As explained earlier, a key premise behind problem-solving is that simply thinking of children's undesirable behaviors as mistakes (rather than as "bad behaviors") is a first step in dealing more constructively with them. Thus it is helpful to remind ourselves, *often,* that children—in fact, all of us—make mistakes. "Mistaken behavior is a natural occurrence, the result of attempts by the inexperienced, developmentally young child to interact with a complicated, increasingly impersonal world" (Gartrell, 1994, p. 37). Our response to children's social mistakes can be a critical turning point in the educational path. As teachers and parents, we have a choice—we can respond to these mistakes as events that require punishment or as opportunities for new learning.

Mistakes and new learning

To clarify the effects of punishment on learning, let's look at some typical mistakes made by children and consider how the child could best learn new skills in these situations.

- *Raj lays his coat on the floor and flips it over his head in an effort to put it on. The coat is now upside down and he struggles to zip it.* Should the adult tell him that because of this mistake, he should "stay inside and think about it?" Or should the adult instead ask Raj if he would like to see another way of putting on his coat so that it can be zipped?

- *Kazumi is painting at the easel and puts the red brush in the blue paint pot.* Should the adult tell him, "Stop painting until you do it right," or should the adult watch to see if Kazumi notices how the color has changed and corrects his own mistake?

- *Takisha finishes a puzzle all by herself and jumps up excitedly exclaiming, "I did it! I did it!" As she jumps, she backs into a tall block tower being built by Anna.* Should the adult remove Takisha from the area, saying she can come back when she learns to be more careful, or mediate a discussion between Takisha and Anna about what happened?

Most of us would agree that children should not be punished for making mistakes like these. Having a clear intention to support children in solving their own problems in all situations can guide adults as they change from punitive to mediation approaches. Consider two more examples:

- *Jessica is quietly wandering around the classroom, repeating a curse word in a low voice. Some children look up and listen.* Should Jessica be told to stop and sent to time-out? Or should the adult instead say to Jessica "It sounds like you're trying out a new word. There are some words that people don't like to hear. Since that's one of them, I'm going to ask you to stop saying it. New words are fun, though. Shall we read a book together and see if we can find some?"

- *Kwame sees Katie playing with the new fire truck and goes over and grabs it from her. She yells, "You stupid dummy!"* Should the adult take the truck away from both of them and tell them to "be friends and share" or approach the children calmly and ask to hold the truck while Kwame and Katie talk about the problem?

Punishing children for mistakes like these is incompatible with an *active learning* approach. Based on child development research and theory, this approach tells us that young children do not learn new skills through abstract lessons, but rather, through *experiences* in which they are actively involved with people, materials, and ideas (Hohmann & Weikart, 2002). It follows from this that children who are involved in disputes are more likely to learn new behaviors if we engage them with, rather than remove them from, the source of their difficulties. Since young children can hold only one or two things in mind at a time, children who are punished focus on the adult's immediate reactions of anger or blaming, retaining the message that they are "bad" or "selfish." On the other hand, if we

A child's interest in developing new skills is most keen at the very moment a conflict occurs.

immediately involve children in problem solving, we are encouraging learning just when they are motivated intrinsically to find new ways to solve a dispute. Thus, a child's interest in developing new skills is most keen at the very moment a conflict occurs.

Responding punitively may meet the needs of adults for order and control, but this not only results in a missed opportunity for new growth but may also change the tone of their relationship with children. When adults do not accept children's mistakes or take time to attentively listen to their feelings and ideas, the relationship may become adversarial. However, when adults see mistakes and conflicts as opportunities for new learning and stronger relationships, the choice to support children's solutions can benefit everyone.

> "For decades, researchers have consistently found that children subjected to physical punishment tend to be more aggressive than their peers, and will likely grow up to use violence on their own children....But it is not only physical punishment that proves ineffective in the long run....All punishment, by which I mean any reliance on power to make something unpleasant happen to a child as a way of trying to alter that child's behavior, teaches that when you are bigger or stronger than someone else, you can use that advantage to force the person to do what you want ....To the extent that helping children develop good values depends on establishing a caring relationship with them, the use of punishment makes that much less likely to happen."
>
> —Alfie Kohn (1993, p. 167)

Why do adults punish?

Considering the doubtful effectiveness of punishment, we may wonder why it is still used in schools and homes. There are many reasons why adults punish children. As discussed earlier, the most common is that this is the approach that adults themselves experienced as children. Without role models for conflict mediation, or for constructively expressing anger or frustration, adults follow the approach that was modeled for them. Instead of supporting "out-of-control" children to learn how to regain control, adults often take over control while venting their own intense feelings.

Another reason adults punish is that they feel responsible for children's actions and words. In public situations, they may even feel social pressure, in the form of dirty looks and rolling eyes, to end the "unpleasantness." They may worry that if they do not respond to a child's mistakes with firm action and very memorable consequences, the child will repeat the behavior.

This well-intentioned concern comes from a sincere desire to do what is best for the child, preventing him or her from growing up "bad" or even criminal. However, the resulting punishment in itself may create low self-esteem and increased hostility (Kohn, 1993).

As we explore the disadvantages of punishment and other forms of extrinsic motivation (such as reward), it becomes important to consider our goals. Do we want long- or short-term results? Is our goal to be in control of the child's behavior or to help the child learn to choose appropriate behavior independently? Part of the appeal of punishment and reward systems is that they appear to work, at least in the short run. Punishment, or the threat of it, does stop some inappropriate behaviors, temporarily, but does not often change the behavior patterns (Kohn, 1993). Unless the child's *interest* in the undesirable behavior changes, the punishment must be repeated again and again. This is often the drawback to popular punishment techniques such as time-out and "1-2-3 Magic"; in order to maintain the behavior changes imposed by such systems, adults must constantly repeat the cycle of punishment. Children acquire lasting social skills only when they are allowed to explore their own ways of expressing their feelings and ideas. Social behaviors coerced by adults are not likely to be repeated by the child without constant reinforcement, and at best this produces only mindless obedience. As Jean Piaget wrote, "Punishment renders the autonomy of conscience impossible" (1965, p. 339).

Coerced outcomes versus child-chosen solutions

If one of our long-term goals is a desire for children to make a *conscious choice* to be cooperative and friendly with others, then we need to adopt interactive strategies that promote the child's *initiative* as an essential element of the learning process. Let's now consider a conflict between two children, both nearly 3 years old, but developmentally more like toddlers. Two possible endings to the story (one is the true one) are provided to illustrate the potential results of (1) coerced and (2) child-chosen approaches.

Lila wants to pet Jack's Queen Bee

Jack pulled the bee toy across the floor. A small plastic crown sat on the bee's head and the words "Queen Bee" were written across its back. Its fluorescent orange wings fluttered so fast that the delicate gold lines on them blurred. The bee's multi-colored body looked like it might come unglued as it moved. As Jack pulled on its knotted plastic string, he watched the bee with fascination. Its wheels squeaked. Two springs sticking out of the bee's head wobbled wildly as Jack and the bee wove their way among the other children.

Jack's belly button showed beneath the curled hem of his shirt as he toddled sideways, watching the bee's progress behind him. He reached for my hand. "Betsy, Betsy, let's go for a walk." With his warm little hand held tight in mine, we began our walk. Jamie crawled on all fours near us; she stopped and meowed. Showing no interest, Jack walked on, his eyes on the bee. Water splashed us lightly as children washed baby dolls in the water table, but Jack, whose eyes stayed fixed on the bee, didn't notice. As we passed the cubbies, we approached Merrilee, my teaching partner, who was reading a book to Lila.

Jack spotted them. "Merrilee, Merrilee!" he said. "Wanna pet the bee?"

Merrilee looked up and smiled at him, "Yeah, I'd like to, Jack."

She reached out and touched the bee's wooden body and smiled once more at Jack. Lila reached out to do the same, but Jack suddenly yanked the bee away. It flipped over several times, landing on its side. The wheels spun uselessly in the air. Lila sat back with surprise, then turned and laid her head on Merrilee's shoulder and began to cry.

Possible Ending #1:

My grip on Jack's hand suddenly changed from gentle to tight as I pulled him toward me. "Jack, that wasn't very nice! We're all friends here and the toys belong to all of us. Let Lila pet the bee."

Jack made a loud grunt and pulled the bee farther away. I could feel anger rising up the back of my neck. I reached over and took the bee from Jack's hand. "Jack, if you're not going to share, I'm going to put this away."

Jack let out a loud shriek and threw himself on the floor. Lila watched him, confused by his reaction and frightened by the tone of my voice. She leaned in closer to Merrilee. Jack continued to shriek.

I put the bee up on a high shelf and turned back to Jack. "That's **enough**, Jack. Merrilee and Lila can't read while you're screaming." Jack's screams became sobs; big tears rolled down his cheeks. As I picked him up, his body stiffened with resistance and he began to pound my back with his fists. "Jack, don't you hit me! Stop that!!" I said angrily.

I took him to the coatroom and sat him down in the time-out chair. He became suddenly silent and still. "You need to stay here and think about what you did. I'll be back," I said. I left, confident that I had shown him that it was not okay to be selfish with his toys. While I was gone, he took every piece of clothing off the coatroom pegs and threw them on the floor.

Later, after I had forced Jack to pick up all the clothing, I saw him stomp angrily through the room until he came to Lila. He found her dressing a doll in the playhouse. Loudly he told her, "You can't come to my birthday. I have even better toys." She looked up at him, confused, and then she yelled, "Get out!" Slowly Jack turned and left.

◆

Possible Ending #2:

I knelt by Jack and told him quietly, "Lila's really sad. She wanted to pet the bee."

Jack answered sternly, "We're going for a walk."

He reached for my hand and pulled as he watched Lila crying. I stood without moving, watching as Merrilee held Lila close, telling her softly, "Lila, you're feeling so sad. You wanted to pet the bee." Lila's face stayed pressed to Merrilee's shoulder and I wondered what I could do to support Jack and Lila in solving this problem. Jack began to pull at my hand again. He had set the bee upright. As I stood up I asked Jack, "She's feeling sad, Jack. She's crying. Can Lila pet the bee before we go on the walk?"

Jack looked closely at Lila, then told me, "No, we're going for a walk right now." He tugged on my hand again and I followed, wondering what would happen next, but also certain that there was nothing to be gained by forcing a solution.

No longer watching the bee that he dragged along, Jack led the way across the Block Area and we entered the playhouse. Jack turned and told me, "We went for a walk right now. We will come back and we…I will let her pet it in a **little while.**"

I sat on the floor as he searched the cupboard. I asked him, "I wonder if she'll stop crying when you let her pet the bee? I wonder if she'll smile?"

But Jack ignored this question as he set two tea cups in front of the baby doll in the high chair. Then suddenly he turned and picked up the yellow plastic string once again.

"Let's go for a walk now," he told me. Holding my hand tightly, Jack led us back to Merrilee and Lila. The bee, which had again rolled off its wheels, tumbled along behind us. Jack didn't notice this.

As we approached, I could see Lila sitting snugly in Merrilee's lap, looking at a book. Jack let go of my hand and stopped in front of them, pulling the bee up close and setting it upright. Jack and Lila looked at each other closely, silently. Merrilee and I waited. Then I knelt down by Jack and explained to Lila, "Jack told me he just wanted to walk the bee for a **while,** and then he would bring it to you to pet. Right, Jack?" Jack nodded and smiled slightly. Tentatively, Lila reached out to touch it. Jack watched her with the same sharp attention he had earlier given the bee. Lila touched the bee lightly, then sat up again, a little smile crossing her face as she squirmed with pleasure and pressed herself back against Merrilee.

Jack turned and pulled Queen Bee away, "Let's go for a walk now," he said softly. He reached out for my hand.

As we walked away, I spoke to Jack, "You solved the problem, Jack. Did you see Lila smile?" He looked up at me with a smile that seemed to move through him like a wave, loosening his whole body.

Later, as the children prepared to go outside, Jack stood by Lila and asked her, "Lila, are you coming next day?" She nodded and beamed a smile at him.

◆

The second response, of course, is the true ending to the story. It is an ending that surprised me, the kind of ending that makes mediation pure joy. Solving problems with very young children is a bit like juggling eggs. It requires tenderness, timing, and very careful attention to body language. But when the result is successful, the satisfaction for everyone involved can be immensely sweet.

Young children are just beginning to understand how their actions affect other people. As a result, they often exaggerate and draw out their actions in order to fully see and understand the reaction. Such exploration of reactions can be very upsetting to adults who want to "teach" caring behaviors.

> "Learning and development are facilitated by the participation of the developing person in progressively more complex patterns of reciprocal activity with someone with whom that person has developed a strong and enduring emotional attachment and when the balance of power gradually shifts in favor of the developing person."
>
> —*Urie Bronfenbrenner (1979, p. 60)*

We may be tempted to tell preschool children like Jack *how* to behave, but caring, responsive behaviors cannot be taught by directing children. We can, however, allow children time to explore various ways of responding to others, as long as children's behavior is not overly hurtful. In accepting children's explorations, we demonstrate our confidence in their emerging ability to choose cooperative actions independently. Such supportive, patient adult responses facilitate, often delightfully so, children's learning of caring behavior.

 *The problem-solving steps are not magic; the process can be complex, though it is actually made up of relatively simple strategies. These strategies enable adults to support children when they are most in need of help, without making them forever dependent on that help. Like a box of tools, some or all of the steps may be needed as adults guide and encourage children during conflict mediations. Throughout this process, children are active—expressing their feelings and ideas, listening to others, and making choices. Over time, this is a process that children come to trust, one that enriches relationships and promotes increasingly complex thinking. Mistakes and differences become the catalysts for growth, providing the opportunity for change. The problem-solving approach enables children to handle disputes constructively and creatively as they become independent problem solvers together.*

The chapters that follow guide the reader to a deeper understanding of the problem-solving steps introduced here. The discussion will continue to center on real stories from the preschool classroom and home. Chapter 2 discusses the first two steps in mediating conflicts: **approach calmly, stopping any hurtful actions,** *and* **acknowledge children's feelings.**

2

 **A Supportive and Safe Beginning to Problem Solving**

If we want children to feel safe in expressing their feelings, it is important to create a non-threatening, supportive tone from the start of a conflict mediation, letting children know, right away, that we recognize their strong feelings. The first two steps of problem solving provide for such a beginning. In these steps, the adult communicates calm reassurance that the problem will be resolved and shows support and respect for children's feelings. This chapter takes a close look at **step 1, approach calmly, stopping any hurtful actions,** and **step 2, acknowledge children's feelings.**

Step 1: Preparation, Perspective, and Strategies

The first step in problem solving is to approach children calmly, stopping them from hitting, calling names, or any other hurtful or destructive behaviors. Though *approach calmly* sounds simple, it can be very difficult to be remain calm when a favorite book is being torn or when children are hurting one another. In such situations, we often feel personally responsible for children's actions or upset by the disruption that the conflict is creating. The need to get to children quickly at the start of a conflict often makes it especially difficult to remain

Six Steps in Conflict Mediation

1. Approach calmly, stopping any hurtful actions.
2. Acknowledge children's feelings.
3. Gather information.
4. Restate the problem.
5. Ask for ideas for solutions and choose one together.
6. Be prepared to give follow-up support.

calm. When a conflict erupts, there may be hurtful behaviors that require our immediate attention, with little time to calm ourselves.

Because of the intensity of children's conflicts, teachers and parents are often unable to respond calmly unless they have thought through some strategies ahead of time. This section presents issues adults can reflect on to prepare themselves for a calm approach.

Seeing children's actions as social mistakes

One helpful thing to remember at the start of a conflict is the premise that hurtful actions are *mistakes* that are about to become a starting place for new learning. If we can see children's offensive behaviors as understandable mistakes, we can often diffuse our own emotional reactions to them. Educator Daniel Gartrell spent many years observing young children in classrooms and developed a model for understanding young children's behavioral mistakes that identifies three "levels" (or categories) of mistakes (1994). These levels and some helpful ways adults can respond to mistakes of each type are described next.

Experimentation-related mistakes. Children are naturally curious and have a strong desire for autonomy ("I want to do it myself!"). This curiosity and need for independence foster both new learning *and* the mistakes that inevitably go with it. For example, a child who is curious about a toy may reach out and take it from another child, or a child may try to impress a new friend by knocking down his building. Understanding the reasons for these mistakes, we can respond helpfully by discouraging the actions while encouraging the *intentions* behind them. One way to do this is to engage children in problem solving, which gives them an alternative way to express their curiosity and need for independence.

Socially influenced mistakes. Children are influenced by the actions and words of family members, neighborhood acquaintances, and characters from television and movies. In an effort to understand these new (and sometimes offensive) words and

In the first two steps of problem solving the adult communicates reassurance and calm acceptance of children's feelings, setting the stage for a discussion of the problem.

actions, children actively explore what they mean and the impact they have on others. For example, an angry child may call someone a "stupid dummy," a name she has heard at home, or a frustrated child may karate-kick another child as seen on his favorite superhero show. To promote more direct and verbal expression of feeling, we can discourage such hurtful words and actions (keeping in mind that they stem from a natural tendency to imitate others) and acknowledge the feelings behind those actions and words. This provides children with a more constructive model to imitate and enables them to explore the source of their feelings. We may also decide to give closer consideration to the children's television and movie selections.

Mistakes resulting from strong needs. There are many reasons why children may develop "strong needs" mistaken behavior. There may be short- or long-term stresses in children's lives, ranging from common family events (a new sibling at home, a divorce, a lengthy illness) to more serious situations such as the abuse and neglect of a child by family or friends. Children who are suffering from any of these stresses may frequently become frustrated with simple tasks. They may cry easily or throw objects, or they may repeatedly taunt and tease other children and otherwise be unable to play constructively. In these cases, it is best to respond to the immediate situation in the same way we respond to other kinds of mistakes—by discouraging the inappropriate words and actions and engaging the child in problem solving. Particular attention to acknowledging feelings may give the child some relief, even if we can't change the situation that is the root cause of the child's distress. If the pattern is chronic, the adult may need, for safety reasons, to give the child close supervision and limited choices for play. When children exhibit strong needs, we must also consider seeking other assistance for the child through a pediatrician or psychological referrals.

With the insights offered by Gartrell's levels of mistakes, it becomes easier to understand the child's perspective. This enables us to redefine children's misbehaviors, seeing them not as intentional wrongdoing but as youthful attempts to actively explore and understand their world. Viewed in this way, children's mistakes are an opportunity for growth. Gartrell's mistake cate-

Daniel Gartrell's Levels of Mistaken Behavior*

"Mistaken behavior is a natural occurrence, the result of attempts by the inexperienced, developmentally young child to interact with a complicated, increasingly impersonal world. When mistaken behavior occurs, adults significantly affect what children learn from the experience. Guidance-oriented responses that encourage children to keep trying and to continue learning empower healthy self-concepts and full personal development. On the other hand, punitive responses coerce children to abandon the need to experience fully and to adopt defensive behaviors, usually in compliance with the teacher's expectations. Punishment can even create a well of unmet emotional needs and lead to survival level relational patterns: withdrawing from situations, reacting with overt and covert hostility, or showing anxiety" (Gartrell, 1994, p. 37).

Level one: Experimentation

"Experimentation…mistaken behavior occurs when the child reacts to one of two motives: curiosity—the child acts to see what will happen; or involvement—the child's actions in a situation do not get the results expected (an 'experiment' in daily living does not work out)" (p. 37).

Level two: Socially influenced

"Socially influenced mistaken behavior happens when children are reinforced in an action, sometimes unintentionally, by others important to them" (p. 37).

Level three: Strong needs

"Children show level three mistaken behavior as a reaction to difficulty and pain in their lives that is beyond their capacity to cope with and understand. Most often, strong needs mistaken behavior occurs because of untreated health conditions or painful life experiences. …[This] behavior in the classroom happens because a child is reacting to strong unmet needs, acting out against a perceived hostile world" (p. 38) …."The primary sign of the strong needs level is dysfunctional behavior with a definite emotional underlay that tends to be repeated—in short, extreme behaviors, repeated over time" (p. 43).

---

*From *A Guidance Approach to Discipline*, 1st edition, by D. Gartrell ©1994. Reprinted with permission of a division of Thomson Learning. Fax 800-730-2215.

gories can also help us determine what kinds of intervention, in addition to conflict mediation, are needed to address children's mistaken actions. These other interventions are summarized in the chart, "Levels of Intervention," on the next page.

As the chart indicates, it is often useful for teachers to use staff meeting time to discuss socially influenced mistakes (such as repeated conflicts arising from children's imitation of television superheroes). Repeated strong needs mistakes often call for all four levels of intervention: mediation at the time of the incident, discussion at a staff meeting, a conference with the child's parents, and possibly referrals to outside agencies or professionals.

Types of Mistakes	Levels of Intervention			
	Conflict mediation steps	Staff meeting	Special parent conference	Referral
Experimenta-tion mistakes	Yes	Possibly		
Socially influenced mistakes	Yes	Possibly	Possibly	
Strong needs mistakes	Yes	Yes	Yes	Possibly

Keeping the past in mind

Even when we understand the reasons for children's social mistakes, we may still find it difficult to respond patiently at the outset of a conflict. Conflict can bring up all sorts of experiences and emotions from our own lives. We may have childhood memories of frustrating and painful conflict episodes that ended in exasperation and sadness. As a conflict mediation trainer, I have heard adults tell intense, hurtful stories of how conflicts were handled when they were children. Often these adults experienced either authoritarian or avoidance approaches to conflict, resulting in memories that are at best unpleasant, at worst, downright horrible. Unfortunately, many of us can recall such painful incidents. As adults we may hope to forget these unpleasant memories, but when conflicts occur at home or at school, the feelings imprinted from our early experiences return, uninvited, to our present situation and interfere with our ability to stay composed and patient.

To begin the process of change, it can be very helpful, at non-conflict times, to think through our childhood experiences with conflict. It can be useful to ask ourselves: What was my model for solving conflicts? Was it punitive or supportive? How does that model affect my usual response to children's disputes? What do I want my response to be?

If our parents or teachers used either an authoritarian or an avoidance approach, our "gut instinct" may be to imitate this model. The decision to try a new approach often requires an awareness that the old one may be hard to change. Change is uncomfortable, and habitual responses are easy to repeat. Only when the new problem-solving approach has been practiced on many occasions will it become comfortable and easy.

Remembering the learning value of conflict

Another thing to keep in mind at the onset of a conflict is the importance of problem-solving skills for young children. If we value the learning that happens during these challenging moments, this may help us find the patience to respond. It may also be helpful to remind ourselves that children do not have conflicts in order to make our lives miserable; nor should we see their conflicts as evidence that we have failed as teachers or parents. Conflict is a predictable, useful part of life. While there

If we remind ourselves of the learning that happens during these challenging moments, we may find it easier to respond with sensitivity and patience.

is a great deal we can do to reduce the number of conflicts, we are not responsible for the mistakes children make. We are, however, responsible for supporting children as they learn from those mistakes. If we walk toward a conflict thinking to ourselves "Children can learn new and important life skills from this," we can set the stage for problem solving as a learning opportunity. Such mental and emotional preparation will make it easier to stay calm.

Preparing for neutrality

Once we have thought over relevant child development and personal issues, a final question to ask ourselves as we approach a conflict is, "Am I ready to be a *neutral facilitator* of problem solving?" A commitment to neutrality is essential if we want to support all the children involved. Neutrality is the ability to be interested in and supportive of the wants and needs of all the children *equally.* In other words, we must approach any conflict without assumptions about who is at fault or without an agenda for the outcome. If we are thinking "It's probably Bobby's fault; he's a bully who's always causing problems" or "I've got to make these children be nice and be friends," we are not approaching neutrally.

Several factors can affect our ability to be neutral: our present mood, presumptions that result in labels such as "bully," "mean," or "bad," and assumptions about what happened. Any of these factors can short-circuit the problem-solving process. Whenever a conflict occurs, approaching with an open mind helps us to be receptive to whatever the children have to say. Perhaps we have seen the beginning of the conflict, perhaps not. But *no matter what we have seen,* all children need to be heard, without judgment, as long as limits have been set on unsafe behavior: "Bobby, pushing must stop. You're feeling upset. I want to hear what happened from you both, one at a time." This neutral stance increases the probability of positive outcomes for everyone.

Once we have carefully considered our current beliefs about children, our past experiences, and the need to be impartial, we are better prepared, both emotionally and intellectually, to approach problem solving with a positive, neutral attitude. Communicating this attitude to children is our next challenge. In the following section we take a detailed look at the ways that we communicate with body language to create a successful beginning for problem solving.

Body language: Communicating calmness and neutrality

As soon as we see children being hurtful to one another or materials, it is important for us to move quickly, focusing on remaining calm and communicating neutrality. We must stop hurtful behavior immediately, and as gently as possible. Body language is the key; it communicates our intentions, saying without words *either* that we are here to express *our* feelings *or* that we want to hear about the *children's* feelings. Intense, loud, dominating body language can frighten and/or distract children. A loud voice and *abrupt* physical intervention may escalate the problem by focusing children's attention on our reaction rather than on the problem. If our approach is very dramatic, children may even forget what was happening or become reluctant to talk. They may assume that we have arrived to punish them and are not interested in hearing from them at all.

On the other hand, calm, collected body language can soothe children, while communicating neutral support of all the children involved. Such body language helps us focus on the children and the details of what is happening for them. Even after a discussion has begun, most of what children come to understand about our feelings is communicated by our gestures and actions.

Strategies for a Calm Approach

Things to keep in mind

- Children's hurtful actions are *social mistakes*.
- Feelings from the past may resurface—avoid being thrown by them and resolve to think through childhood conflict experiences at another time.
- Conflict is a positive learning experience for children.
- Problem solving may feel awkward at first, but will become comfortable with practice.
- Be neutral—don't take sides.

Things to do

- Stop hurtful actions and words; continue to gently restrain children if necessary.
- Place yourself between children, on their level.
- Use calm body language to soothe children and convey your neutrality: comforting gestures, eye contact, soft voice, supportive facial expression.
- Be "fully present" for children.

A commitment to neutrality is essential for effective mediation. This sequence begins with a child, left, who is distraught because he wants a block another child has. Below, Chantal calmly approaches the two boys.

Chantal positions herself between the children, on their level. Her calm, collected body language soothes the children, communicating neutral support for them both. Often, adults insist that children look at them, which can communicate that the adult is directing the situation. A more effective way of gaining children's attention is for the mediator to stay in a neutral, in-between position, offering eye contact and gentle comfort and speaking in a calm tone of voice, as Chantal does here.

At left, Chantal conveys reassurance by gently reaching out, putting her arms around both children. Her facial expressions reflect the concern she feels as well as the sadness and anger the children are expressing.

Chantal's body language gives the children the reassurance they need to feel safe in fully expressing their feelings, engaging in the negotiation, and deciding on a solution.

Problem solved! ◆

Following are body language strategies that help to create a calm and neutral climate at the beginning of a mediation. As described here, the strategies assume a typical dispute between two children; they may be adjusted if more children are involved.

Neutral position. Position yourself between the children, on their level. This position helps you give equal attention to both children, making it easier to make good eye contact, to touch gently, or to physically intervene if it is necessary. This position also makes it easier to hold any objects that are part of the conflict (see "Neutralizing Objects in Dispute," p. 76). Since this in-between position communicates that you are a partner in the negotiation, it should be used whenever possible. Sometimes, however, it may be necessary to comfort a child in your lap or to restrain a child who is expressing feelings physically and cannot stop. If you cannot place yourself between children, it is important to use other strategies to communicate neutrality. These might include leaning toward the child not being held, making very steady eye contact, and giving plenty of speaking time to that child. As the child you are holding becomes calm, you may even shift to a more neutral place by repositioning yourself between children.

Comforting gestures. Once you are on the children's level, gentle, non-intrusive contact communicates in a very concrete way that you are there to give support and comfort, not to take over and solve the problem for them. When appropriate, you can convey reassurance by gently reaching out to each child, for example, putting your arms around both children, placing a hand on each child's shoulder, or even holding one of each child's hands. When you reach out to children, watch closely for their response. If children withdraw from your touch, respect these feelings by staying close but not touching. It is important to be sensitive to personal or cultural factors that may affect children's response to touching.

Comforting physical gestures at this point help to focus children's attention on the transition to a cooperative discussion. If there is an object in dispute, it may be necessary to initially place your hands on the object as you tell the children that you would like to hold it until the problem is worked out.

Eye contact. For effective mediation, be prepared to offer steady eye contact to the children. This tells them concretely that you are really listening.

Children may or may not make full eye contact in return. This is okay! Individual or cultural factors may affect children's response to steady eye contact, and these preferences should be respected. Children can listen without making eye contact. Often adults insist that children look at them; some adults may even grasp a child's chin and turn the child's face to theirs. This will not help the problem-solving process. Such physical intervention communicates that the adult is directing the situation, and children may consequently become more passive. A more effective way of gaining children's attention is to stay in a neutral, in-between position, gently reaching out to each child, offering eye contact, and speaking in a calm tone of voice.

Tone of voice. Frequently, the beginning of a conflict can be very loud and full of emotion. The challenge for the mediator is to use a voice level and tone that is loud enough to be heard without being scary. If children's voices are loud, briefly speak just above their level, using only one or two words (such as "STOP" and the children's names) while intervening physically with gentle restraint, or with your hands on an object in dispute. As the children become quieter, your voice can reflect and encourage this by quieting as well.

If children are not loud at the outset, a calm voice communicates neutrality and a willingness to support the children in staying in charge of the problem. Be mindful of your tone of voice; if your voice is sharp or loud, it may seem domineering or shaming to children. This may derail a respectful problem-solving process.

Facial expression. What you show on your face is another important factor in how you convey your support to children. If a child is upset, it is important for your facial expression to reflect the concern you feel as well as the sadness or anger the child feels. To do this, make an effort to be fully "present"; in other words, focus your thoughts, feelings, and full attention on the problem at hand. If your facial expressions reflect some of the intensity of what is happening for the child, this can be very comforting because it communicates that you understand the child's feelings. This gives the child the reassurance needed to feel safe in fully expressing any feelings and in engaging in the negotiation.

> "One rule of thumb used in communications research is that 90% or more of an emotional message is nonverbal. And such messages—anxiety in someone's tone of voice, irritation in the quickness of a gesture—are almost always taken in unconsciously, without paying specific attention to the nature of the message, but simply tacitly receiving it and responding."
>
> —*Daniel Goleman (1995, p. 97)*

To summarize, the first step in problem solving involves preparation and perspective-setting. When a conflict begins, obstacles to problem solving may arise due to our concern over children's physical impulses, our own habitual ways of reacting to conflict, and/or our leftover feelings from past experiences. To counter these problems, we can examine our own reactions, inwardly assume a positive, neutral stance, and use a soft voice and gentle body language to calm and reassure ourselves as well as children. The next step in problem solving, *acknowledge children's feelings,* can now begin.

Step 2: Acknowledging Feelings— What Is It?

To acknowledge means "to express recognition of or to report the receipt of" (*American Heritage Dictionary,* 1985, p. 75). To acknowledge feelings means to say and reflect what we see by describing and showing, both verbally and non-verbally, the feelings we think the child is experiencing. When we describe or label a feeling for a child who is using harmful actions or words, the child realizes that we have received and understood the feelings. It may help to imagine this feeling expression as a ball that the child is trying to throw to us. When we have sensitively acknowledged the feeling, we have "caught the ball," and the child can stop trying to "throw" it. Children are often able to describe the concrete details of their problems, but find it much harder to express their emotions. When we label their feelings for them, showing empathy with our tone of voice and facial

Acknowledging feelings is like catching a ball.

expression, we communicate that their feelings are accepted and understood. Once feelings have been acknowledged, or received, the child becomes more aware of those feelings, and better able to use appropriate words to describe similar feelings in the future.

Understanding how children express their emotions

"I hate you! You can't come to my birthday party!" "You're a stupid dummy and my brother is going to beat you up! He's really strong with big muscles!" "This is a dumb school and I'm not ever coming here again!" Emotional exclamations like these are commonly heard from young children who are involved in disputes. An understanding of why they use such negative and dramatic language can help us carry out step 2 with sensitivity. The child development theories of Jean Piaget (Piaget & Inhelder, 1966/2000) suggest that this kind of language results from young children's concrete understanding of the world. According to Piaget, young children (aged 3–7 years) are in the "preoperational" stage of development. This means that they base their understanding of

To acknowledge feelings means to say and reflect what we see by describing and showing, both verbally and non-verbally, the feelings we think the child is experiencing.

Feelings are the foundation on which learning takes place, which means that being emotionally literate is as important as reading and math.

the world on obvious physical characteristics, making the concrete details of the world enormously important in their eyes. Thus it makes sense they would be physically active and/or use physical language to express their feelings. For example, if Hillary is very angry but is unable to name the feelings she is experiencing, loudly shouting "I want it!" and following this with a punch communicates her feelings very clearly. Exclamations like "You can't ever come to my birthday and you're not my friend!" "I'm going to break this house down and kick everything!" and "You can't ever play with my Barbie dolls again!" express deep hurt, anger, and frustration in a very literal way. Such verbal outbursts give specific, physical shape to feelings.

The adult's response: Communicating that feelings are understood

The aggressiveness and intensity of children's expressions can be startling to adults. The challenge is to find a constructive and helpful way to respond so that children learn to control their hurtful impulses while also learning how to express emotions safely. When children express feelings in very physical terms, they need adults to acknowledge and reframe these expressions using feeling words. By responding with a name for the feelings, *not* a question, we communicate understanding and acceptance. Questions address thoughts, not feelings. If we say, to a crying child, "Are you feeling sad?" we are not giving clear recognition to what is obvious. Instead, we are asking the child to *think* about the feeling. By contrast, saying sympathetically "You're feeling really sad," clearly tells the child that we understand the feeling. When we respond in this way, children experience support and respect for their feelings, while learning the names of feelings. Once children's emotions have subsided, questions about *what happened* are appropriate and necessary.

It is curious that when adults introduce new objects to children, they always tell them the name of the object; yet when children experience strong emotions, adults rarely label the feelings for the child. This may be because adults are anxious to

Stan: How the Ability to Express Feelings in Words Develops

It is vital for adults to label children's feelings from birth on. Hearing a wide range of emotions named in a variety of situations helps children begin to use feeling words themselves. These true stories of Stan's development illustrate his stages of growth and the supporting interactions. (All of these stories are told from memory by his parents.)

▲ **At 3 months,** Stan screams when his mother gently positions him on the diaper changing table. She reassures him gently, "You're feeling really upset, Stan. You don't want to have your diaper changed. I know you're feeling upset. I'll be as quick and gentle as I can." She continues to talk to him soothingly. Stan does not yet understand her words. But his mother's tone is calming, and he *will* learn the meaning of the words as his feelings, happy and mad, are described in words every day.

▲ **At 10 months,** Stan begins to cry at the sound of loud thunder and lightening. He runs to his father, who holds him tightly, calmly telling him, "You're feeling really frightened, Stan. That's thunder. It's very loud and you're feeling very frightened." He clings to him until it passes. Each time Stan experiences fright, over thunder, airplanes, or other loud noises, his feelings are acknowledged in this way.

▲ **At 14 months,** Stan is startled by toast suddenly popping up in the toaster. He toddles quickly to his mom, grabs her leg,

"I happy, Daddy," Stan says.

and says, "Frightened." This is the very first time Stan himself has used a feeling word. His mother kneels down and reassures him, "You're feeling frightened, Stan. The toast popping frightened you." Inwardly, however, she is also delighted that Stan is learning to express his own feelings in words.

▲ **At 16 months,** Stan's feelings have been acknowledged on numerous occasions. In addition, challenging situations such as conflicts with friends, difficulties with toys, and other emotional experiences are consistently identified as "problems," and then, if needed, problem solving begins. One morning Stan's mom has had some sad news. Stan enters the kitchen and sees tears running down his mother's cheeks. He moves close to her and says quietly, "Mama. Sad. Problem." Stan's mom smiles, then cries even more, moved by Stan's speaking to her so sensitively.

▲ **At 22 months,** Stan is riding on the back of his dad's bicycle. After riding a good distance, his dad gets off to talk with Stan. "How are you doing, Stan? I'm feeling worried this is getting boring for you." "I happy, Daddy," Stan quickly replies. Expressing feelings with words and identifying problems have become part of Stan's everyday language.

avoid conflict ("Uh-oh, Chris looks like he wants that ball all to himself—here comes trouble!") or because they are afraid that they will name the wrong feeling. However, for children to acquire useful emotional skills, they need to know the names of feelings (see "Stan," opposite). As children's language abilities mature, they will correct an adult who has mislabeled their feelings. ("I'm not sad. "I'm mad!") If the adult is really unsure of what the child is feeling, acknowledging by saying "You're really upset!" can be helpful.

Children (and adults, too!) can be greatly helped by such acknowledgments when strong feelings overwhelm their ability to think. The diagram, below, demonstrates this visually. Most of the time, children move through their days with their thoughts and feelings in balance (1). But crises and conflicts are part of everyday life and sometimes they overwhelm children's thinking abilities. At these times, they are "flooded" with feeling, unable to think easily (2). If they are fortunate enough to have someone to acknowledge their feelings, accepting them as important, they can "empty out" those emotions (3). Once they have fully expressed their emotions, they can let go of them and their thoughts and feelings can return to a functional balance. It becomes possible for them to think *and* feel once again (4).

For some adults, acknowledging children's feelings may initially feel awkward—adults may feel they are simply stating the obvious. It can be a bit uncomfortable at first to interact in new ways, but this approach usually becomes more comfortable when adults see that children feel supported by it. Adults who combine respectful body language with sensitive responses

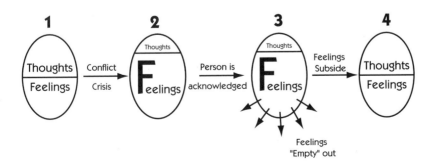

"Remember, the child is dependent on others (usually his parents or caregivers) to help him elaborate a rich world of connections between ideas and wishes. To the degree that caregivers accurately understand the child's communications and elaborate on them in the direction the child is moving, the child's internal world keeps expanding, forming an even more logical and refined network of thoughts and images that gives structure and meaning to his inner life."

—*Stanley Greenspan (1997, p. 99)*

will observe children becoming emotionally literate people who know the language of feelings and can express them in constructive ways.

The power of acknowledging feelings

Acknowledging feelings is a simple technique that has enormous impact, not only at conflict times but during all kinds of life situations. Following are two true classroom stories that illustrate the effects of acknowledging feelings. Although the first story does not describe a conflict situation, it is included here because it illustrates so dramatically the power of this technique. Kristy, the preschooler in the story, suffered from chronic stress due to challenging life circumstances. Kristy's home situation could not be altered, but in this incident the emotional landscape of her day was reshaped, however briefly, giving her some relief from the stress that at times paralyzed her.

Kristy: Overwhelmed by sad feelings

Kristy came to school each day and wept. She wept for large parts of the day. Her teachers knew that her home life was unstable and, for the time being, unchangeable. At school they had tried to console her by sitting with her and asking questions: "Are you sad, Kristy?" "Why are you crying?" "Wouldn't you like to play?" "What can we do to help you feel happy?" Kristy didn't respond to this and her sadness continued for weeks, dominating most of her time at school.

One day Rachael, an early childhood mediation trainer, came to the school as a consultant. She had been asked to observe the teachers and children throughout their daily routine. Very quickly she became painfully aware of Kristy's sadness. At the end of the day, most of the children had left and Rachael talked to Lynn, one of Kristy's teachers, about Kristy's needs. Lynn described their efforts to console Kristy by asking questions about her sadness. She admitted that it was not working at all and asked Rachael for help. Rachael asked to speak to Kristy, recommending that Lynn be available to give back-up support if needed. Lynn agreed.

Kristy sat alone in the book area, crying softly by herself as Rachael approached and sat down very close to her. Very gently and with sadness in her voice and face, Rachael told Kristy, "You're feeling really sad." Kristy began to cry louder. "You're feeling really, really sad," Rachael said. Kristy began to cry uncontrollably. Her whole body began to tremble and Rachael put her arm around her. "You're so sad that your whole body is trembling." Kristy, between sobs, called out for Lynn who came to her. Kristy got on Lynn's lap, still crying loudly, large tears rolling steadily down her reddened cheeks. Rachael whispered to Lynn, "Tell her, 'I see you're feeling really sad.' Keep telling her." Slowly, uncomfortably, Lynn repeated, "You're sad...you're feeling so sad." At first Lynn's words sounded flat and mechanical, but as Lynn continued to tell Kristy about the feelings she was seeing, Kristy curled in closer to her. Kristy continued to cry, but stopped trembling. Lynn repeated the same words, reflecting more of Kristy's sadness in her voice tone and her face as she said, "You're feeling really sad."

Kristy's crying quieted. After a few minutes it stopped. She sat in Lynn's lap for a few moments longer. Lynn held her and rubbed her back. Kristy began to look around the room. Nearby, Rajiv was playing with play dough as he waited for his mother. He looked up and noticed that Kristy was watching. He held out a piece of dough to her. Slowly, like someone waking from a long sleep, Kristy slid off Lynn's lap and put out her hand. Rajiv dropped a small ball of green play dough in her hand and Kristy gently closed her fingers around it. Rajiv rolled his play dough on the table. Kristy, still in slow motion, rolled hers. Lynn and Rachael watched silently as she played, in awe of the change in Kristy and the power of connecting with another person's feelings. Quietly Lynn told Rachael, "This is the first time I've seen Kristy play all year."

Through Lynn's acknowledging words, Kristy was released from her sadness—not forever, but for the time being. The source of her sadness was still there and would require more attention from the teachers in the days that followed. But at this moment at least, Kristy knew that someone else recognized her sadness and that it was safe to fully express it; she was not suffering alone. Kristy experienced this because the adults took a few simple actions: Rachael, and then Lynn, showed with their voice tones and expressions that they understood Kristy's emotions; they simply *made statements* about what they thought she was feeling instead of *asking questions* about those feelings.

◆

Intense feelings like those Kristy experienced can absorb all of children's capabilities, making them unable to think or respond. To a child in this state, adult questions offer no comfort, no empathy; the child feels even more miserable because the older, wiser adult does not understand what she is feeling. On the other hand, each day that the child's feelings are shared and understood by an adult whose every expression—face, voice tone, comforting gestures, *and* words—reflects this understanding, on that day, the child can experience some relief. For a time at least, someone else is helping her carry the heavy burden of sadness. At these times, the child can move on—to play and perhaps experience life beyond the sadness.

Other occasions for acknowledging feelings

The story of Kristy is a very dramatic example of the impact of acknowledging feelings. However, most of the occasions when adults acknowledge children's feelings are of a simpler, less intense nature. For example, a child might run excitedly to the teacher, calling out, "Look, look, I made a picture!" Wanting to support the child without evaluating the creation, the teacher might respond, "You are really happy with this picture! Tell me about it." Or, a child might shout to an adult on the playground, "Look at me, look at me!" as she pumps the swing, to which the adult might respond enthusiastically, "Wow, you did it! You're pumping so high! You worked really hard at this and now you're doing it!"

In situations like these, the adult uses acknowledgment as a way of affirming children's feelings of excitement or pride. In conflict situations, acknowledging feelings plays a somewhat different role: it allows children to release intense feelings and move on to the cognitive work of problem solving. The following story of a conflict in my classroom illustrates how ineffective questions about feelings can be and how the simple technique of acknowledging feelings can play a pivotal role in helping children resolve a dispute. My acknowledging words are underlined throughout the story.

Alan: "Just let nobody have a turn!"

At recall (a part of our daily routine when children share their experiences) I hand out felt pieces shaped like various facial features to the children in my small group. This is part of a recall game in which the children add their felt features to a blank felt face as they individually tell what they did during work time. The recalling begins with everyone picking a felt piece.

Alan:	Hey, I wanted a white piece!! I wanted to make an eye. (*I notice that Alan has a small black circle and that both Lakisha and Evan have white pieces.*)
Betsy:	You really wanted to do an eye. So what can we do to solve this? There aren't any other white pieces. (*Holding out the remaining pieces*) Do you want any of these pieces?
Alan:	Nooo. (*Slumps in the chair.*)
Betsy:	You're really frustrated. So what are we going to do to solve this, Alan?
Alan:	Just let **nobody** have a turn!
Betsy:	I can see you're very upset about this. (*Pauses.*) You think that nobody should have a turn. Hmmm. If nobody has a turn, how are we going to get recall finished so we can have our snack? (*Alan doesn't respond.*)

Douglas: Well…well…Alan called me…well, he…last night he called me a name and…and he throwed a block at me. *(Douglas shows no emotion as he tells this, but something has triggered his memory of a recent conflict he had with Alan.)*

Betsy: How did you feel about that, Douglas?

Douglas: *(Ignoring the question)* He throwed a Bristle Block at me…and banged them.

Douglas's description of yesterday's unresolved conflict suddenly seemed important. His story, told in the midst of another conflict, meant he still had concerns about it. However, my questions had not helped him with those feelings. This was feedback for me. As mediators, we do not always know which responses will be the most useful. Children's actions and words (or their silence) give us a continuous flow of information about what is working and what isn't. To mediate effectively, we must be willing to take in that feedback and adapt our responses. I decided to acknowledge what I thought Douglas might be feeling, even though now, a day later, it was unclear. As a result, both boys fully described what happened with remarkable honesty.

Betsy: <u>You were upset about that,</u> Douglas.

Douglas: *(Sadly)* Yeah.

Alan: I was throwing everything…'cuz he was calling names at me.

Betsy: <u>You were feeling upset too,</u> Alan, and it sounds like you were both calling names. *(Alan nods.)*

Douglas: *(Smiles.)* I said "stupid Alan." Now he called me stupid, too.

Betsy: So if somebody calls you a name, Douglas, what can you do?

Douglas: Well, he just shoots bullets at me…and I shoot my gun at him.

Betsy: *(Gently)* Did that work—did that solve it?

Douglas: No.

Betsy: So if you don't like people calling you names, what can you do so they will stop, Douglas?

Douglas: Say "Don't call names."

Betsy: Say "Don't call me names"?

Douglas: *(Nods yes.)*

Betsy: And Alan you could say that too if you don't like it? *(Alan nods.)*

Lakisha: *(Enthusiastically)* Here, Alan, you can have my white piece!

Alan: Thanks! *(Looking pleased, he straightens up in his chair.)*

Betsy: You solved Alan's problem, Lakisha! *(Lakisha smiles with pleasure.)*

Everyone looks ready to move on. With Alan's initial problem of the white piece solved, the group continues with recall time. Still unsure that the name-calling issue has been solved, I decide to speak to my teaching partner about doing a problem-solving discussion the next day at small-group time. Name-calling has been a recurring issue in the classroom and it seems that talking about it as a group may be useful. This results in a very productive small-group discussion, held the next day. [The use of small-group discussion for such recurring problems is explored in Chapter 6.]

◆

Children express feelings with shouting and name-calling because they are still learning how to identify feelings and how to express them constructively. By recognizing and accepting their feelings, we can help children become self-aware and support them in moving on from hurtful words and actions to an honest rendering of what happened. In the next section we describe strategies for acknowledging feelings.

Whether we are working with preschoolers or school-aged children (as here), children's actions and words (or their silence) give us a continuous flow of information about what is working and what isn't.

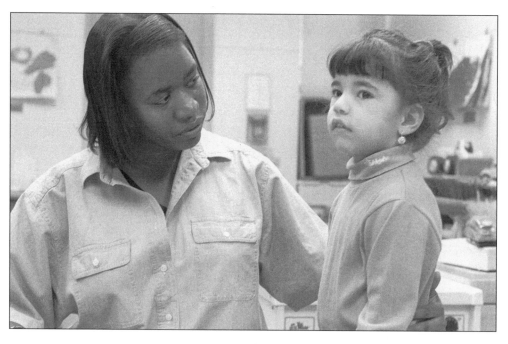

Simple recognition and acceptance of children's feelings helps them become self-aware and supports them in moving on from hurtful words and actions to an honest rendering of what happened.

Strategies for Acknowledging Feelings

Reframing children's strong feeling words

When children are very upset, they often express their feelings in very forceful ways. If we take their aggressive-sounding statements literally, we will misunderstand their feeling messages and "miss the ball." If children feel misunderstood, their feelings and hurtful actions may intensify *or* they may withdraw and give up. Thus it is important for us to quickly respond with body language and words that show we understand. To do this we reframe what children say and do while physically stopping their unsafe or destructive actions. *Reframing* means putting children's intense verbal and physical expressions into more specific and appropriate language, removing the original threats, accusations, or judgments about people and stopping and setting limits on any aggressive behavior. Reframing helps to separate people from problems by clearly stating needs and wants only. After children's feelings have calmed, problem solving can continue. The following examples illustrate the use of reframing and acknowledgment with children who are at different levels in their ability to express feelings. The examples illustrate only steps 1 *(approach calmly, stopping any hurtful actions)* and 2 *(acknowledge children's feelings).*

- A child wants a truck that another child is playing with. She grabs the truck away and says, "I hate you! You can't come to my birthday party, you stupid dummy!"

  Adult response: The adult places himself between the children, gently restraining the child who is grabbing, and says, "Stop. You're feeling really angry that you can't have a turn with the truck. Grabbing the truck is not okay. I know you're really angry and you want a turn with it." As the child calms, the adult begins a discussion about taking turns with the truck: "Tell me what happened…."

- A child wants to go out on a rainy day but his teacher says it's too wet. The child says to the adult, "I hate you! You'd better let me go out or my big brother is going to beat you up! He's really strong with big muscles!" The child pushes the adult.

  Adult response: "You're feeling very upset that you can't go outside. Name-calling and pushing must stop. I know that you are very upset. Let's talk about this problem." The name-calling and pushing stop, and discussion begins about what the child wanted to do outside.

Strategies for Acknowledging Feelings

- **State feelings concretely:** ("You are feeling very upset." "I can see you are really, really angry.") Do not ask questions about feelings.

- **Reframe children's hurtful words as you acknowledge feelings** (If Ofelia has called Juan a "stupid dummy," say to Ofelia: "You are feeling very angry with Juan. It's not okay to call people names when you are upset. I know you are very angry.")

- **If necessary state a limit as part of your acknowledging statement.** ("Mun, stop hitting. You are feeling very angry because David has the truck and you want it. It's not okay to hit. I know you really want the truck.")

- **Let children know you need to hold any objects in dispute** until an agreement is reached ("I need to hold this while we talk.")

- **Watch for signs that children have fully expressed their feelings** (body relaxes, crying stops, voice tones become lower and softer, children's actions or words change); then move on with problem solving.

- **If necessary, acknowledge feelings throughout the problem-solving discussion.** If a child refuses every solution offered with a loud "no," this is a clear indicator he or she is still upset and feelings need to be acknowledged again.

- A child, when not chosen to pick the book at story time, begins to cry and says to her teacher, "This is a dumb school and I'm never ever coming here again!"

    Adult response: "You're feeling very frustrated that you didn't get to choose the book and you're feeling angry at me." The child stops crying; a discussion begins about the book choice and when the child will get to choose the book.

- A child grabs a doll out of the arms of another child who screams loudly and hits the child on the back.

    Adult response: "Hitting must stop. You're feeling really angry at her." The child begins to cry sadly, and tells the adult, "Yeah, she took my doll." Together, with the other child, they problem-solve.

- A 4-year-old child (who is beginning to be aware of and able to name feelings but who still needs to attach concrete expressions to those feelings) says, "I'm angry as a cockroach as big as this house!" (Yes, a child really said this!)

    Adult response: (The child's words are not hurtful to anyone and consequently do not need reframing as shown in the previous examples.) "Wow, your anger is as big as a cockroach and this house! You're feeling very, very angry. Your anger is sooo big." The child then repeats that he is angry, without cockroach references, and begins to describe what is happening that is upsetting him.

When young children are expressing strong feelings, they often use concrete, physical language (about big houses, mean brothers, and birthday parties, for example) to get across the full force of their feelings. Such details are their unconscious way of "beefing up" their feeling messages.

Avoiding getting derailed by children's strong feelings

In situations like these, where children's actions and words are quite intense, we may be tempted to put children in time-out or tell them to "calm down and be nice." Or, we may try to discuss specific details they have mentioned in their angry outbursts. However, we do not need to comment on the details of birthday party rejections, muscular brothers, or dumb schools to communicate our understanding of the children's feelings. Children's bold and colorful language expresses the intensity of their emotions in very concrete (and creative!) ways, but their specific words are usually not related to the actual problem. Young children use such details to get across the full force of their feelings. Such phrases are their unconscious way of "beefing up" their feeling message. However, if we respond by discussing party invitations, the kindness of brothers, the virtues of schools, and the absurdity of house-sized cockroaches, we risk getting mired in semantic arguments that miss the point. As a result, the children will not feel that their emotions have been understood. A sim-

Birthday parties are powerful events for young children, so it's not surprising that they express their strong feelings in terms of these important events: "You can't come to my birthday party!"

ple statement describing what we see ("You're feeling *so* upset!") is a better way to "catch the ball" and let children know we understand.

Responding to "I hate you, you're not my friend"

Another common feeling message heard from children is "I hate you, you're not my friend." Often adults try to correct children by saying things like "Of course John is your friend. You play together every day." This kind of response may only intensify the problem. From the child's viewpoint, the adult is not only refusing to receive the anger message but also arguing that the message is not true. In other words, the adult has "missed the ball" and the child must now try harder to "throw it." To get the message across, the child must now insist that the statement is true, responding "I do too hate him...hate, hate, hate! I'm never, ever going to play with him again!!" For children, anger or sadness and "You're not my friend" often mean the same thing. If we respond by reframing such messages into acceptable language that names wants, needs, or feelings (Adult: "You are very angry at her!" or "You really want to play alone right now!"), children can usually express themselves fully, their feelings will subside rather than intensify, and the offending behavior will stop.

Hurtful behavior: Setting limits

Before and during the initial two steps in problem solving, children may show the intensity of their feelings by name-calling, pushing, hitting, grabbing, and/or biting. Adults must clearly and firmly stop these actions while acknowledging feelings and listening for information about the conflict at hand. Doing all this at once requires quick thinking and action. To de-escalate physical conflict, we may find it helpful to position ourselves between children, holding their hands and/or gently placing children on our laps while we simultaneously state limits and acknowledge feelings. For example, if Jesse has just said, "You're a stupid idiot!" and is hitting Leela, we may intervene by kneeling in front of Jesse, holding his hands, and saying firmly "Name-calling and hitting must stop. I know that you're very, very angry. It's okay to be angry. It's not okay to name-call and hit." And, when Jesse stops, we would add, "Let's talk about what is happening." In this example, the mediator, in quick sequence, stops the hurt, acknowledges feelings, sets limits, and begins the problem-solving dialogue. When conflicts break out, all this can and should be accomplished as quickly and calmly as possible to insure children's safety and reassure children that their feelings are recognized.

Adults must be ready to clearly and firmly stop hurtful actions while acknowledging feelings and listening for information. Doing all this at once requires quick thinking and action.

Limit-setting statements should be simple, clear, and specific. Mediators should avoid statements like "Be nice" or "Let's all be friends." Such comments are vague and miss the source of the problem. Children need to know what specific actions are being discouraged, with the offending action named clearly. ("Hitting must stop" is clearer than "You must stop.") However, conflict interventions can do much more than stop hurtful behaviors. Punishment systems, while they may succeed in stopping hurtful behavior temporarily, do not help children learn new skills. Consequently, children who are punished are likely to respond hurtfully the next time, or they may withdraw, repressing strong emotions that can erupt later. Clear limit-setting, by calm, neutral adults, sets the stage for acceptance of feelings, mutual solutions, new skills, and long-term change.

Neutralizing objects in dispute

When children are fighting over an object, it is usually very difficult for them to discuss possible solutions as long as one of the children is holding the object. If one child has possession of a disputed toy, that child often has little reason to be concerned about the problem. And, without possession, the other child may not feel hopeful about getting a turn with the toy. Because young children think concretely, they need to see the disputed object in neutral hands as they are discussing it. Thus the mediator needs to hold the object until the dispute is settled, keeping it *within view* to maintain the children's interest in the possibility of getting a turn. For example, during the conflict of Lakisha and Seth discussed in Chapter 4 (pp. 125-28) both children wanted to use the swing. While we talked out the problem, I held the disputed swing. Since the swing was in neutral hands, the children could focus on the negotiation, rather than the swing itself.

Conflict mediation is a process of balancing power or control. As mediators, we need to "neutralize" any object in dispute by *telling* the children we will hold it until the problem has been solved. (If we *ask* for the object, children may say no.) First the mediator says, "I am going to hold this until we've solved the problem." It may also be necessary to reassure children by adding "We're going to talk about ways you can both have a turn." Then, with the children's agreement, the mediator gently takes the object and holds it in view. If one or both children will not agree to release the object, as it is likely to happen with toddlers, the mediator and the children can all hold it together, agreeing to hold it gently as the problem solving continues.

Holding the object for children stabilizes and refocuses the problem solving. When children have agreed upon a plan, the mediator restates the solution and releases the toy to one of the children. This process of placing disputed objects in safe and neutral custody until a solution is found gives both children an equal measure of control in the situation, motivating them to stay with the discussion. The children are now partners in finding a solution, and as a result, the negotiations are likely to move along much more quickly.

As mediators, we need to "neutralize" any object in dispute by telling the children we will hold it until the problem has been solved. Here Betsy holds the chalk in view of the children.

Watching for signs that feelings are fully expressed

Children express so much of what they feel with their bodies that it is usually quite easy to observe when the "feelings stage" of problem-solving is over. Some signs we can watch for include a change in the pitch, tone, or volume of children's voices, a relaxation of their bodies, and/or a shift to slower or more gentle actions and words. When children are finished with an expression or idea, they will often move on in such an obvious way that there is no missing it. For example, in the story of Bobby and Jerome in Chapter 1 (pp. 32–34), it was easy to see the change that occurred as soon as I named their feelings. Bobby's voice tone shifted from sad to frustrated, he straightened his body, took a deep breath, and relaxed. Jerome, whose back had stiffened with frustration, also relaxed, and he very quickly suggested a way to share the computer that was agreeable to Bobby.

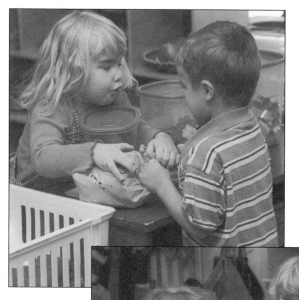

If one or both children will not agree to release a disputed object, the mediator and the children can all hold it together, agreeing to hold it gently as the problem solving continues. This strategy is often necessary with toddlers or younger preschoolers.

Sometimes, however, children's feelings are not completely resolved, even when feelings have been acknowledged (step 2) and children have begun to discuss solutions. In such cases, a current of feeling continues to run through a conflict mediation, and these feelings must be named whenever they surface or they may interfere with children's ability to come to an agreement. If children vehemently refuse all solutions, this is a sign that they are still upset. Sometimes the adult will need to name children's feelings several times in the course of a mediation. The teacher did this repeatedly in the incident with Lakisha, Alan, and Douglas in the "He's shooting" story told in the next section. (The teacher's words and actions throughout this conflict are highlighted on p. 84.)

These repeated acknowledgments allow the solution-seeking process to succeed. It is hard for children to reach a mutual decision if one child is still feeling angry or hurt. When we observe children continuing to name-call, hit, growl, or make fierce faces, we can assume they are still upset. The adult can gently but firmly respond: "Jack, it's not okay to call him a dorkhead. You do seem angry still. It is okay to tell us what you're angry about." Such statements, which name feelings while clearly setting limits, help children know exactly which actions need to stop *and* that their feelings have been heard. The search for a solution can then continue.

Children who express emotions intensely and often

In every classroom there are children who become very emotional, even hysterical, over difficulties other children respond to with little or no emotion. Three children from my classroom—Lakisha, Alan, and Douglas—often became very upset over "little things"—someone brushing against them, a puzzle that wouldn't fit together, a snack that crumbled. (These children were introduced in the story "Just let nobody have a turn," pp. 67–69.) Lakisha, Alan, and Douglas were not always so emotional, however. Much of the time they played happily. However, when they did experience frustration, anger, or sadness, they expressed it very intensely.

It can be challenging for us as teachers and parents to respond to children's frequent emotional outbursts—we may wonder if their strong feelings come from a "bottomless pit." However, in an environment where feelings, no matter how chronic, are named and accepted, children become more and more capable of expressing emotion without becoming hysterical. This was true of Lakisha, Alan, and Douglas; over time, their hurtful actions and words were gradually replaced by constructive dialogue and resolutions. As all three children became more verbally expressive, their difficult behaviors became less frequent: Lakisha became less tearful, Douglas screamed less, and Alan did less "shooting"—the behavior that led to the conflict in the following story.

Lakisha, Douglas, and Alan: "He's shooting at us!"

One morning, 3-week-old bunnies had been visiting the preschool. The children had held them gently in their laps, stroking their soft, fluffy fur. Some of the bunnies had been put back in the basket where they had immediately curled up together and gone to sleep. Lakisha and Douglas began to play "mommy and daddy bunny," crawling about on all fours, returning to check on the bunnies, lifting the blanket, patting them gently, tucking them in, and crawling away again.

At 10 o'clock the baby bunnies were taken home by a parent. Lakisha and Douglas, however, were still playing bunny parents. They crawled into the Block Area where Alan was sitting inside a block structure. He had a "gun" (a long block), and he began to shoot at them with it. Lakisha left the area crying in shrieks and Douglas began screaming very loudly at Alan. My co-teacher, Merrilee, intercepted Lakisha as she crossed the room. Putting her arm around Lakisha, she listened as she walked with Lakisha back to the Block Area. Lakisha tried hard to tell her what was happening.

"He's shooting at us and...." Her words became unintelligible sobs.

"Hmmm," Merrilee responded as she continued to hold Lakisha's shoulders gently.

As Merrilee and Lakisha came into Alan's view, he put his "gun" down and yelled, "I already know! I already know!"

Merrilee described the situation for Lakisha: "Alan did something that upset you...that made you feel sad."

Lakisha, speaking more clearly, answered, " Yeah, it made me **angry** and upset."

"Angry and upset," Merrilee repeated.

Alan pointed his block at them and made shooting noises through puckered lips.

Douglas screamed at him, "No! Noooo!"

Merrilee knelt by Douglas just a couple of feet from where Alan sat in his block structure. Lakisha moved in close to her. Merrilee turned to give Douglas her full attention, and he told her, "He's shooting our bunnies."

Alan quickly responded, "Well, I'm not going to stop! He kept yelling at me."

Merrilee acknowledged Alan by stating, "You're feeling upset, Alan. You don't like the yelling." Alan shook his head no and put his block down.

Lakisha answered, "Well, I don't like to get shot at!"

Douglas added softly, "And he kept doing it."

"Hmmm," Merrilee responded, acknowledging all of them. For a few seconds everyone was quiet.

"Well, well...I want to tell you something...," Lakisha said to get everyone's attention. "If...if you stop shooting, we'll stop yelling."

"Yeah!" Douglas added emphatically.

"But I want to be by myself here," Alan told them.

"So the problem is, you really want to be by yourself and that's why you were shooting," Merrilee restated.

Alan nodded, "I won't [shoot] if they stop yelling."

Merrilee, knowing that English was a second language for Douglas, encouraged him to say what he was feeling, "Douglas, do you want to tell...you were feeling really strongly about something."

She put her hand gently on his back as he began to speak. "Yeah, I was 'cuz...yeah, 'cuz he was shooting at us out there," Douglas said.

As she began to walk away, Lakisha quickly suggested, "So let's move out to Art and draw a picture of both of us being bunnies. Okay, Douglas? Let's draw a picture."

Douglas started to answer: "No, let's..." but he saw that she was gone and he followed.

Merrilee moved closer to Alan, staying to support him as he watched Douglas and Lakisha leave. "Is this problem solved for you, Alan?" she asked. He nodded yes. Merrillee continued, "It worked when you told them you wanted to be alone. When you were shooting, they didn't know what you were upset about. I'm glad you told them." Alan listened and then began to work on his structure. Feeling that Alan was ready to be alone again, Merrilee followed Douglas and Lakisha to the Art Area. They had gotten out paper and markers and were drawing. She sat down next to them and asked, "Lakisha and Douglas, is this problem with Alan all solved for you now?"

Lakisha answered, "Yeah, we didn't want him to shoot us."

Merrilee repeated, "You didn't want him to shoot you."
Douglas added, "Yeah, 'cuz we were bunnies."
"And you didn't like that shooting and you told him.
Telling him solved the problem. He listened to you." Lakisha
and Douglas nodded and turned their focus to drawing.
Merrilee watched for a bit until she felt sure they had noth-
ing more to say. They began to chat about their drawings
and she moved on.

◆

Children learn to problem-solve in stages, just as they
learn to walk, to draw, and to read in stages. The adult's role
is to support children at each stage, encouraging their problem-solving *efforts* by being fully "present," using body language to communicate support, and using active listening and
close observation to stay in touch with children's needs and
wants. As children try to work out their difficulties, their first
efforts to say what is wrong or how they feel may be muddled
and confused. It's a bit like watching a child scribble, knowing
that eventually, out of the scribble, a unique vision will emerge
that will explain more about who that child is. Likewise, children first express their feelings and thoughts with some difficulty. Our acceptance and respect for these first attempts are
the key to encouraging children's continued efforts. (See the
chart in Chapter 4, p. 154, for a summary of the typical stages
in the development of problem solving and strategies for the
adult to use at each stage.)

The "He's shooting" story shows all three children at a tran-
sitional time in the development of their problem-solving skills,
when they were just discovering that they could resolve disputes
in a new way. With Merrilee's help they could express their feelings and needs in words, but with some effort.

Lakisha, had been new to the program that year. After two
short months of having her feelings acknowledged many times,
she was now quite capable of naming her feelings (as when she
said, about the shooting, "It made me *angry* and upset"). For
Lakisha at this time, getting through the first, most emotional part
of a conflict mediation was the biggest challenge. This is true for

many children learning to problem-solve; solutions sometimes come quite easily after this "feeling work" is done. This was what happened with the problem of Alan's "shooting": once Lakisha was helped to say how she felt about it, she immediately saw the solution ("If you stop shooting, we'll stop yelling").

Douglas, also 4 years old, was at about the same stage in the development of his problem-solving skills as Lakisha. Although he was still struggling with English (his second language) at the time of this incident, he had learned to trust the problem-solving process and now would usually stay engaged in working things out. Like Lakisha, Douglas most needed support in the "feeling steps" of problem solving, but was usually quite capable of deciding on solutions independently. In this incident, he became quite composed once Merrilee had supported him in fully expressing his feelings. Although he did not participate verbally in Lakisha's decision to start drawing, his actions showed agreement and Merrilee's final check-in helped to verify that the solution was okay with him.

The resolution of the bunny incident showed that Alan, too, was maturing. Alan was also 4 years old. He liked to play alone or with one other child and often appeared to be feeling fearful and anxious. He was very interested in "power play" that included shooting and fighting and was still working at finding new ways to show his feelings. His use of "shooting" in this incident showed that expressing himself in words was still a struggle for him. However, with patient adult support, he could say what he wanted. Thus it was particularly important that Merrilee accepted his first explanation of his problem ("He keeps yelling at me!"), even though in the end he explained the real reason for his anger—that he wanted to be left alone. In the months following this conflict he used his "gun" less and less for expressing himself and he found it more and more satisfying to try to *say* what he needed.

Merrilee's role: Observing, facilitating, acknowledging

In the bunny incident, Merrilee acted as a gentle, observant facilitator, primarily relying on steps 1 and 2 *(approach calmly* and *acknowledge children's feelings)* to support the children's problem solving. This is an effective way to support children at this stage in the development of problem solving, when they are fairly skilled in finding solutions but are still struggling to express feelings constructively. Once children have learned what to expect from mediation, adults may need to give support only with these two steps. At this point, with little adult help, the children can usually negotiate solutions on their own. To highlight Merrilee's facilitating role and her reliance on acknowledging feelings throughout the dialogue, below we list Merrilee's words and actions only from the story. Each of her actions is labeled with the relevant steps.

Merrilee's Role in the Bunny Story

Below are listed Merrilee's **words and actions only** from this story. Note that she does not need to provide support with all the problem-solving steps, and that the steps are not always used in a 1–6 sequence.

- Merrilee listened as she walked with her arm around Lakisha to the Block Area. **(step 1)**

- "Hmmm," Merrilee responded as she continued to hold Lakisha's shoulders gently. **(step 2)**

- Merrilee described the situation for Lakisha: "He did something that upset you…that made you feel sad." **(step 2)**

- "Angry and upset," Merrilee repeated. **(step 2)**

- Merrilee knelt by Douglas, just a couple of feet from where Alan sat in his block structure **(step 1)**. Lakisha moved in close to her. Merrilee turned to give Douglas her full attention as he spoke. **(step 1)**

- Merrilee acknowledged Alan by asking "You don't like the yelling. Hmmm." **(step 2)**

- Merrilee, knowing that English was a second language for Douglas, encouraged him to continue: "Douglas do you want to tell…you were feeling really strongly about something?" She put her hand gently on his back as he began to speak. **(steps 1, 2, and 3)**

- Merrilee moved closer to Alan, staying to support him as he watched Lakisha and Douglas leave. **(step 6)**

- Merrilee said, "Is this problem solved for you, Alan?" He nodded. "It worked when you told them you wanted to be alone. When you were shooting, they didn't know what you were upset about. I'm glad you told them."…"Lakisha and Douglas, is this problem with Alan all solved for you now?" **(step 6)**

- Merrilee repeated to Douglas, "You didn't want him to shoot you." When he replied, she said, "And you didn't like that shooting and you told him." **(step 2)**

- Merrilee continued, "Telling him solved the problem. He listened to you." **(step 6)**

The Effect of Mediation on Social-Emotional Development

As we look back on the stories told in this chapter, the effect of mediation on relationships is another valuable outcome to consider. In each of these stories, children and adults are learning to trust and respect one another. Can the course of children's social-emotional development be affected by experiences in the block area or at the swing set? The answer is an unequivocal yes. Children's social competence is like a cloth whose essential fibers are being woven in these early years. The conflict lessons of our childhood can become the very foundation for how we relate to others, now and in the future. As children negotiate, they are learning to recognize and respect differences among people.

Development of emotional skills as violence prevention

Over time, through many successful problem-solving experiences, children learn that directly expressing their feelings, without physical hurting or verbal threats, is the quickest, most effective way to make their feelings known. As children are learning to do this, adults can help by responding to their young expressions of feeling in respectful, rather than puni-

"Preschoolers' social relationships and capacity for initiative benefit from children's growing ability to talk about their ideas and represent them in play. Using words they know, they can begin to recognize and name their own emotions. 'I'm happy. My daddy's coming home today!' They can also begin to recognize and name the emotions they see in others. 'Betty looks happy. She'll be fun to play with.' 'Sammy's crying. He's sad because he wants his mom, but she has to go to work today.' This emerging ability to identify their own and others' moods and emotions helps young children decide with some success when and how to approach their peers. Along with language, preschoolers' developing social ability and capacity for initiative are also characterized by *intentionality,* a desire for *friendship,* and a struggle to resolve the *conflict between 'me' and 'we.'* As preschoolers gain experience in dealing with these social issues, they exhibit a growing *social competence."*

—Mary Hohmann & David Weikart
(2002, pp. 375–376)

"Much evidence testifies that people who are emotionally adept—who know and manage their feelings well, and who read and deal effectively with other people's feelings—are at an advantage in any domain of life, whether romance and intimate relationships or picking up the unspoken rules that govern success in organizational politics. People with well-developed emotional skills are also more likely to be content and effective in their lives, mastering the habits of mind that foster their own productivity; people who cannot marshal some control over their emotional life fight inner battles that sabotage their ability for focused work and clear thought."

—*Daniel Goleman (1995, p. 36)*

tive, ways. Respect, acceptance, and simple acknowledgment of children's feelings in these early years will help children develop the ability to express feelings appropriately, without violence, as they grow older. Children who experience such responses from adults grow confident in verbally expressing their sadness, pain, and frustration before these feelings intensify and become hurtful. They learn to express feelings with clarity and proportion, controlling their impulses to be hurtful and learning to make choices and to negotiate differences. When a young child's block tower is knocked down, the child may respond by screaming and hitting. With our support, the child can mature from screaming and hitting to "You can't come to my birthday party" and eventually to "I'm angry that you knocked my building down. Don't do it again!" We can assist in this development by recognizing and naming children's most obvious feelings of sadness or anger, as well as their subtler, more complicated feelings.

Once children can say when they are angry, we can also help them identify the feelings that are sometimes beneath the anger. Anger is often an extension of pain, sadness, or frustration, feelings that we can point out to more experienced problem solvers. Through these experiences in hearing feelings named and in naming their own feelings, children are becoming emotionally skilled people who are capable of fully communicating their feelings, nonviolently. These are skills that children will need and use as they build relationships throughout their lives.

With our support, the child can mature from screaming and hitting to "You can't come to my birthday party" and eventually to "I'm angry that you knocked my building down. Don't do it again!" These school-aged children are able to talk over differences calmly and respectfully.

Effects of emotional support on learning

In considering the value of time spent on supporting children's emotional development we must not only consider the long-term benefits of emotional skills but also the role of feelings in the immediate learning process. Strong feelings, whether they be angry, happy, or sad, affect children's ability to concentrate and learn as well as their capacity to form relationships. Strong feelings may either enhance or detract from children's motivation to learn and relate to others.

Children who enter the classroom still upset by events or interactions that occurred at home or in their neighborhood will often have difficulty focusing on the day's tasks. While we may

Two children work out turn-taking with a bunny. Such conflict lessons in childhood become the very foundations for how these children will relate to others, now and in the future.

not know the specifics of what has happened for these children, and while we should not try to be their therapists, we can, simply, be there to accept children's feelings. By offering this support and understanding as children make the transition from home to school, we can help children let go of their feelings and move on with the day. If we observe children who cannot move on from their emotional distress, we can take steps to respond to behaviors that are "red flags" (see Chapter 4, pp. 151-58, for advice on identifying children who need extra support). Children will struggle to be capable learners and friends unless they feel emotionally as well as physically safe with the people and events in their lives. Feelings are the foundation on which learning takes place, which means that being emotionally literate is as important as reading and math.

*In this chapter, we've explored the first two steps in conflict mediation, which support children in expressing feelings. Conflicts among people, whether young and old, involve strong feelings, and these feelings have a healthy and useful function: to signal distress (or joy!) over differences in values, needs, wants, and perspectives. Strong feelings let us know that something is stirring our passions, calling in question our beliefs, or perhaps endangering our very being. Such feelings are too important to ignore; their exploration can lead us to greater knowledge of the world and ourselves.*

As mediators in children's conflicts, we have an opportunity to recognize and address strong feelings. Strong feelings are a signal that children's motivation to learn is high and that a moment of intense interest is at hand. At these times, children need our support. They are learning how to express emotions constructively, a skill required for them to grow into sensitive, responsible adults. This learning begins with our supportive responses, which let children know that strong feelings are not only acceptable, but essential to a happy, full life.

3

Getting to Solutions

One of the important goals of conflict mediation is for the children to find a solution that works for everyone. During the first two steps of mediation adults create a "safe opening" for discussion by acknowledging and accepting children's feelings. During the remaining four steps, adults guide the solution-seeking process by encouraging children to describe what has happened and to decide together what can be done to solve the problem. During **step 3, gather information,** the adult solicits the details of the dispute from each child's point of view. During **step 4, restate the problem,** the adult repeats or reframes what the children have said, ensuring that each point of view has been understood. During **step 5, ask for ideas for solutions and choose one together,** the adult communicates to the children that they are in charge of the outcome and supports them as they find a collaborative solution. During **step 6, be prepared to give follow-up support,** the adult affirms the children's accomplishments as problem solvers and keeps a watchful eye on the results for a short period. Each of these steps plays a unique role in getting to solutions.

Step 3: Gather Information

Gathering information about what has happened during a conflict is critical to finding a solution that will work for everyone. In fact, the children's descrip-

Six Steps in Conflict Mediation

1. Approach calmly, stopping any hurtful actions.
2. Acknowledge children's feelings.
3. Gather information.
4. Restate the problem.
5. Ask for ideas for solutions and choose one together.
6. Be prepared to give follow-up support.

*Gathering informa-
tion about what has
happened during a
conflict is critical to
finding a solution that
will work for everyone.
Like mining for pre-
cious nuggets, the
adult's careful listen-
ing helps everyone sort
through all the details,
revealing the special
bits that will lead to a
successful outcome.*

tions of their dispute often contain information which may be
the starting place for the solution. Like mining for precious
nuggets, the adult's careful listening helps everyone sort
through all the details, revealing the special bits that will lead
to a successful outcome.

When the emotions of the conflict have calmed, we can initiate step 3 by asking the children questions about the conflict,
making sure to begin these questions with *what* rather than
why. "Why" questions ("Why did you do that?" "Why did you hit
her?") can sound accusing and are often too vague to evoke detailed responses. Asking "What happened?" or "What is the problem?" is an effective way to elicit the specific details needed for
a resolution. As children respond, it's important for us to listen
for each child's perception of the problem so that we may repeat or restate relevant details for the children to consider. Our
key role in this step is to continue to listen neutrally, avoiding
taking sides or forming opinions about the situation.

The children's descriptions of the problem may range from
simple to puzzling to downright complicated. In any case, the
mediator's role is simply to be a conduit and facilitator. A child
may state the problem simply and clearly—"I want some of that
play dough"—and the other child may then hand some over. Or
a child may say something like "I don't like her yelling at me!"

providing information about what happened *during* the conflict, but not about the original problem. Or, the children may go back and forth several times with exclamations like "I had it first!" In all these instances, we simply need to repeat the information ("You're telling me you had it first"), not debate it. Children's answers may not initially give us direct information about the problem, but it is still important to receive whatever they say without judgment and with attentive listening and respect. This reassures children that it is safe to continue communicating and encourages children to carry on with their explanations until all the issues have been explored. This approach usually leads to a more complete and candid picture of what has happened.

Step 4: Restate the Problem

After children have shared all their information about the situation, our next step is to restate the problem. In most situations, this means we simply repeat back what the children have said, reframing any hurtful words and resisting any judgments or quick solutions. The phrase, "So the problem is…" can be a helpful beginning to the restatement. If it is a particularly confusing situation and there has been a lot of explanation, we can start by saying "Now let me see if I understand all of what happened. The problem is…" This longer lead-in can help to get everyone's attention focused on the details of the

To restate the problem means simply repeating back what the children have said. Keeping track of all the ideas suggested and repeating them for the children is the adult's key role in this step.

situation. It also can be helpful to restate each child's explanation right after we hear it. This strategy gives the child immediate confirmation that we have listened and understood.

Here are a few examples of how restatements of different situations may sound:

- "So the problem is, Owen, you want to paint on this side and Chris, what about you? You want to paint on this side too?"

- "So the problem is, Brianna, you're telling me you had it first, and Raymond, you're telling me you had it first."

- "Now, let's see if I understand what happened. The problem is that Sam was playing next to the block shelf and Patrick was trying to get a block, but Olga wanted the same block, and Sam's building got knocked down. Is that what happened?"

As discussed earlier, children sometimes correct us when we acknowledge their feelings ("No, I'm not sad, I'm mad!"), and the same can happen when we restate the problem. A child may say, "No, that's not it—Olga pushed me and then Sam's building fell down." In such cases, we should then restate the correction. This may lead to more discussion, and perhaps even more acknowledging of feelings: "Ohhh, you got pushed and then Sam's building fell down. It sounds like you're feeling upset about being pushed." If there have been any safety issues, it is necessary to make a statement of limits at this point, then quickly move on to helping children learn new skills: "It's not safe to push. Instead of pushing, let's think of a safe way to solve this."

Step 5: Ask for Ideas for Solutions and Choose One Together

After children have expressed and explored their feelings, needs, and wants and have talked about the factual aspects of the situation, they are ready for step 5 of problem solving, in which they discuss possible solutions and choose one that is agreeable to everyone. A simple way to get this started is to ask the question,

"What can you do to solve this problem?" Children must then think carefully about the wants and needs of others as well as their own. This step is challenging for young children; it is difficult for them to keep more than one or two things in mind at a time and to consider, from their egocentric perspective, what others want. The adult's restatement of the problem (step 4) helps to make this easier.

Despite the challenges of thinking of appealing solutions, many children really do enjoy this stage of the discussion. In fact, this part of problem solving is sometimes so interesting that children looking on are often eager to join in with their own suggestions. The search for a solution is similar to the fun that children have in finding the final piece to a puzzle. Sometimes the children having the dispute need to consider just one or two ideas before deciding on a solution that works for everyone; at other times, they need to consider many more possibilities. Keeping track of all the ideas suggested and repeating them for the children is our key role in this step. If children become stuck, we can sometimes remind them of a suggestion made earlier that was not fully considered. (See the list at right for more ideas.)

As the children discuss suggested solutions, we may ask for clarification and specifics: How will that work? What will each of you do? How long will that take? Usually, the solutions that turn out to be successful are those that are clear and concrete. When an idea appears to be agreeable to all, it is useful to check in with each child individually, restating what will happen for that particular child. "So, Olga, you're going to help Sam fix his building so it's not so close to the shelf, and Chris, you're going to get one long block for your road."

What to Do If Children Are Not Agreeing on a Solution

1. First, ask children involved in the dispute for solutions: "What can you do to solve this problem?"

2. Next, ask children nearby for ideas: "We have a problem here (give brief explanation). Do you have ideas for what they could do to solve it?"

3. Tell the children that you have an idea, and ask if they want to hear it: "I have an idea for solving this. Do you want to hear my idea?"

4. Give limited choices: "It's almost time to clean up. You need to choose one of the ideas we've talked about, or you need to choose something else to do."

5. Tell the children you will need to decide the outcome: "If you don't choose, I'll need to choose for you." (This is absolutely a last resort and is rarely necessary.)

Step 6: Be Prepared to Give Follow-up Support

Once children have all indicated their agreement to a solution or set of solutions, we can give further support to the children's ideas and efforts by making a simple affirming statement. "You thought of ideas and decided what will work for all of you. You solved this problem!" Such statements let children know that they really did solve the problem themselves. Otherwise, the presence of an adult may cause children to think the adult solved it. As we point out what the *children* did, it is important to avoid evaluative comments like "You did a great job!" instead stating specifics: "Olga, Sam, and Patrick, you thought of a way to fix the building so it won't get knocked down, *and* that will make it easy for Patrick to get his block. You solved the problem!" Recognizing children's accomplishments with detailed encouragement, rather than praise, builds understanding and confidence in problem-solving skills, empowering children to use them again in the future.

We can give further support to the children's ideas and efforts by making a simple affirming statement. "You thought of ideas and decided what will work for all of you."

A second important follow-up strategy is to stay nearby briefly as children re-engage in their activities. As we observe, perhaps from a distance, we must remain vigilant. This way, we are available to help if there is any confusion about the solution or if unresolved feelings flare up once again. This is especially needed with children who are new to problem solving or children who may have difficulty fully expressing themselves.

Right before small-group time, Rosie mediates a conflict, top and right. Noticing that one of the girls may still need support, Rosie seats herself next to the child as they begin the small group, left.

The Rationale for Child-Made Solutions

Why is it so important to support child-made solutions? In an "active learning" approach, this practice is consistent with a strong belief that adults can best support children's development by encouraging children's initiatives in all areas of learning (Hohmann & Weikart, 2002). If we accept this tenet, we would, for example, take a similar supportive approach whether children are drawing a picture or resolving a dispute with peers. When children are busy drawing, as supportive adults we would not intervene to tell them what to do, nor would we draw the picture for them. Instead we would encourage them to use their own ideas and to draw in their own way as we comment in a matter-of-fact way on what we see them doing. In this active learning

Fortunately, child-made solutions are most often the ones that work best. These children have worked out a way to use the tape together.

approach, *what* the children make, in fact, is not as important as the *process* of making it. Likewise, when children are trying to resolve a conflict, we would encourage, rather than direct, their efforts at problem solving. This way, the *children* can think about the situation, creatively designing their own solutions and, with mutual agreement, making choices about which solution they will try. Again, the process is even more important then the end result.

As we support children in the process of exploring solutions, the resulting cause-and-effect thinking can be full of challenges. Often, new problem solvers have difficulty coming up with solutions; their solutions can be unrealistic, cumbersome, and/or egocentric. Sometimes when we ask children for solutions, we get silence. Sometimes the evaluating and choosing of a solution can take time. In spite of these difficulties, the time invested in exploring solutions is well spent. When children discuss different ways to solve their problem, they are learning to express feelings construc-tively, to see things from others' perspectives, and to engage in the back-and-forth of negotiating together. And fortunate-ly, children's solutions sometimes prove to be surprisingly inventive and perfect for the situation. On many occasions, children's solutions extend play to a whole new level of complexity or inclu-siveness, leading to results that delight everyone. To see this happen, adults need only open themselves to the possibility.

When children discuss different ways to solve their problems they are learning to express feelings constructively, to see things from others' perspectives, and to engage in the back-and-forth of negotiating together.

Even though children's solutions do not always seem "fair" or logical to us, to become independent problem solvers, children must be given the chance to think things through from their unique perspective and to independently try out the solutions they have created. In other words, they need the chance to practice. In contrast, when we impose solutions on children, we are stealing a learning opportunity. The experience of deciding on solutions and consequently learning what makes a solution successful is critical to the development of children's independent problem-solving capabilities. As children learn to problem-solve, the support of a neutral adult, who can facilitate a process that allows children to *remain in control of solutions,* is a necessity.

Facilitating Creative Solutions: Six Stories

The stories that follow show how adults can facilitate the discussion as children create solutions, and they illustrate how this experience helps children to build confidence in their abilities. In all the incidents described, the search for a solution was important not only because of the successful outcome but also because of the learning that occurred along the way.

Learning to see things from others' perspectives: Whose keys are they?

In the incident in the first story, very intense feelings arose at the beginning of the conflict. The mediator, José, was very soothing as he acknowledged the children's feelings. Consequently, the children's emotions de-escalated quickly. As this change occurred, José sat down and stretched out his legs, a simple gesture, probably made without thinking, that told the children that he would be staying until the problem was worked out. The children knew, from José's reassuring body language, that they would all be heard. Coming up with solutions was now up to them. This conflict happened 7 months into the school year in a classroom of 3-year-olds. By this time, José had decided it was important to encourage the children to say "I don't like that" rather then stating limits himself.

Natalie, Kristie, and Tommy: "I want the keys!"*

In the corner of a Head Start classroom Natalie cried and struggled to free herself as Tommy held her tightly from behind. Kristie, who had been playing with Tommy, watched nearby. Natalie was still struggling to get free when José, her teacher, came over. Calmly he told them, "Hold on a minute." He knelt down by them, putting his hand over Tommy's hands and saying "What's going on?" Tommy did not let go of Natalie. Calmly, José told Tommy again, "One minute— let go." As soon as Tommy let go, Natalie tried to hit him; Tommy then tried to hit her back. José quickly placed himself between the two children, stopping them both while quietly saying "No, no…one minute, hold on." He stroked Tommy's arm gently as he held him away from Natalie. Tommy and Natalie's expressions immediately reflected a change from fierce anger to listening. José supported Natalie as she sat up straight. "Hold on, sweetie, let's see what's going on. You're both very upset!" José said, making eye contact with both of them.

As José acknowledged Tommy and Natalie's feelings, Kristie had been trying to tell José something. He looked up at her and Kristie said, "I want the keys from her hand."

"You want the keys from her hand?" José repeated.

"Yeah…that was Tommy's!" Kristie said, patting Tommy on the head with one hand and holding her own set of keys with the other.

"Oh, that was Tommy's," José repeated.

José spoke to Tommy, "You wanted the keys?"

"He was using it," Kristie explained as she sat down by Tommy and Natalie.

"He was using it," José repeated. Sensing that the anger had dissipated, José settled into a more comfortable sitting position and stretched out his legs.

Natalie crossed her arms across her chest in imitation of how Tommy had held her. "He was going like that to me."

José repeated to Tommy, "You were going like that to her?" also crossing his arms as Natalie did. Tommy looked at José and nodded his head yes.

---

*Some of the dialogue in this story has been translated from Spanish, which was the home language for many of the children in this classroom. Both Spanish and English were used throughout this incident. The conflict may be viewed in its original form in the High/Scope video *Supporting Children in Resolving Conflicts.* (1998).

Natalie continued, "I don't like him doing that."

Looking back at Tommy, José held his arms across his chest again and repeated, "She doesn't like it that you did that."

Tommy said, "She can't hit me. I don't like that."

José looked back to Natalie and repeated, "Tommy says don't hit him—he doesn't like that." Natalie looked closely at José and listened.

Kristie had listened patiently but now reached suddenly for the keys in Natalie's hands. "I want the keys 'cuz…" Natalie quickly held them out of Kristie's reach.

José reached out for the keys, "Could I hold the keys for a minute, please?" Natalie immediately handed them to him. He cradled the keys in his hands and held them snugly to his chest.

"You both want the keys, so what are we going to do?" José looked at all three children and waited.

"I really want these," Tommy told him as he reached out and gently touched the cradle of José's hands.

"You really want these, yeah," José acknowledged. Turning to Natalie, he repeated this: "He really wants these keys."

"He could use mine," Kristie offered, holding up a different set of keys.

"He could use yours?" José repeated. "Tommy can use your keys?"

Tommy responded, "This is finished."

José asked him, "What's finished?"

Tommy told him, "Her keys finished."

"Her keys finished?" José repeated, confused about what this meant. Tommy nodded yes.

"He could use his," Kristie suggested.

José clarified, "He could use his?" He opened his hands and held up the keys. Kristie nodded.

"But Natalie, do you want these keys?" José asked. Natalie nodded yes. José turned back to Kristie and Tommy. "Natalie says she wants these keys." He pointed to the ones in his hands again. Tommy gently touched the keys in José's hands. "I'm going to hold on to them," José reassured Tommy.

Jingling the keys as she talked, Kristie offered again, "He could use mine, but he can't have it. He could use mine."

"He could use yours but he can't have it?" José repeated. Kristie shook her head to indicate a yes.

"He can use mine," Kristie repeated as she handed the keys to Tommy.

As Tommy took the keys, Kristie reached out gently, sympathetically, and placed her hand on Natalie's head.

"Tommy, you can use hers," José repeated to Tommy. He then paused a few seconds as this solution was absorbed. "Is that okay?" José asked. Tommy nodded. "And can we give these back to Natalie?" José asked Tommy and Kristie. Tommy and Kristie looked at each other and nodded their heads.

"Yes?" José asked, looking carefully at both of them. They nodded again and José handed the keys to Natalie. "There you go."

As soon as the keys were in Natalie's hands, all three children jumped up and left the area. José smiled as he watched them go.

In this mediation, José, in quick succession, acknowledged feelings, gathered information, restated the problem, and asked the children for solutions. He asked to hold the keys and then said, "You both want the keys, so what are we going to do?" After asking this question, he simply repeated children's ideas, clarified Natalie's interest in the keys, and checked that the solution worked for everyone. This successful outcome shows that children *can* move on from their egocentric viewpoints. In the end, Kristie had moved from "That [the keys in Natalie's hands] was Tommy's" to "He could use mine."

◆

Friendship and the importance of being "in control"

The next story depicts a group of 4-year-old girls who were struggling with the difficulties of friendship and play. The conflict reflects a very common issue in early childhood classrooms—"Are you my friend?"—while shedding light on the deeper issue of what friendship means to the young child. At this age, friends are defined as the people you are playing with, the ones you are having fun with right now. Such a fluid definition can often result in exclusion of those who are not "friends" at the moment.

Grace, Niki, and Aja: "Stop following us!"

Grace and Niki were drawing at the small table in the Art Area when Aja got a piece of paper and came over to sit near them. Niki and Grace looked at each other. Niki said to Grace, "We don't want to be with her, right?" and they got up and moved to the larger table nearby. Aja moved as well.

"Stop following us!" Niki told Aja loudly. Aja didn't answer, but continued to follow. Looking carefully at them, she slowly put down her things, and took a marker from the box.

"We don't want her to follow us, right?" Grace said to Niki. They picked up their paper and the box of markers and moved again. Aja picked up her paper and marker and followed them back to the small table.

"We don't want you to follow us!" Niki repeated to Aja who, looking more determined than upset, watched them cautiously again as she slowly sat down near them and put down her paper. Niki and Grace looked at each other angrily. Niki picked up her paper once again and reached out for the marker box just as Aja reached for a marker. Niki yanked the box away. Aja stood up and planted herself in front of them as they headed for the bigger table.

"You can't keep that necklace I gave you!" Aja said to Grace.

"What necklace? " Grace asked with concern.

"The one from the party—and I'm not gonna be your friend!" Aja told Grace angrily. Aja reached for the marker box, and she and Niki began to pull it back and forth. Leaving the two struggling, Grace went and sat down at the large table. Chloe came over to the small table and took a marker from the box Niki and Aja were struggling over.

"We're using these!" Niki yelled at Chloe.

Chantal, their teacher, heard their rising voices and approached the group. She placed a hand on Niki and Aja's arms and Aja let go, leaving Niki with the box.

"All right, let's talk about this problem," Chantal told them as she knelt down on one knee. She reached her arms around them. Calmly, she recognized feelings: "Aja, you look upset—and Niki, you look a little bit upset."

With these simple actions, Chantal set the stage for solutions. Understanding that Aja's threats (to take back the necklace and stop being friends with Grace) were her way of expressing anger, Chantal had acknowledged the upset feelings only without repeating the threats.

> "What happened?" Chantal asked them.
>
> "Niki wouldn't let..." Aja's voice became low and garbled; her words trailed off.
>
> "Take your time to tell me 'cuz I can't understand you," Chantal reassured her.
>
> Aja took a breath and told her, "I want to stay with her and she wouldn't let me stay."
>
> "Niki?" Chantal said as she turned to her.
>
> "She took the marker and she won't give it to me!" Niki told her.
>
> "And Chloe?"
>
> "I want a marker," Chloe replied.
>
> "So the problem is: Niki, you're saying you don't want her to take the marker [Niki nodded], and Chloe, you want her to give you a marker [Chloe nodded], and Aja, you want to work with Niki but she won't let you [Aja nodded]."

As each child stated her individual perspective, Chantal listened very carefully, demonstrating this when she clearly restated the various problems. This restatement helped the children by letting them hear about the problems again, free of emotion. Since keeping several things in mind at a time can be challenging for young children, this is a critical step. Chantal did not state any opinions about any of the actions or perspectives, and she resisted giving suggestions at this point. Instead she remained neutral, showing confidence that the children, who had been problem-solving with her for about 3 months, would come up with a solution.

> "We have a very big problem. What are we going to do about this problem?" Chantal asked them all. Niki looked at the box of markers and shook it. The other children watched her and Chantal's question went unanswered.

Chantal put her hands under the marker box, saying "I'd like to hold this box for a minute until we solve this problem, Niki." Niki released it into her hands.

Children involved in the majority of conflicts where control is an issue will be distracted by one child having more control than another. By taking the box into her own neutral hands, Chantal put all the children on equal footing.

As soon as Chantal had the box in her hands, the children looked back to her. Their faces showed relief, perhaps because they anticipated and trusted what would happen next.

"So what are we going to do to solve this?" Chantal asked them.

"Chloe and Aja can go to that table [the small one]," Niki told Chantal.

"Chloe and Aja can draw at the small table? What about the box of markers? How will that idea work for the others?" Chantal asked them.

"She [Niki] can use the crayons," Chloe told Chantal.

"Nooo!" said Niki emphatically.

"I can stay with Niki…and use markers," Aja offered.

"You want to stay with Niki and use markers. What about Chloe?" Chantal asked. The children were silent for a few seconds. Chantal waited. Then, speaking very gently, Chantal turned to Niki, "Niki, do you have another idea about what we can do about this problem?"

"Maybe I can give 'em some of these and we can go over there [the big table] and have some room…and sit next to Grace and that would make 'em feel much better."

"Aja and Chloe, did you hear Niki's idea about sitting over there where there's more space, and everybody can sit there and have some room and feel better? What do you think about that?"

"Yeahhh," said Aja. Chloe nodded. Chantal looked at each child and checked for agreement again: "Is that going to solve this problem?" Chantal made eye contact with each child, and they all nodded again. "So, I'm going to give you the markers and you're going to work over there where there's more chairs. That's the way you're going to solve this problem!" Chantal summarized and encouraged. Niki took the markers from Chantal and they all joined Grace. Niki placed the markers in the middle of the table and they all began to draw. Where once there were two "friends" playing, there were now four. Chantal watched from nearby as they began to talk about the colors and the people in their drawings.

◆

Young children have a natural interest in control; to become independent, they need lots of opportunities to make choices on their own. When children explore issues related to control and friendship they are better able to construct their own ideas about what it means to be a friend. Their conflicts over friends sometimes result in exclusion behavior like Niki and Grace's ("We don't want you to follow us!"). When dealing with such behavior, it can be particularly challenging for adults to remain neutral. It is so easy to empathize with the rejected child; but while we may be tempted to force children to "be friends" or "be nice," friendships cannot be dictated. By remaining impartial and putting the children in charge of finding a solution, Chantal accomplished a number of things. Instead of forcing everyone to play together, she supported their interest in control by keeping them in control. She maintained their responsibility for the problem by asking them to think of ideas that might solve it. Finally, by accepting their solution, she expressed her trust in their abilities. Fortunately, child-made solutions are most often the solutions that work best. If Chantal had forced Niki to play with Aja, the likely result would have been more rejection of Aja, perhaps concealed from adults. However, since Niki was permitted to *choose* to alter her behavior and included Aja as a result, the outcome was more likely to have a positive effect on their play and their relationship.

> "One of the basic principles of human relationships is that you can change only yourself; however, when you change yourself, you change the relationship and the other person must respond somehow."
>
> —*Elizabeth Crary (1993, p. 7)*

Solutions are worked out based on children's ideas. Mediators often find that a simple "hmmm" is a useful thing to say. This kind of comment expresses interest while giving the children time to formulate their ideas.

Fairness and sharing: Their role in the mediation process

Adults can best facilitate the justice of the *mediating process* by remaining neutral and making sure that all children are heard. This will not necessarily result in a just *solution*. The goal of the solution-seeking process is to find a solution that all the children will agree to, whether it seems fair to the adult or not. The adult's role is to facilitate fairness in the *process,* rather than in the *solution*. The following story illustrates this.

Christian, Mark, and Alex: "I need only one more!"

Christian, Mark, and Alex, all 4 years old, were pretending to be dogs as they played with marbles from the Marble Chutes construction set. Christian was holding a small collection of

marbles in his right hand, while Alex and Mark each had larger collections (of at least 10) in separate bowls. Rose, the
teacher, was sitting nearby. Mark reached over to Christian
and tried, gently, to take one of his marbles. "No!" Christian
told him assertively, closing his hand tightly and leaning back
against Rose's leg.

"What's the problem?" Rose asked.

"I just want four," Christian told her calmly.

Rose looked over to Mark, who immediately told them,
"I know…but I…I just want lots of medicine to help the little
dogs."

Rose repeated, "You want lots of medicine to help the
little dogs." Turning back to Christian, she said, "And you
want four marbles. How many do you have?"

Christian opened his hand and looked, answering, "Four
marbles."

Rose looked back to Mark, who was rattling his marbles
loudly in his small blue bowl. "I need only one more," he
told them in a pleading voice.

"You feel you need one more. Hmmm… where could
one more marble be?" Rose said thoughtfully as she looked
around.

As this mediation began, the children showed very little
emotion, so the exchange moved right along to Mark and Christian stating their wishes. Rose facilitated this without making a
judgment about the disparity between the two boys' collections
of marbles. She listened to and respectfully repeated each child's
wishes. Her quiet "hmmm" was a simple but pivotal expression
at this turning point in the mediation. Using this expression can
be helpful in several ways: it is a soothing sound that lets children know we are there and thinking along with them, and it
also communicates that we will not jump right in with a solution. For Rose, saying "hmmm" was a natural, subtle, expression
that showed patient concern for their quandary.

"Hey Christian, I know," Alex excitedly told him as he put
his bowl close to Christian's hands. "Put 'em in here so we
can save 'em." Christian responded immediately by opening
his hand. Everyone was quiet as his four multi-colored marbles clinked repetitively into Alex's bowl.

"You want your four marbles to go with Alex's?" Rose said quietly. Christian nodded. She looked back to Mark, "And Mark still wants one more."

Looking over to Alex, Christian immediately responded, "Is it all right if we give him one more of those?" Without hesitation, Alex picked one marble out of his bowl and handed it to Mark.

"Mark, do you have enough marbles now?" Rose asked as she watched this exchange. Mark looked back at her, still a bit surprised to have gotten one more. Rose repeated, "One more—that's what you asked for."

Mark finally nodded and began to get up with his bowl. Turning back to Christian, Rose asked, "And you put your four with Alex's and you and Alex are going to use those marbles?" Christian nodded happily, stood up, and began to talk to Alex about his "Benji the dog" videotape. Rose watched as the three re-engaged in their dog play.

It is important to note that even though Christian had refused to give Mark a marble at the beginning of the conflict, the negotiation ended with Christian giving Mark one more (from Christian and Alex's combined collection). Rose did not impose this solution; Christian had freely chosen it. Behavior changes that adults choose for children are usually not repeated unless the adult repeatedly enforces them. Because Christian eventually chose to share, and experienced success when he did, it was more likely that he would share independently in the future. Mark, who got his "one more marble," was also likely to benefit from this peer model of sharing behavior. In the end, harmony and play were restored with a creative outcome that would have been very hard to predict at the outset.

Before moving on to the next conflict story, let's contemplate the role of fairness and sharing in the marble dilemma. Why didn't Rose ask Mark to give up any of his larger set of marbles? We know it is unlikely that any adult would have suggested the solution Christian chose—first giving all his marbles to Alex, then giving Mark one marble from his and Alex's joint collection—especially since Mark had originally tried to take one from Christian. Typically, adults in these situations often think a child like Mark is being "selfish." Mark, however, was simply acting his developmental age; he was acting on behalf of his wants alone because his thinking was still egocentric. Wanting to promote "fairness," adults might have been tempted to impose a solution like dividing the marbles evenly or asking Mark to share. True sharing, however, requires willing cooperation.

Can adult-dictated solutions actually teach fairness or sharing? Children who are forced to "share" may be learning the mechanics of sharing (dividing materials or taking turns), but they are not likely to acquire a *willingness* to share. When sharing is imposed, children learn mindless obedience rather than a gen-

Children who are forced to "share" may be learning the mechanics of sharing (dividing materials or taking turns), but they are not likely to acquire a willingness to share. As a result, struggles like this are likely to recur.

uine desire to respond to the wants and needs of others. Children may also become resentful or distrustful of adults who direct their use of materials. If adults can support children's solutions, no matter how uneven the results, they will strengthen the children's interest in real sharing, that is, sharing that is child-chosen.

Reaching mutual agreements is a primary goal of mediation. Even though Christian ended up sharing his marbles, he was satisfied with the result; he had been given the chance to make choices about what was most important to him, and he had agreed with the others on the final outcome. Mark, for his part, had experienced the difference between egocentric and collaborative action—that is, between trying to take a material from someone without asking, and simply stating his wish for the material and having that wish be respected as well as met. This successful result was likely to make collaboration a lot more appealing to him in the future.

◆

In any conflict mediation with young children, the solution-seeking process may eventually lead to a fair solution, but this is not its primary goal. Fairness is a difficult concept for young children because it involves keeping the wants and needs of everyone in mind. Since preschoolers view things from an ego-centric perspective and find it hard to focus on more than one or two things at a time, they are mostly focused on their own wants and needs. Ultimately, at this developmental stage, the "fairness" of the solution is less important than the experience of exploring solutions together. This exploration, when supported by patient, neutral, adults, will achieve *mutual agreement* among children as they choose solutions that are appealing (rather than fair) for all of them.

The challenge of exploring all the options

This next story, from my classroom, is an example of the patience that is sometimes required as children explore all the choices that arise as they try to reach a mutual agreement. Sylvia and Josh were experienced problem solvers who were very interested in the opportunities for dialogue and control that problem solving presents.

Josh and Sylvia: "I had it first!"

Josh, aged 3½ years, was holding a small pink and purple plastic toy that his classmate Simon probably got from a cereal box. The toy looked like a helicopter propellor, without the helicopter. Josh had picked up the toy where Simon had left it. Sylvia, aged 4 years, had become interested in it, but Josh told her he was using it. Hearing Sylvia's voice rising sharply, I went over to the children.

"You sound upset, Sylvia. It seems like there is a problem over this toy. Can you tell me what the problem is?" I asked.

"I want to carry it to Simon!" Sylvia told Josh.

"I had this first," Josh told me as he spun the toy in his hand.

"This right here you had first?" I asked, touching the toy in Josh's hand.

"Yeah, and he wants to bring it and he's not letting me do it!" Sylvia added.

"So the problem is that Josh, you want to have this, and you want to have this too, Sylvia?"

"Yeah, and bring it to Simon," Sylvia responded emphatically. Josh nodded.

"Bring it to Simon because it belongs to Simon?" I asked.

"Yeah," Sylvia confirmed.

"Hmmm. That's the problem. What do you think you should do?"

"Both carry a wing!" Sylvia suggested enthusiastically.

"Both carry a wing so you'd carry it together?" I repeated.

"No—I have a better idea," Josh told us. "I can do it first and then if it…and then it will be your turn to pick it up."

"Do it first?" I asked Josh. "What does that mean…what are you going to do to it?"

"Well, I want to do it first!" Sylvia said, her voice rising to a frustrated pitch.

"Like this," Josh said as he tried to spin it.

I said to Josh, "So you're not wanting to take it to Simon, Josh. You're wanting to play with it, it sounds like." Josh nodded yes.

"No! I wanna…I wanna take first…I wanna take it to Simon first!" Sylvia pleaded as she looked at Josh holding the toy.

"You know what, Josh? I think I'd like to hold it for a minute, until we figure this out," I told Josh gently. He handed me the toy right away.

"So what are we going to do about this problem?" I asked again.

"I don't know…," Sylvia began, "well, he found it so I'll carry it."

"I had it first!" Josh responded.

"Sylvia is suggesting that she carry it to Simon and you're saying that you had it first. So how are we going to solve this?" I asked them all.

"Well it's a good idea because…because, he gets to do one thing…he gets to find it and I get to carry it," Sylvia told us earnestly.

"Ahh. So because he got to find it, now you get to carry it to Simon. You think that's how we should solve this?"

"Yeah!" Sylvia responded brightly.

"What do you think of that idea, Josh?" I asked. Josh hesitated. I restated, "You got to find it, so now she gets to carry it to Simon?" Josh shook his head no.

"You don't like that idea. Hmmm. Have you got any other ideas, Josh, of what we can do?"

Josh paused and spoke slowly, "Umm, well…that's okay if we can hold on to each wing."

"So we're back to Sylvia's idea that you both can carry it, each of you holding on to a wing and carrying it to Simon?"

"Well I go back," Sylvia told us, smiling, "now I don't think my own idea is very good."

"You don't like your own idea anymore," I repeated, laughing a bit with her. "So do you have another idea, since you don't like that idea anymore?"

"The only idea I have is…is that I carry it," Sylvia said quietly.

"But Josh didn't really like that idea," I reminded her. I looked over to Josh, who was beginning to look closely at Tomas's purple stuffed Barney, which was lying on the floor. The stuffed dinosaur was covered with pink Band-Aids.

"Well what can we do about it?!" Sylvia said with some exasperation.

"Boy, I don't know!" I told her, reflecting back that feeling.

"Hold onto each wing," Josh said, looking up from Barney.

"Josh wants to go back to that idea of holding onto each wing," I repeated. Sylvia shook her head. "But you're not liking that idea," I reflected back. "What shall we do? Could we ask somebody else for ideas?"

We all looked around but there was no one nearby. "I don't see anybody else around to ask."

"I have an idea," Josh told us.

"You have another idea? What's your idea, Josh?" I asked.

"Sylvia can go first if Simon losed it, then I...it will be my turn to pick it up."

"Your idea is that Sylvia will have a turn...."

"Okay! Okay!" Sylvia began to exclaim excitedly.

"Wait a minute, Sylvia. Let me just make sure I understand this idea. He's going to have a turn and then you're going to have a turn. And then what are we going to do after you're both finished?"

"Tell Simon to keep it in his hands," Josh wisely suggested.

"Tell Simon to keep it in his hands, or maybe in his cubby," I responded, smiling.

"I'll bring it to him," Sylvia said quietly as she took it from me and began to leave with it.

At this point I realized that I had not been very clear about the agreement—Sylvia was confused. I had thought that they both wanted to try the spin toy before Sylvia would return it to Simon, but I had said, "You're going to have a turn." Sylvia had taken this to mean that they would each take a turn carrying it back to Simon. I needed to be clearer. What I should have said was "You're each going to have a turn to *use* it."

"Wait a minute, Sylvia," I said. "The idea was that you were going to use it first and then Josh was going to use it, and then you were going to take it to Simon."

"No, no, I don't want to do **that** idea," Sylvia told us matter-of-factly.

"Oh, well, wait a minute, you need to give it back to me. I thought that was the idea that we just agreed on," I said

"I don't want to!" Sylvia said, as she handed me the toy.

"You don't want to, so then we'll need to figure out another idea," I said.

"Yeah!" Sylvia responded enthusiastically.

"Yeah!" I said back to her.

"But what is it?" Sylvia asked.

"See, Josh wanted to have a turn using it before he took it back to Simon. So you didn't want to have a turn with it. I thought you wanted to have a turn too, Sylvia?"

"No, I want to have...I don't want to have a turn to play with it. I want to have a turn to **bring** it," Sylvia told us calmly.

I noticed Josh eyeing the dinosaur again and wondered if we would lose him soon. "Oh, so you just want to take it back. So can Josh have a turn trying it first before you take it back then?" I asked.

"Yeah!!" Sylvia answered excitedly.

"Okay, there you go." I handed the toy to Josh, "You need to go ahead and try it and then Sylvia is going to take it back to Simon."

"I'm going to go," Josh told me.

"Where are you going to go with it?"

"Uh...Simon."

"Oh. You know, the idea was that you were going to have a turn trying it, spinning it, and then Sylvia was going to take it back to Simon. Is that okay?" I clarified with him.

Josh nodded in agreement. He spun it and it fell to the floor.

"That's it?" I asked. Josh nodded and moved toward Tomas's dinosaur. "Okay, Sylvia, he tried it. Now you can take it back," I said, waiting. She picked it up off the floor.

As I turned to talk to Sylvia, Josh was asking Tomas about his stuffed Barney. "Why does it have bandages all over it?"

"You might suggest to Simon that he put this in his cubby," I told Sylvia.

"Yeah," Sylvia said with a sigh of relief.

I turned back to Josh, "Well I'm glad you solved that problem! You figured out a lot of different ideas before we solved it, didn't you!" I told Josh enthusiastically.

"Yeah," Josh said, looking at me with a smile. "Why does that Barney have a lot of bandages?"

This exchange lasted only about 5 minutes (though it may seem longer to those reading it). It was a rich language experience for Sylvia and Josh and a very fruitful and enjoyable 5 minutes. In fact, as I look back on it, I think Sylvia and Josh also enjoyed the back-and-forth of evaluating and clarifying ideas as much as I did. The mediation of a conflict can often seem like a ping-pong match, with the mediator going back and forth between the two children to facilitate their discussion. These rapid exchanges are an indicator of spirited, and usually successful, negotiation.

Josh and Sylvia both seemed to enjoy conflict discussions in the classroom, often joining in to help others find solutions. Talking over problems held benefits for each of them. In this propellor-wing conflict, Josh, a young 3-year-old, had an opportunity to stretch his thinking, language, and self-assertion skills. Sylvia, a verbally and emotionally expressive 4-year-old, gained practice in using thinking and listening (instead of loud demands) as strategies for meeting her needs and wants.

◆

When conflicts begin to resolve more quickly and easily

Once children have had some experience in finding solutions with adults facilitating the process, they begin to move more and more quickly from their own egocentric points of view to an understanding that solutions must (and can) work for everyone. Having choices about that solution is the incentive that encourages children to make this transition. These next two conflicts illustrate how quickly solutions are found after children have had a few months of problem-solving experience.

In the incident described next, Stephie and Tamika were playing with dolls in the Playhouse. They were able to agree on a solution to their problem very quickly. Once I helped them clarify the problem, they solved it.

Tamika and Stephie: "She won't let me hold the doll"

Tamika comes to get me and says she is having a problem with Stephie. We go to find her.

Tamika: There's Stephie.

Betsy: Stephie, Tamika seems to think there is a problem here and I don't know what it is. So Tamika, tell me again what it is.

Tamika: She won't let me hold the doll.

Stephie: Well I like it, too.

Betsy: Is this a school doll? *(They nod. I turn to Tamika.)* So the problem is, she won't let you hold

> the doll. We have lots of other dolls, but it's this doll in particular you want to hold.
>
> **Tamika:** Yeah.
>
> **Betsy:** Hmmm.
>
> **Stephie:** We can take turns!
>
> **Betsy:** You're going to take turns? *(They both smile and nod.)* I don't think you needed me. You figured this problem out all by yourself!

The speed of this exchange made it clear that Stephie and Tamika had moved on in their ability to problem-solve. The inclusion of an adult in the process merely reminded Stephie of what she needed to do. She immediately stepped into the role of problem solver and suggested a solution that worked. In the incident in next story, from another classroom, the children settled their problem with only a little help from Eileen, their teacher.

◆

Lydia and Jesse struggle over a stroller

Eileen sees Jesse and Lydia struggling over the stroller and approaches them. She kneels by the stroller, putting her hands on the handle.

> **Eileen:** It looks like you have a problem. I'm going to hold this. *(Jesse keeps one hand on the stroller and Lydia sits on the floor next to it.)*
>
> **Jesse:** *(Turning to Eileen)* She's trying to take it from me!
>
> **Lydia:** *(Looking at Jesse)* Hey! I know an idea! How 'bout I have five…how 'bout we have it for five minutes and you have it for five minutes?
>
> **Jesse:** *(Emphatically swinging his head)* NO!
>
> **Lydia:** How 'bout two minutes. *(Jesse looks at Lydia, immediately nods yes, and releases the stroller.)*
>
> **Eileen:** So Lydia says she'll have it for two minutes and then you and that's okay? *(Jesse nods again and Lydia stands up and moves to the stroller handles.)*

Eileen: *(Gently touching each child)* You guys solved the problem! Lydia's going to use it for two minutes and then Jesse's going to use it for two minutes. You're going to take turns. You worked it out!

Both Jesse and Lydia look pleased with their accomplishment and Lydia pushes the stroller away. Jesse asks Eileen if she will tell him when 2 minutes is over. She says yes and checks her watch. In 2 minutes she tells Jesse it's time for his turn. He goes to Lydia and she immediately gives him the stroller.

As a mediator I look forward to the discussions that occur during the solution-seeking steps and the child-made solutions that are the result. I love the surprise of children's ideas and the earnestness of their efforts. I see this part of mediation as an occasion for hope that conflicts can be solved respectfully and creatively, now and in the future. As impartial mediators who support rather than control children's search for solutions, we can clear a safe opening for communication and cooperation. With a belief in the capabilities of children, we can facilitate a stimulating, hope-filled process—a deliberation that weighs needs and wants, sequence and circumstances, and so much more. Mediation invites children to find real solutions to real problems as they mature from egocentric to more inclusive perspectives and actions. As they do this, we will see them grow into individuals who can get to solutions on their own.

When Adults or Children Feel Upset: Responding to Strong Emotions

onflicts can result in very strong feelings, not only for the participants in the dispute but also for the mediator and any observers of the conflict. These intense emotions may be constructive catalysts that generate dialogue, clarify issues, and strengthen relationships, or they may be obstacles that block communication and divide people from one another. Strong emotions may ignite verbal abuse and physical violence, or they may stimulate deep caring and connection. Sometimes the emotions of a conflict may generate a mixture of these results. One of the challenges of mediation is to encourage all parties to fully express their emotions, without verbal abuse or violence. Without this full expression, there can be no true resolution to conflict, yet the strong feelings themselves can interfere with problem solving. Mediators need to know what to do when either they or the children are feeling such strong emotions that successful problem solving could be compromised. The rest of this chapter describes ways to prepare for and respond to these challenging situations.

Children hit and yell hurtful things because they have yet to learn other skills. Through mediation, they learn to express emotions fully, without verbal abuse or hitting.

Intense emotions can be constructive catalysts that generate increased awareness of feelings...

...careful thought about what is wanted...

...expression of those wants to others...

...and eventually, a connection— communication that resolves the feelings and the issues.

Children's Emotional Expressions: What to Expect

To be prepared for the strong emotions that sometimes arise during children's conflicts, we need to know more about what to expect when children become upset. There are four basic, immediate ways that children express strong feelings:

- **Noises**—loud screams, grunting, shouts, or crying:

  Keegan is playing with a toy truck when Jesse comes by and grabs it. Keegan screams and then begins to cry.

  Chris wants to paint and there is no space for her. She cries.

- **Physical actions**—hurtful or expressive:

  Angelica is playing with a toy truck and Jill grabs it. Angelica hits her on the back.

  Cory is carrying a toy truck and Dana grabs it. Cory kicks the blocks on the floor nearby.

- **Words**—appropriate or hurtful:

  Xavier is playing with a toy truck and Luke grabs it. Xavier says, "Hey, I was using that!"

  Dynell is painting and Wendy grabs his brush. Dynell says, "I'm not ever going to be your friend, you stupid dummy!"

- **Withdrawal**—silent, or with quiet tears:

  Lilly is playing with a toy truck and Pat grabs it. Lilly gets up and walks away.

  Sadie is painting at the art table, and Leela pours some paint on Sadie's picture. Sadie cries quietly without moving.

Sometimes there is a combination of these emotional responses, such as shouting followed by quick withdrawal, hitting while shouting hurtful words, or a constructive verbal response followed by a hurtful action. If we keep in mind that all of these responses are possible, and fully accept these possibilities, we will be less upset or surprised by children's words and actions at conflict times. Such intense responses are developmentally appropriate for young children: *children hit and yell hurtful things because they have yet to learn other skills.* Keeping this in mind can help us resist labeling such mistaken actions or the children as "bad" or "selfish," judgments that can impede problem solving.

Responding to Children's Emotional Outbursts

There are children in every classroom who cry easily, have tantrums, scream frequently, or become rigid with anger in a wide variety of situations. Adults who work with them can become exasperated with the frequency and intensity of these behaviors (especially if the issues appear minor) and consequently may not acknowledge their feelings adequately. The children may then become more and more upset, and soon a recurring cycle of children's strong feelings and adult frustration has begun. In these emotional situations adults may sometimes be tempted to tell children "Stop all that fussing" or "Be nice, we're all friends here." To a child who is "acting out" strong feelings, adults may say "Excuse me!" or to a sad child, they may say "Calm down—it's okay" and attempt to draw the child's attention to something interesting. In reality, at such moments, things are not okay for that child. Strong feelings are not calm, and they are usually not "nice." We cannot simply tell children to exchange one set of feelings for another, though this in fact is what such approaches ask for.

When children's strong feelings go unacknowledged as a result of such avoidance practices, it is likely they will simply be repressed, reappearing in a disproportionate way on some other occasion. Such repressed feelings are often the root cause of "strong needs" mistaken behavior. The child who frequently hits or hurts others for no apparent reason is usually a child who has been discouraged from fully expressing feelings.

Another way that adults may respond to strong feelings is by attempting to direct children to "be friends." However well intentioned, this response negates the emotions and problems that children are experiencing, sending a message that strong emotions, and their sources, are undesirable. Actually, the truth is that strong emotions, and our ability to express them, are central to the human experience. If we can avoid sending a message that intense feelings are not okay, children can learn to express strong feelings in ways that are creative and genuine. Most often, conflicts are resolved because people find constructive ways to express their strong reactions to events or people. If we can respond to children's disputes by accepting their feelings rather than punishing their actions, we can support children in learning to solve their own problems.

Children who have had 2 to 3 months of problem-solving experience begin to develop a trust in this process. After witnessing or participating in a number of mediated conflicts, they know that adults will listen to everyone involved, no matter how upset they are or what has happened, and will not take sides. Through this experience children come to know that their feelings are valued and that they can say what they feel without being told to "calm down" or "be nice."

Perhaps this sounds too easy, and sometimes it *is* this simple. Frequently problems go unresolved because we don't listen to and notice feelings enough. Unsettled by children's intensity, we may try to fix problems without addressing emotions. If we can move past these barriers and simply give children in distress 2 to 3 minutes of our full attention, we can profoundly change their emotional experience (and our own) in the classroom or at home.

Noticing and naming strong feelings

In the incident in the next story, Lakisha (whom we got to know in Chapter 2 in the "He's shooting at us!" story, pp. 80–82) continued to show her growth as a problem solver. She still became teary easily, but her intense reactions passed much more quickly and she articulated what was happening much more confidently. Her outbursts had become less and less extreme as she had come to accept her emotional reactions in the way that the adults in her life did. Adults had noticed and named her feelings many times, modeling how to describe those feelings in words. This adult support had not been intended to change or suppress what she was feeling but rather to let her know that she was understood.

At the outset of this conflict over a swing, Lakisha's emotions were very intense. This intensity may always be part of who she is and will likely enrich her life in very valuable ways. In this situation, as in other conflicts, the most important experience for Lakisha was my acceptance of her first flash of feeling—an acceptance that would help her to carry that emotional energy *positively* into this and other problem-solving experiences she would encounter throughout her life.

Lakisha and Seth: "I wanted the swing!"

It was near the end of the day and we were all outside playing. Some parents had begun to arrive. Lakisha walked over to where Douglas and a friend were swinging. I had just given him an "underdog" (a push from underneath the swing).

"I want to have a turn," Lakisha told us.

"You could talk to Douglas about that," I suggested to Lakisha.

"Douglas, when can I have a turn?" she calmly asked.

"When I'm done," Douglas responded cheerfully. He flew back and forth, pumping his small legs with the rhythm of the swing, sending himself arcing through the air. Lakisha waited.

A few moments later Lakisha's mom walked up behind her and Lakisha turned and gave her a big hug. As they hugged, Douglas got off the swing and Seth, another 4-year-old, climbed on. Lakisha turned just in time to see this and shrieked. Tears instantly flowed from her eyes. As Seth tried to get started, Lakisha began to pull on the swing. Seth yelled no. Lakisha's mom looked beseechingly at me as I approached. Lakisha saw me, opened her arms, and as I knelt down, she fell into my lap, crying loudly.

"Lakisha, you're feeling really sad." I hugged her tightly and she laid her head on my shoulder and cried louder. "You're feeling so sad, Lakisha."

"What for?" Seth said from a few feet away as he dangled his feet from the swing, waiting for a push.

"I'm not sure, Seth. When she's finished crying, maybe she'll tell us what happened."

Lakisha's crying began to quiet. She had calmed quickly, I thought to myself, at least compared to the beginning of the year. Lakisha lifted her head up and looked over at Seth, big tears still rolling down her cheeks.

"I wanted the swing and Seth got it!" Lakisha cried out.

"Wuull, I'm on it," Seth told us softly, still looking a bit confused by Lakisha's intense reactions.

With my arm still around Lakisha, I moved closer to Seth and knelt down again between them.

"Seth, we have a problem with the swing. I need you to get off for a few minutes while we talk about it."

Seth calmly slid off the swing. I looped my arm around the swing's chain and reassured him, "I'll hold onto it while we're talking."

Seth looked ready to listen so I asked Lakisha what happened. "I wanted the swing and he got on!" she told us loudly.

"You were really wanting the swing. You were waiting for Douglas to finish. And what about you, Seth? What happened?"

"I saw the swing and I got on 'cuz Kioko's on that one." We all looked over at Kioko sitting on the other swing and dragging his feet in the wood chips.

"So Kioko is on there. Was this empty?"

"Yeah," Seth told us quietly.

"But I wanted it next!" Lakisha protested loudly.

"You're feeling really upset, Lakisha. You wanted a turn on the swing and Douglas had told you that you could go after him, but I'm not sure if Seth knew that. Did you know that she was waiting for it, Seth?"

"No," Seth said softly.

"See, Seth didn't know, Lakisha. So the problem we need to figure out is that there is just one swing open and there are two of you who want to swing." I looked back and forth at them both as I asked, "What do you think we should do?"

Seth spoke right up. "I think I can have a turn and she can after."

"Noooo," Lakisha responded loudly, close to tears again. Seth turned to watch Kioko.

"Hmmm. Look at Lakisha, Seth. I don't think she wants to do that idea."

Lakisha, can you think of another idea to solve this?"

"I can have a turn and Seth can go after me."

"No, I don't want that," Seth said quietly, his eyebrows scrunching together.

"Hmmm. So we still have the problem. What else can we think of to do?" I looked toward Seth.

"How 'bout I have a quick turn, then she can have it," Seth told us.

"Ahhh, a quick turn," I answered. "What do you think, Lakisha?" Lakisha studied Seth closely. Now calm, she was clearly thinking this over carefully. I repeated Seth's idea, "So Seth, you would have a quick turn right now and then Lakisha would have a turn?" Seth nodded. Lakisha still seemed to be thinking. I looked up at her mom who nodded that she could wait.

"Just quick," Lakisha told Seth.

"So Seth, how will we know when a quick turn is over?"

"Just quick," Seth repeated. I was worried that this was too ambiguous, but I saw Lakisha nod yes so I checked in with her, reminding myself that I needed to support *their* solution. If she trusted his solution, so should I.

"So that's okay with you, Lakisha?" I asked. She nodded as Seth got back on the swing.

Seth asked me to give him an underdog and then he began to pump. We all watched. After a few minutes Lakisha asked him, "Seth, when will it be my turn?"

Seth didn't answer, so I restated the question. "Seth, how will Lakisha know when a quick turn is over?"

"Count," Seth told us.

"How many will I count?" I asked.

"Three," Seth answered.

"I'll count to three," I agreed.

"Three, four, five," Seth added.

"You want me to count to five? Shall I do it slowly?" Seth didn't answer so I began to count, worrying again about the solution, wondering if he would be upset if the count was over too quickly. I counted using the rhythm of the swing, counting each kick of his legs at the end of the arc. On hearing me count, Seth made no protest—a hopeful sign. At the count of five, Seth put his feet down on the woodchips and slowed himself to a stop. With a smile, he slipped off the rubber seat and moved away as Lakisha got on. Kneeling down, I put my arm around Seth. As he turned to watch Lakisha, I told him enthusiastically, "You thought of a way to solve this problem, Seth! You took a quick turn and now Lakisha's having a turn!"

Looking pleased, Seth watched as I gave her a starting push.

"Betsy, give me an underdog!" Lakisha said excitedly.

"You mean a toe-touching, sky-scraping underdog?"

"Yeah!" she said with a broad smile. Seth watched, smiling too, as I lifted Lakisha high over my head, and she began to fly through the air in rhythmic arcs.

I remember really enjoying Lakisha and Seth's back-and-forth negotiation as they carefully considered each other's suggestions. Lakisha had expressed her frustration without letting it immobilize her; she had been able to move on to thinking critically about a solution. And Seth had remained remarkably calm and trusting. Though confused at first by Lakisha's strong feelings, he had found a way to get what he wanted as well as a solution that satisfied Lakisha. Sometimes the most tender point in a conflict is the moment when a solution like Seth's is suggested—at once conciliatory, fragile, and surprisingly simple. Such moments make me stand back in awe of children.

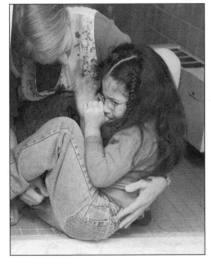 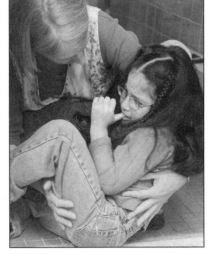

By accepting the intense outbursts of feeling children often express at the onset of a conflict, adults help children carry this emotional energy positively into this and other problem-solving experiences they will encounter throughout their lives.

Reflecting the intensity of children's feelings

Children who are expressing intense emotions need adults to acknowledge them by reflecting the *intensity* of their feelings. This shows children that their feeling message has been completely received. Recently, I was reminded of what a difference this can make while visiting a friend and her 5-year-old son, Dean. Like Lakisha, Dean could become quickly and intensely upset when there was a problem. Just as I arrived, Dean came out of the shower, dripping wet, with a towel wrapped loosely around his waist.

Children who are expressing intense emotions need adults to acknowledge them by reflecting the intensity of their feelings. Rachael's facial expression shows the children that their feeling message has been completely received.

"Mom!!" he shrieked, "Jeffrey used up all the hot water!!" Dean stood there, waiting for a response, his body rigid with fury as he dripped water all over the floor. His mom, continuing to fix breakfast, responded matter-of-factly that he could solve his problem by getting up earlier and getting to the shower first. Dean continued to stand, transfixed, and yelled, "I hate him! Stupid idiot! He hogs all the water!" His mother responded again with possible solutions; for a few more minutes, Dean and his mother went back and forth like this. Dean didn't move from his very wet spot and soon there was silence between them. As she left the room, I reframed what I'd heard, reflecting Dean's intensity, "Boy, Dean, you sound *very* angry. That must have been **really awful** to get covered with cold water!" Dean's body suddenly relaxed, "Yeaaah," he said, with a big sigh, as he came over to the breakfast table and sat down. He poured himself some juice and began to tell me about his plans for the day.

How can acknowledging children's feelings in this way help so dramatically? This technique is not a magic cure-all. Sometimes children's emotional outbursts are not simple; they may result from a complex web of frustrated, sad, and angry feelings that have been ignored for a long time. Such feelings do need acknowledging by teachers and parents, on a daily basis. Occasionally, a professional child therapist may also be needed to help a child explore the source of repeated outbursts or withdrawn feelings. Most children, however, do not need professional intervention. Acknowledging a child's feelings, immediately and sincerely, can help most children to empty out the feelings right away. Children who grow and learn with the support of adults who accept and respect feelings are better equipped to become emotionally healthy adults.

The key to supporting children who are very emotional is knowing that the child's feelings will need to be acknowledged *often,* perhaps throughout the whole problem-solving dialogue, and that the acknowledging statements will need to reflect the *intensity* of the child's feelings. The adult can match the child's intensity by using facial expressions, by emphasizing certain words ("You are **really, really angry!**" "You **really** want that truck ***now!***"), and by patiently listening to the child's feelings. In other words, the adult will need to reflect and notice the child's feelings for a longer period of time. When we are working with children who frequently become very emotional, this may initially seem very time-consuming. However, as children become more skilled at expressing feelings and more confident that the adult will accept all feelings as okay, the frequency and/or intensity of the upsets will decrease.

The following story of 4-year-old Ian demonstrates another way a child can express strong feelings throughout problem solving. Ian was a child who became frustrated easily. When he didn't get what he wanted right away, his body would stiffen, the pitch of his voice would rise, and he would loudly state or shout his demands. At the beginning of the school year, Ian had cried, screamed, and run away whenever anything frustrated him. By the time of the following incident, he had been at preschool full-time for about 3 months. He had begun to trust that the adults in the classroom would respond to his strong feelings, which, though still intense, no longer overwhelmed him to tears or screaming. It was still just as important for us to acknowledge his feelings, and now, with this support, he could fully express how he felt and move on to the "thinking" part of problem solving.

In the incident with Ian and Carl described next, it was necessary to acknowledge Ian's feelings throughout most of the problem solving. I did this by saying "You're feeling really frustrated" as well as by frequently reflecting the intensity of his tone as I repeated his wishes. [Note: In the following story, my acknowledging comments to Ian are underlined.]

Ian and Carl: "I want it RIGHT NOW!"

During greeting time, Carl and Ian got out the fire trucks in the Block Area, near to where I was sitting. After using his own truck briefly, Ian moved toward Carl and tried to take the fire truck he was using, demanding "I want this."

Carl answered quietly, "No" and pulled it away.

Knowing that Ian's feelings and actions could escalate quickly, I watched closely.

Ian reached out to try again to take it away so I scooted closer to sit between them. Quietly I asked them, "It seems like there's a problem here. I heard you ask Carl for the truck, Ian."

Ian took his hand off the truck, and I saw his back stiffen. He shouted, "I got this first and I get it!"

As I restated this, I tried to reflect some of Ian's intensity and to show him that I was really listening to the problem. "So the problem is you're **really** wanting this. I saw Carl using it and you asked him for it. What did he say when you asked him?"

Quietly Carl answered, "I needed it."

"You need it, Carl. You're using it," I repeated. Carl nodded yes.

Ian spun on his knees, moved quickly away from Carl's truck, and went back to the other truck. He picked it up and told us emphatically, close to tears, "This one doesn't work right!"

I told him, <u>"You're feeling really frustrated with that one."</u>

A little more calmly, he told me, "Yeah, but mine doesn't work right."

I took a deep breath, relaxing as well now that Ian's strongest feelings seemed to be easing. I touched Ian's shoulder gently, made eye contact, looked at him with concern, and told him, "It doesn't work right and <u>that's very frustrating.</u> It doesn't work right."

"I need that one!" Ian told us firmly as he pointed to Carl's truck.

<u>"You really need **that** one,"</u> I repeated back, rubbing his shoulder gently.

Almost sounding relieved now, Ian repeated, "Yeah, this doesn't work right."

I asked him, "What's wrong with that one?"

"The wheels don't work right," Ian explained.

I picked the truck up and tried to spin its sticky front wheels with my fingers. "Hmmm. Something keeps the wheels from turning."

Ian repeated again, urgently, "So I **need** that one."

"Could you work out a way to solve this problem?" I asked.

"No, I want it **right now!** I have to play with it first," Ian told us in a high-pitched voice.

<u>"You really want it **right now.**</u> You want to play with it first," I repeated with his urgency.

Ian's voice, getting louder, told us, "He can have this [truck] and I'll have that!"

Gently I reminded him, "Hmmm. Your idea is that you would have that truck and Carl would use the one you're holding. <u>I know you're **really, really** wanting it,</u> and Carl has said he's using it right now."

"Yeah, but I want it right now!" Ian yelled loudly as his body stiffened and his chin lifted up.

I told him, <u>"You're **really** wanting it **right now**</u> and he's still using it. Carl, Ian's really wanting a turn with that truck. Do either of you have any ideas about what we could do?"

Carl calmly suggested, "We could put the timer on." (Large salt timers are frequently used in our classroom for turn-taking. One turn of the timer takes about 3 minutes.)

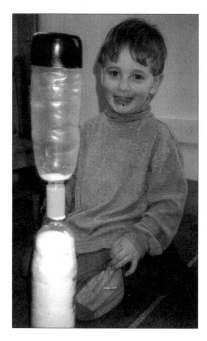

Large salt timers may be used for turn-talking.

I repeated this idea: "Ian, Carl suggested you could use the timer, and then he'd give you a turn after the timer." Ian listened. "How many times, Carl?" I asked.

"Three," Carl told us.

"No!" Ian answered with frustration.

"You're really wanting it right away... Three is pretty short, Ian," I tried to reassure him.

Ian folded his arms across his chest. "I want to only turn it one," he told us firmly.

I repeated this, "You want to turn it just one time, Ian?" He nodded. "Carl, Ian wants to turn the timer over just one time. Would that be okay?"

Still with unwavering calm, Carl replied, "Two."

"You're saying you want it longer. You want to have him turn it over two times?" I asked Carl. I repeated to Ian, "Two times? What about two times, Ian?"

"Okay," Ian agreed.

"You solved this problem, Ian and Carl. Carl will use it now and Ian will turn over the timer two times. It's solved!"

Ian got up, brought the timer close to the truck he had been using, and sat with it across the rug from Carl. Carl moved the other truck around the rug, making soft siren noises. Ian watched the salt flow through the large timer. Before he finished the second turnover, Carl brought the truck over and handed it to him.

Matter-of-factly Carl told him, "Here Ian. I'm done."

Once again, the children's resolution of the problem was a pleasure to watch. As I considered my role as their mediator, I thought that reflecting the *intensity* of Ian's feelings, and doing this whenever he expressed them, had been a key factor in letting him know that I really understood how he felt. This understanding made it possible for him to continue with the problem solving (rather then become overwhelmed). In such situations, acknowledging feelings is only effective when the mediator's body language and verbal language are congruent. In other words, to say, with a completely flat tone and an expressionless face, "You're really, really wanting this" will not work. Unless the adult also uses expressive body language and voice tone, children will not believe that their feeling message has really been received and they will continue their attempts to communicate it through angry words and actions. Adults need to name children's feelings *and* show they understand them. This approach to naming and reflecting feelings was probably also very helpful for Carl, enabling him to feel less intimidated by Ian and to be clear and assertive about what he wanted.

One of the challenges of supporting children like Ian is to *respond to the strength of the child's feeling rather than the size of the problem.* Children can become upset over issues that adults might consider unimportant. It can be very hard to tell if the child is truly upset about the details of the problem, or is upset about something else and is using the issue as an outlet. In the heat of the moment we may not understand *why* a child like Ian is reacting so intensely, and very likely he does not know why either. At these times, it can be very reassuring to have adults simply respond with empathy.

Adult Emotions and Conflict: The Role of Experience

One useful step in preparing for emotionally charged conflict situations is to consider the typical ways we as adults respond to conflicts—as observers, participants, or mediators. As we work with children, we need to remember that our conflict experience is much more extensive than children's and this personal experience profoundly affects our emotions as we participate in or mediate conflicts. Let's first consider our experience simply as *observers* of conflict. Many of us witness conflict as a constant part of our jobs—as customer service representatives, as airline ticket agents, as police officers, as marriage counselors, or as teachers. But those of us who have less conflict-ridden jobs also see disputes, and the strong emotions that can go with them, in everyday occasions in the workplace, at the mall, at the bank, or during busy commutes. Whenever there is conflict and expression of strong feelings, we turn our heads to watch. Anxiously we wonder: What will happen? How will people respond? Will the conflict become physical? As observers, we often feel anxiety, even fear, and usually, a desire to get away. From past conflict experiences, we know that we can expect results that will at best be unpleasant, at worst, even deadly.

In addition to our everyday experiences as conflict observers, the other, more important, influence on our adult conflict behavior is our experience with conflict as children. As described earlier (pp. 51–52), it can be helpful to reflect on these experiences: When we fought with our siblings and friends, how did the adults in our lives react? What role models (authoritarian or avoidance) did we have for responding to conflict? How are these role models affecting us now? If we remember frightening arguments, violence, or stony silence, how does this experience affect our feelings during children's disputes, now that we are the responsible adults?

If we grew up with adults who used an authoritarian approach, we may feel anger or fear during children's conflicts and have difficulty regarding children's hurtful words and actions as mistakes. Like our role models, we may often respond by punishing children. On the other hand, if conflict avoidance was the approach used by our parents and teachers, this may affect our ability to fully engage with the children during a dispute. We may feel uncomfortable or anxious; like our role models, we may try to bring conflicts to a quick end by fixing the problem ourselves, or we may try to ignore conflicts altogether.

Many of us have had few, if any, constructive role models for positive responses to conflict situations. Thus, the strong feelings triggered by conflicts may cause us to revert to the same ineffective approaches we have seen others use. As a result, disputes may escalate or the parties may withdraw without a satisfactory resolution. In either case, we tend to perceive conflict as failure—failure to communicate, failure to get what we need or want, failure to respond to the emotions of others. In this perception, conflict is seen as an *ending* rather then an opportunity.

The effects of such negative conflict experiences can make it challenging to respond to conflict in a patient, calm, and optimistic manner. For most of us, dealing in positive ways with our own strong emotions requires some introspection and practice. Even when we have done this "background work," we may still become rattled by our own strong feelings or those of the children. *The emotions of both the adult mediator and the children, rather than the specific issues of a conflict, are usually the most difficult obstacle to constructive resolution of conflicts.* For those times when emotions are overwhelming, making it impossible for us to approach calmly and mediate in a neutral way, it is important to have clear alternative strategies prepared. Some strategies for such times are presented next. These techniques are also effective when children are feeling too overwhelmed to begin the mental work of problem solving.

Strategies to Use When Either Adults or Children Are Too Upset to Begin Problem Solving

Delaying problem solving

Strong emotions can derail successful problem solving if the child is feeling too upset to begin to problem-solve; if the child is ready, but the adult is feeling overwhelmed; or if both the adult and child are simultaneously feeling very emotional. At the start of a conflict, if we have acknowledged children's feelings and/or tried quickly to calm ourselves but either we or the children are still not calm enough, mediation should be briefly postponed. *Adults should avoid trying to initiate problem solving if they or the children are feeling too emotional.* Emotions can overwhelm the ability for rational thought and sensitive listening. If we try to talk through what happened when we are highly emotional, it is possible that we may shame, punish, or label

1. *Two boys quarrel over using a large cardboard tube. The dispute escalates and they begin to wrestle.*

2. *Merrilee quickly intervenes and speaks calmly to each of the boys.*

3. *The child begins to say his strong feelings…*

4. *…and she listens patiently as he empties out his frustration.*

5. *Merrilee gives him time to calm as she takes a moment to be near the other child. This kind of short break is intended as a time for feelings (rather than a time to "think about" misbehavior).*

6. *Once the first child is calmer, they begin to try talking about what happened. Merrilee continues to acknowledge the upset feelings of both boys.*

7. *At right, the boys describe their ideas for solutions, and Merrilee listens to them both…*

8. *…and they agree on how to share the tube.*

9. *She stays with them, assisting as they each get into the tube.* ◆

children unfairly. Likewise, if we try to begin a problem-solving discussion with children who are screaming, flailing about, or hitting, we are unlikely to succeed. A brief pause, allowing a bit more time for feelings to calm, can make all the difference. (This story is retold from memory without a recording transcription.)

Stan: "I want whack it!!"

Rachael and 2-year-old Stan had planned to take a train to the science museum with friends. Rachael suddenly realized that they needed to leave quickly to meet the friends and catch the train. She rushed to get Stan's coat and told him it was time to put it on. Stan refused, telling her "I want whack it!!" (meaning he would throw it down if she tried). Feeling very frustrated by his reaction and very worried they would miss the train, she decided to pause rather than try to talk this through with him.

She left the room, thinking to herself: "Blankety, blankety, blank!!! Why are we taking this trip—it would be easier to stay home! Blankety, blank! Phew...I need to calm down ...breathe. Okay, so it's below freezing and he has to wear his coat—I'll gather our things and when I'm a bit more calm, I'll try again."

Having taken a few minutes to gather their things for the trip, Rachael was feeling a lot less rattled. She went back to where Stan was playing and quietly told him, "Stan, it's time to put your coat on and go to the train."

"Okay," he said agreeably and slipped his arms in the sleeves. The pause had given Rachael and Stan the break they needed. An emotional confrontation was avoided.

◆

There will always be times like these when either the adult and/or children are not ready or able to problem-solve together. At these times a short "breather" is very helpful. In fact, adults who feel overwhelmed by anger, frustration, or other feelings during a conflict should take time out—literally—to breathe. This kind of habit can give adults something to do until the intensity of their emotions eases. Some adults and children have spontaneous ways of soothing themselves during sensitive situations.

To regain composure, adults may speak quickly to a colleague, take a few deep breaths, gaze out the window for several moments, or engage in a bit of reassuring "self-talk" ("Keep calm, breathe—I can handle this!"). Children also may have unconscious, but very helpful, habits for soothing upset feelings—sucking a thumb, twirling their hair, snuggling with a blanket, or leaning up against a comforting adult.

Adults may also suggest that very emotional children take a few minutes to calm down. Depending on the situation and the child, going to a "calming place" (such as the book area or the water or play dough table) can be offered as a choice. Unlike the common strategy of "time out," this kind of short break is intended as a time for feelings, rather than a time to "think about" misbehavior or a punishment. Offering children time to fully express and recover from strong feelings communicates to children that the feelings are okay. Occasionally adults may need to decide for children that they need to take a break to calm. In these instances, adults can help children continue to feel in control by encouraging them to choose a calming place and to decide when they are ready to come back for problem solving. (This story is retold from memory without a recording transcription.)

George: Finding a calming place

Three-year-old George was often tired and easily upset at school. He lived with his mother who had recently separated from George's father. He reacted quite intensely, screaming and crying, to even minor conflicts. The first few times this happened, acknowledging George's feelings had not helped him to calm enough to begin problem solving right away. When given limited choices ("Are you ready to problem-solve or do you want to take some time to calm down?"), George usually couldn't decide, so his teacher would suggest that he take a little more time to calm down: "Let's see if we can find a place for you to be while you are feeling upset. When you're calmer, we will problem-solve." Although he resisted this at first, he usually would begin to calm as soon as they went together to find a "calming place." He often would choose to look at a book by himself and would ask for his bear and pacifier (these were kept in his backpack for rest time).

Soon he began to choose to take this time on his own. As the adult would begin to problem-solve with him, he would say, "I'm not ready," and he would go to his backpack and take his pacifier and bear to the book area. He'd select a book, and sucking and snuggling his bear, he would read for 4 to 5 minutes. Then he would put them away, and come back and quietly tell the adult "I'm ready to problem-solve now." He was a very willing and creative participant in problem solving after these calming moments. Eventually his intense reactions subsided, as he discovered that problem solving resulted in solutions that he liked.

◆

When problem solving must be delayed due to the overwhelming feelings of either the child or adult, two additional strategies may be necessary, *making "I" statements* and *giving limited choices.*

Calming Places

They are

- Places for children to go when acknowledging feelings is taking some time and they are not ready to problem-solve

- Places that have soothing things to do (e.g., play with books, sand or water, play dough)

- Places for children to be alone or with an adult until the child and the adult are ready to problem-solve

- Places where children feel safe and are not shamed or punished

"I" statements: Constructive communication about strong feelings

"I" messages describe the adult's feelings about the situation, focusing on mistaken actions, not people ("I feel worried because throwing blocks can really hurt someone"). This focus on *actions* is particularly important in working with young children because they are egocentric and therefore vulnerable to feeling responsible for everything that happens. By focusing specifically on problems, not people, we can clarify the issues while avoiding blaming children or labeling them as "bad." Because their thinking skills are still developing, young children can take in only one or two things at a time, especially when confronted with an upset adult. If adults can say what they are feeling and

"I" messages describe the adult's feelings about the situation, focusing on mistaken actions, not people ("I feel worried because throwing blocks can really hurt someone"). Such statements demonstrate to children how to express anger and other strong feelings constructively.

follow this immediately with a concrete description of the upsetting action, the child can more easily focus on stopping the action and moving on to solve the problem.

The structure of an "I" statement is critical to its effectiveness. It is important for us to name our intense feelings and the *actions* that have provoked them without the use of "you," which can result in a blaming tone. Since this statement is being made at an intense time, the structure is simple and requires us only to "fill in the blanks":

"I feel _____ because_____."

(Name feeling.)　　　　　　　　(Describe actions or reasons
　　　　　　　　　　　　　　　　without saying "you.")

"I feel **scared** because **running close to the road is dangerous.**"

"I feel **sad** because **the toy is broken.**"

"I feel **angry** because **hitting hurts.**"

Making "I" statements is a powerful strategy that not only helps adults express emotional messages without blaming or accusing but also teaches children, by example, how to express anger and other strong feelings constructively. A clear "I" message can accomplish a number of things at once.

In making "I" statements, we are essentially acknowledging our own feelings while avoiding statements like "You are making me angry because you are being mean." At such moments, it is absolutely critical to convey that it is not the children we dislike, but the specific actions. We can even state this directly by saying "I really like you. I don't like hitting." Once we have acknowledged our own strong feelings and have calmed down (and children have calmed as well), conflict mediation can begin.

Language that gives limited choices

After we've made an "I" statement, if we or the children need more time to calm, we can give children limited choices with the option of going to a calming place. Often it is necessary to add choices and limits to our "I" messages. These limited choices can clarify what needs to happen next, what the child

What "I" Statements Do

An "I" statement

- Helps adults express and "empty out" their own strong feelings about children's actions, without being hurtful to the children. This gives adults a way to calm down and prepare for neutral problem-solving.

- Stops the offending action in preparation for problem solving, a logical consequence for the child's behavior.

- Gives children choices of safe places to wait while they or the adult are calming down.

- Separates problems from people by avoiding the use of "you" and by clearly describing the upsetting actions that need to be addressed.

- Offers an alternative to blaming, punishing, or labeling children who have made a mistake.

- Models a constructive way of expressing strong emotions.

can do while calming, or what the child can do while the adult is calming. Giving children choices that define the limits on their behavior helps them continue to feel in control and motivated to assist in solving the problem. Following are some examples:

- **Limited choices:**

    "Jane, I feel **very worried** [adult's feeling] because **swinging the block near people** [action] is not safe. Your choices are to build with the block or to find a soft toy to swing instead. Which do you want to do?"

    "Chris, I feel **very frustrated** [adult's feeling] because **Legos are still on the floor and everyone is ready for lunch** [reason]. When the Legos are put away, then we will go to lunch. Your choices are to do this alone or ask someone to help you."

- **Giving children time to calm:**

    "Marina, I feel **concerned** [adult's feeling] because **problem solving is not happening** [reason]. Your choices are to talk this through with me or choose a calming place. When you're calmer, we will talk this out."

"Joe, you're feeling really, really·**angry.** Some calming time will help. Do you want to go look at a book or use the water table as a calming place? When you are calmer, we will problem-solve together."

- **When adults need time to calm.**

"Tasha, I feel **very angry** [adult's feeling] because **biting hurts** [action]. Your choices are to go to look at a book or go to the water table [any two safe places where there are no children]. When I'm calmer, we will talk this out."

"Hyung, I'm feeling **really sad** [adult's feeling] because the **book is ripped** [action]. Your choices are to go do a puzzle or look at the fish [two places nearby]. When I'm calmer, we will talk about how to solve this."

Sometimes when children are very emotional, they find it difficult to make a choice. At these times, their behavior can be "out of control." The best way to help them learn how to *help themselves* is to give them a way to choose to be back "in control." If children do not respond to the choices, we can tell them we will choose the calming place.

In the last two examples, choices are given when the adult needs time to calm. By giving children such limited options when *we* are upset, we let them know they still have some control over the situation. Then, when we are calmer, we can help them take responsibility for the problem.

Preparing "I messages" for personal triggers

For all of us, there are particular situations that trigger very strong feelings—feelings that can result in words and actions that may be regretted later. It is important to anticipate such situations, thinking ahead about the words and actions that really get us "steamed" and preparing "I" messages for those situations. Even experienced mediators sometimes encounter circumstances in which a rush of strong emotion threatens their ability to think rationally. When older children hurt younger children, I sometimes get very frustrated. The following is my story of such a situation. The strategies of postponing problem solving, using

"I" statements, and giving limited choices were all useful to me in this incident, in which I was initially too upset to problem-solve.

Aaron hits Sam: Betsy gets angry

Aaron and Bjorn, both aged 4, sat by the Duplo basket building cars during work time. Nearby, Sam and Raj, two recently enrolled 3-year-olds, looked at a book together, their backs turned to the two older boys. Aaron and Bjorn looked over toward them and began to giggle; then Aaron reached out and lightly hit 3-year-old Sam on the head for no apparent reason. Aaron quickly leaned back by Bjorn, and they laughed together. Sam rubbed his head, looking confused.

Aaron had been involved in a similar incident with a younger child the day before. During problem solving, he had told the younger child that he wouldn't hit again, and in fact he had stayed out of conflict for the rest of the day. After that incident, however, I had not felt sure that I understood what was happening for Aaron. Something about having younger children in the classroom was bothering him.

But these rational thoughts were far away in my mind. Right now I was filled with angry frustration, thinking "Aaron hit him for no reason! He is one of our older kids and he knows he's not supposed to hit children! Not only that, we just talked about it yesterday!" I realized, as I got up and began to walk towards Aaron, that I was too upset to problem-solve. I went over and squatted down by Aaron and Bjorn. For balance, I reached out and grabbed the edge of the large Duplo basket and inadvertently gave it a bit of a shake. Both Aaron and Bjorn looked startled. I was definitely not calm enough for problem solving.

"Aaron, I'm feeling really frustrated because hitting hurts …and we just talked about this yesterday!" I said. "Your choices now are to go look at a book or to go to the Art Area [there was play dough there]. When I'm calmer, we will talk about this again."

Aaron, looking very worried, immediately got up and walked to the Art Area. Merrilee and I quickly made eye contact, but since I didn't ask for help, she understood that I was taking a quick "breather" and that I would problem-solve with Aaron. I walked slowly around to the drinking fountain and took a long drink. I stood up and took a couple of deep breaths while I looked around the classroom. All the other children were working independently. I thought about my initial reaction that Aaron hit Sam "for no reason." Thinking more rationally now, I reminded myself that children always do things for a reason, although the reason may be hard to discern.

Feeling it was now possible for me to be neutral, I began to think about a beginning sentence for problem solving with Aaron. I walked towards the Art Area where Aaron was sitting. He was watching the other children at the table with disinterest and had not gotten out any materials. I approached slowly and gently pulled up a chair near him. He looked up at me anxiously.

"I'm feeling calmer now, Aaron," I quickly reassured him. He continued to look at me and leaned back in the chair. I paused for a few seconds before speaking again. Then I calmly said, "Aaron, we have a problem. Hitting is not okay. It hurts. We talked about this yesterday, but there is still a problem of hitting. What's happening, Aaron?"

Aaron looked down at his hands and slumped in his chair. He looked up at me again, his eyes soft and sad, "You know my brother beats me up all the time." I thought I had prepared myself for whatever might happen next, but I was stunned by his revelation. It is always a surprise when a young child can so quickly and clearly identify the source of a problem. I was glad that I had taken time to move on from my own frustration so that I was ready to receive this painful information.

"That must be really hard for you, Aaron…to get hurt by your brother."

"He says he's just wrestling, but I don't like it," he answered.

"It's no fun to get hurt, Aaron." After a pause with no response from Aaron, I continued, "I don't think Sam likes to get hurt either."

"I won't do it anymore," Aaron told me clearly.

"I think Sam would like to know that. Let's go over and talk to him."

Aaron and I walked over to where Sam was still looking at a book.

"Sam, Aaron wants to tell you something."

"I won't hit anymore," Aaron told Sam. Sam looked at him closely. Aaron reached over toward the Duplo basket and silently handed Sam the car he'd made.

"Is this problem solved for you, Sam?" Sam nodded.

"Is it solved for you, too, Aaron?" He nodded as well and headed back toward the Art Area. This time he got out the play dough. I followed him, watching as he began to roll it. Taking a small piece of play dough out of the container myself, I began to roll it in the same way.

"You thought of a way to solve the problem of hitting, Aaron," I told him as we rolled. He was listening, but didn't respond. "I wonder if you want to talk about how to solve the problem of your brother hurting you?" He shrugged his shoulders. I rolled my play dough into a long snake like his. Aaron's snake broke into two pieces and he exclaimed, "Look, mine's tail fell off!" He got more play dough from the container. "I'm going to make a bigger snake again!"

As Aaron became more animated about the play dough creatures, I realized that he did not want to talk about his brother. For the present time there was nothing more I could say to support him. We played with the play dough until clean-up time. In the following days, Aaron's aggressive behaviors seemed to diminish somewhat.

◆

At a staff meeting later that week I described what had happened with Aaron. The other teachers reported that on two different occasions at pick-up time, they had observed Aaron's older brother hurting Aaron. Their parents had watched without responding to these incidents. We agreed to bring up this problem during a parent conference that was coming up soon. During the conference, we shared anecdotes and our concerns about Aaron being hurtful in the classroom and about seeing Aaron being hurt by his older brother. His parents reported that there was a lot of "wrestling" between the two boys, and that sometimes Aaron did get hurt at the end of the wrestling. They agreed to keep a closer eye on the two boys. The staff also suggested that they might consider consulting a family therapist and suggested a name. The next week, the parents reported back to us that they had seen that Aaron was often getting hurt during the wrestling play. They had talked it over with the boys but were having difficulty getting the older brother to change his behavior. They were supervising them very closely now, never leaving them alone for any length of time, and they had decided to speak to a family therapist.

Over the next couple of months, Aaron's aggressiveness diminished. We noticed his brother still being physical with Aaron on the playground, but the play was more inhibited. Sometimes Aaron's parents would ask if he had had a "good day or bad day." We responded that we were uncomfortable describing his day in those terms. Aaron still made aggressive mistakes but there had also been a big change from earlier. We discussed how mistakes are isolated occasions that require problem solving, after which we all move on with the day, usually very positively. An occasional aggressive mistake does not make a whole day "bad."

When Aaron left preschool for kindergarten, the boys' rough play still seemed to be an ongoing family issue that was going to take some time to resolve. Though his difficulties continued, much progress had been made. This hitting incident was the beginning of change for Aaron; my decision to postpone problem solving until my own angry reaction had passed allowed me to listen attentively and gain a much better understanding of Aaron's needs. Following up with Aaron's parents was also very important.

Aaron's story illustrates the complexity of supporting children both during and after a conflict. To decide what strategies to use to support children's developing social skills, we need to consider not only the immediate facts of conflict situations but also the child's developmental status and situations in the child's home life. This process of evaluating the factors contributing to individual children's conflicts is discussed in the following section. (For a discussion of general strategies that can affect the overall level of conflict in a classroom, center, or home, see Chapter 7.)

Assessing the Sources of Conflict

In addition to responding to children's immediate needs in conflict situations, we also need, at calmer times, to think carefully about patterns in individual children's behaviors to assess whether something can be done to reduce the number or intensity of their conflicts. Most conflicts reflect the normal, healthy issues of childhood—disagreements over materials, space, and friends. Such conflicts are merely the result of children growing and learning together. Sometimes, however, there are conflicts (like the previous incident with Aaron) that are disturbing or repeated, or that reflect a change in the child's usual behavior. These conflicts require closer attention *after the conflict is over.* As we consider the content of the conflict and its possible source, we can take steps that may help to prevent similar conflicts in the future. Some typical sources of children's conflicts are summarized on the chart on the next page.

Conflicts that are disturbing, repeated, or that reflect a change in a child's usual behavior require closer attention after the conflict is over. The first step is a team discussion to assess the problem.

Developmental stages in problem solving and adult responses

In assessing the sources of children's conflicts, it is also important to keep in mind that most children pass through predictable stages as they learn to problem-solve. There are strategies adults can use to support children's learning at each stage. These stages and the appropriate adult responses are summarized on page 154. These general developmental patterns are also affected by many individual factors, which may include circumstances inside or outside the classroom. Individual children's behavior at each stage may vary in intensity as a result of these factors, and

Conflicts: Consider the Source

Some conflicts mainly result from issues originating in the classroom while others originate from (or are influenced by) unresolved feelings about situations outside of school. An understanding of the possible factors contributing to a conflict helps adults not only to respond supportively at the time of the conflict but also to assess what they might do to ease the source of difficulty in the future.

Typical classroom conflict sources

- *Objects*—Children are in conflict because they want to use a particular toy or material at the same time.

- *Space*—Children are in conflict because they want to use the same space at the same time.

- *Privileges*—A conflict occurs because children want a certain privilege: for example, being first in line, doing a favorite task (ringing the lunch bell), or being able to continue an activity when it's time to clean up.

- *Social situations*—A conflict occurs as a result of a social need or interaction, such as two children excluding another child from play or a child misunderstanding something another child has said or done.

Non-classroom conflict sources

Non-classroom sources of conflict may range from extreme problems such as abuse, neglect, and severe punishment to typical family events such as a new baby, a move, or illness. Unresolved feelings from these situations may cause children to express anger, anxiety, or sadness that is not related to any specific incident at school or is aggravated by an incident at school. Examples:

- A child witnesses a violent act at home or in the neighborhood or watches violence on TV. Disturbed and confused by the violence, the child comes to school needing to explore and understand this violent behavior. The child may act out the violent actions, repeatedly and intensely hurting others.

- A child engages in a yelling match with a sibling on the way to school, becomes angry, but is unable to resolve the issue before arriving at school. At school the child may not want other children to play nearby and may yell at them.

- A child is told about an impending event (a move, surgery, divorce), and comes to school feeling anxiety, sadness, or anger. The child may become either more aggressive or more withdrawn in reaction to these feelings.

In identifying the sources of a conflict, it is also helpful to consider whether a particular conflict is the result of "experimentation," "socially influenced," or "strong needs" mistakes (see pp. 46–49 for an explanation of these mistake categories identified by Daniel Gartrell, 1994). For example, most conflicts that originate in the classroom result from "socially influenced" or "experimentation" mistakes. Most "strong needs" mistakes result from factors outside the classroom; however, some children may develop "strong needs" mistaken behavior as a result of being hurt frequently or excluded in the classroom. A chart illustrating the levels of intervention that may be needed to respond to children's mistaken behavior is given on page 50.

the strategies adults use to work with children will vary accordingly. The following stories of Dion, Wally, and others in the rest of this chapter illustrate both the general stages and some of the individual factors adults consider as they support each child. For another perspective on relating children's development in problem solving to adult support strategies, see the chart in Chapter 2 (p. 50), which illustrates appropriate levels of adult intervention for different kinds of social mistakes.

Dealing with intense emotions from non-classroom sources

Children bring all sorts of things to school—bugs in jars, shells from the beach, new shoes. Much of what they bring, however, can't readily be seen: the fight with a brother, the tension between Mom and Dad, the spanking inflicted before bedtime, or the upcoming move to a new house. The weight of these stresses is carried differently by different children; but whether children's reactions are mild or intense, these outside events are likely to affect their behavior at school, exacerbating simple problems or, in extreme cases, causing withdrawal or aggression that lasts all day. The outward signs of difficulty often appear in the children's play and interactions with others. To help, we must observe with care and sensitivity and, when a problem arises, respond with the same acknowledgments and careful listening we would use during any conflict. Even if we do not know the exact source of a non-classroom difficulty, it is still important for us to follow through with appropriate responses, beginning with mediation and possibly initiating a parent conference or some other intervention. Sometimes children will tell us, directly, what is troubling them. In these cases we should accept and respect their disclosures; they signal the child's need for someone's trust and care. The following story illustrates how this can happen.

Spanking and classroom aggression

Dion, aged 5 years, was in his last week at our preschool, where he had been for 3 years; he was scheduled to enter kindergarten in the fall. He had recently returned to preschool

Developmental Stages of Problem Solving and Adult Responses

1. Child is being physically hurtful and/or is expressing very strong feelings.

Adult response: Calmly restrain the child, stopping hurtful actions and acknowledging feelings using a calm voice and giving reasons for the restraint. Ask the child to choose a calming place. If child is unable to, choose the place for the child. When the child is calmer, problem solving begins.

Post-problem solving responses: Write anecdotes, discuss at staff meeting, plan a parent conference, and, if behavior happens repeatedly, consider referral options.

2. Child is being verbally or physically hurtful.

Adult response: Place your body or hands between children and acknowledge their feelings, gently restraining them if necessary for children's safety. When children have stopped the hurtful behavior, begin the mediation, using all the steps.

Post problem-solving responses: Write anecdotes, discuss at staff meeting, discuss at parent conference.

3. Child may become hurtful in an escalating conflict and needs support with some of the mediation steps.

Adult response: Approach calmly and begin problem solving, perhaps using only some of the steps. (After mediation has begun, the child is often able to participate independently in finding a solution.)

Post problem-solving responses: Write anecdotes, possibly discuss at staff meeting.

4. Child has a problem, but cannot get others to listen. Once others are listening, the child problem-solves independently.

Adult response: Encourage all the children involved to pay attention, then stay nearby as children problem-solve independently.

Post problem-solving responses: Write anecdotes.

5. Child problem-solves with others independently.

Adult response: Observe (and quietly celebrate) the children's new skills!

Post problem-solving response: Write anecdotes.

after a 2-week absence. During his first day back, he became involved in two conflicts over objects. In both incidents he had pushed children. The teachers had used problem solving successfully in each of these conflicts but they were disappointed that Dion, an accomplished problem solver, had regressed to using physical tactics again. Although his pushing had not been intense enough to be hurtful, it had been a long time since Dion had acted this way.

On his second day back, another incident occurred. Dion was playing in the block area with Bjorn, also 5. Ian, a 4-year-old, sat down nearby to watch them, and Dion shoved Ian away with his foot, saying nothing. Ian didn't respond, but I went over and told Dion that it was not okay to push people. Ian replied, "It's okay—Dion's my friend." Then I told them both that it was not okay to push anybody, even friends. I asked if there was a problem to talk over, but neither child responded. Dion turned back to his play and Ian started using other materials nearby. A short while later, Bjorn and Dion were using a set of small plastic tools in their block play. When Ian tried to enter their play again, Dion used the plastic hammer to hit Ian on the head, telling him "No, you can't play with us!" Ian didn't react to the hit, which had not been hard, but I felt frustrated seeing one of our more mature children hurt a younger child. Here's how my problem solving with Dion began:

Dion: "Treat me like an older boy."

Betsy: Dion, I can see that you are upset about something. It's not okay to hit people on the head!

Dion: *(Making a face at me, and using a taunting voice)* I won't do it anymore.

Betsy: I don't feel sure that you aren't going to do it anymore by the way you're using your voice and making faces. I need to be sure that the other children will be safe here with you.

Dion: *(Tossing his head and using a silly voice)* I won't do it anymore! *(He looks over at Bjorn and laughs.)*

At this point I felt my own frustration rising, both because Dion was not responding in a sincere way and because his behavior toward Ian seemed like a regression from his problem-solving skills.

Betsy: Dion, I'm feeling upset because I'm still not sure that other children will be safe here with you. I think you and I need to go talk this out away from everyone. *(I take him by the hand and he willingly follows me to the book area. He sits on the small couch and I sit in front of him on the floor.)* Dion, I feel frustrated, because hitting is not okay and we talked about it only a little while ago.

Dion: *(Speaking in a calm, natural voice as he looks at the floor)* I shouldn't even be at this dumb preschool. I'm supposed to be in kindergarten.

Betsy: Hmm—you're wishing you were in kindergarten. *(Pausing as I think about what's happening for him)* It's not time for kindergarten yet. It will start in a few weeks. *(Pauses.)* Right now you're here, and we need to figure out how I can be sure that hitting will stop.

Dion: Treat me like an older boy.

Betsy: I'd like to treat you like an older boy. You are older now, but older people don't usually hit when they have problems. Let's think of some older people and what they do when they're upset.

Dion: *(He pauses for a moment and looks up at me, making eye contact for the first time since the conflict began.)* Yeah...my Dad, he hits me, he spanks me.

Dion's insight, connecting so clearly his home and school behaviors, took my breath away. Suddenly I realized his dilemma:

Betsy: Hmmm. That makes this really hard for you to figure out. I tell you that it's not okay to hit, but your Dad hits you—he spanks you.

Dion: Yeah, I tell him not to, and that if he doesn't stop, I'll hit other kids.

Betsy:	And what does he say?
Dion:	He doesn't say anything. He just spanks me and leaves.
Betsy:	It sounds like that's really hard for you. *(I reach out and hold his hand. There is silence as we both realize that we have reached the source of the difficulty.)*
Dion:	*(Reaching for a book)* Will you read this to me?
Betsy:	Sure. Have we agreed that there will be no more hitting?
Dion:	*(Quietly)* Yeah.

As I sit next to him and begin to read the book, Dion snuggles in as close as he can without getting in my lap—at least as close as an older boy can.

Strategies used with Dion. There were a number of issues here for Dion: playing only with boys his age, hitting versus talking, anticipating kindergarten, and being spanked. I tried to follow Dion's lead about which issue was most important, right then, for him. My role as Dion's teacher was to support him at this confusing moment, knowing that he had encountered a fundamental disparity between what adults say and what they do. A few weeks after this incident, at Dion's parent conference, we discussed mediation versus punishment strategies, but his dad was adamant that punishment was appropriate for Dion. There will always be times when teachers and parents don't agree about strategies. The very best that teachers can do is to try to describe clearly the reasons for the approach used in the classroom and hope that parents will reconsider.

Effects of Physical Punishment

"Research documenting the detrimental effects of physical punishment has been published at least since the 1940s. One interesting study found a clear-cut relationship between the severity of the punishment received by eight-year-olds and how aggressive their peers judged them to be. More than two decades later, the researchers tracked down some of these same subjects and found that the aggressive children had grown into aggressive adults, many of whom were now using physical punishment on their own children (Eron et al., 1987). Even more recent research has found...that toddlers who are hit by their mothers are in fact less likely than their peers to do what they are told (Power and Chapieski, 1986), and that three- to five-year olds who are spanked by their parents are more likely than other children to be aggressive while playing at a day care center (Watson and Peng)."

—*Alfie Kohn (1993, p. 329)*

The use of two "I" statements was very helpful both for Dion and for me in this incident. ("I'm feeling upset because I'm still not sure that other children will be safe here with you." "I feel frustrated because hitting is not okay and we talked about it only a little while ago.") Using this strategy made it possible for both of us to fully experience our feelings. This way, I could express my feelings of frustration without blaming, and the focus remained on the problem, not the person. This allowed Dion to feel it was safe to tell me what was really happening for him— that he was angry about being spanked and wanted to be with older kindergarten children.

Behind Dion's veneer of aggressive behavior I sensed a mixture of feelings: fear about leaving the safety of a school he had known for so long and confusion over what it meant to be older. My hope was that Dion would hold tight to what he had gained from this experience: the understanding, however confused by his father's actions, that it is not useful to hurt others when you are angry and the reassuring knowledge that sometimes you can tell adults your deepest feelings and you will be heard. Though Dion's disclosure did not lead right away to a change in his father's approach to discipline, knowing about this situation had helped me to be sympathetic to Dion's dilemma and aware of his needs during his last few days with us.

◆

Other adult strategies. After a conflict in which either adults or children have been very upset, one useful strategy is to consider the possible sources of conflict as illustrated in the stories just related of Aaron and Dion. This and other strategies for responding to strong feelings have been discussed in the first part of this chapter (see summary, opposite).

Four Challenging Mediations

The rest of the chapter explores how the strategies listed at right are used in a variety of challenging problem-solving situations as illustrated through four stories. As the mediator in each of these episodes, I found once again that there is always something new

Strong Feelings: A Summary of Adult Strategies

At calmer times—

- Review what to expect from children who are very upset. Common ways young children express strong feelings: loud screams, hitting, kicking, hurtful language, silent withdrawal.

- Assess personal factors that affect your responses to conflict. Think over conflict experiences in both adulthood and childhood; know your personal "triggers."

- Assess the sources of disturbing or repeated conflicts. To decide what to do *in addition to* conflict mediation, consider both classroom and outside factors and the types of mistaken behaviors. At staff meetings, explore whether other interventions (parent conference, therapy or assessment referrals) may be needed.

At conflict times—

*Before problem solving, **only** if you or the children are very upset—*

- Immediately state limits for hurtful behavior. ("Stop hitting. I know you are really upset. It is not okay to hit.")

- Use "I" statements to express strong feelings about children's behavior, focusing on the problem, not the person. ("I am really worried because swinging the block near people is not safe.")

- Offer limited choices and time to very upset children. ("You're feeling really frustrated. You want to go outside in your tee-shirt. [Pause, giving the child time to calm.] You're **really** not wanting to wear a jacket, and I'm worried you'll be cold. You can wear your jacket or this school sweater.")

- If the children are too upset to problem-solve, provide "calming places" for them to go to for a few minutes. Always follow this with problem solving.

- If you are still too upset to problem-solve, postpone problem solving for a few minutes. ("I am feeling too upset to problem-solve right now. When I'm calmer we will talk this out.")

During problem solving—

- Notice and name all strong feelings without judgments about the source of the feeling.

- Reflect the intensity of children's feelings by using your voice tone, words, and facial expressions. ("You are **really, really angry."** "You **really want THAT** one. You're feeling so sad.")

- Even if children are very upset over a seemingly minor issue, respond to the size of the feeling, not the size of the problem. ("You are **really, really upset.** You **really wanted** to pass the snack basket.")

- Acknowledge feelings frequently and throughout the problem-solving discussion, if necessary.

- Use problem-solving strategies with patience and persistence—you may not see results right away, but you will see them.

Most conflicts are primarily about people finding ways to express and respond to strong feelings.

to learn. In the first two incidents, children were very resistant to problem solving: in one, a child hit me; in the other, a child refused to discuss his unsafe behavior. In the last two incidents, my own personal values were challenged. The children raised questions of life and death in the animal world, and as the children made some mistakes, so did I. Fortunately, *perfect* mediation is not necessary. Meaningful dialogue and thoughtful resolutions are the goal as children explore their world, and in the end, that is what we achieved in each of these situations.

Wally's story: Problem solving when both adult and child are very upset

Some of the most challenging conflicts are those in which, without warning, both the child and then the adult become emotionally overwhelmed. Conflict situations that provoke such strong feelings may lead to "lose-lose" outcomes; the adult angrily blames the child, the child's feelings and needs are not heard, and there is no resolution that reconciles the adult and child.

Some of these challenging situations arise when children become suddenly and unexpectedly angry. This can happen at awkward times, when the group is busy or in the middle of a transition to another activity. In fact, transitions are prime times for angry outbursts. When children's anger flares up suddenly, it can be difficult for adults to maintain the neutrality they need to help resolve the issue. They, or the children, may need to take a break before trying to problem-solve. Once problem solving begins, these intense conflicts can become "win-win" encounters, deepening the trust and bond between adults and children.

Sometimes, outside factors contribute to these especially difficult conflicts. So much happens in children's lives before they come into the classroom. Though it may help us to be more sympathetic if we know about a child's circumstances, much of the time this is not possible. Our knowledge or lack of knowledge about the source of the intense feelings should not change the way we respond. ***All strong feelings need to be noticed without judgments about the problem or the source of the feelings.***

In the conflict in the following story, Wally, a child in my classroom, experienced intense anger, ostensibly over a sweater. His anger might also have been related to an earlier incident as well as the stress of having a new baby at home. I found Wally's anger so unsettling that both Wally and I were initially too upset for problem solving. The story, though lengthy, is included in its entirety to illustrate the challenges of such situations and strategies for resolving them.

Wally hits Betsy, over an itchy sweater

Wally's outburst began during the transition to outside time, as children dressed and stood on the ramp by the coatroom, waiting to go to the playground. Wally bolted for the door and stood defiantly at the end of the entry ramp. Spinning to look at me, he shouted, "I'm not wearing that itchy sweater!" I looked at his thin blue tee-shirt and his furrowing eyebrows. It was a gray, 55-degree spring day. I looked at the rest of the children putting on their coats, once puffy and bright, now faded and slack from the constant wear of winter. We had already told several children that, because of the cool air, long sleeves were required for the playground today, but observing Wally's defiant stance, I wished that I could make an exception.

"Wally, it's chilly today. Everyone needs to have their arms covered in order to stay warm," I told him as calmly as I could manage. He latched his hands tightly around the railing.

"No! I hate that sweater. My mom doesn't make me wear it if I don't want to!"

"Wally, your arms need to be covered. It's chilly out. Come back in and we'll look for something else."

"No! I hate everything else!" he yelled back.

Other children began to spill out onto the ramp as I wove my way through to him. Gently putting my arm around his shoulders, I told him, "Wally, I know you're upset about this. We need to go inside and find something to cover your arms."

In a furious explosion, he turned and began hitting me with both fists. I quickly reached for his wrists, but as soon as I held them, he leaned back against my grasp and began kicking me with both feet. As I turned him around in an embrace, I told him firmly, "Wally, it's not okay to hit me! I know you're upset. Hitting and kicking need to stop." He screamed and went limp, putting his weight fully into my arms. I moved with him towards the door, his feet kicking lightly at the children as we passed. They quickly moved out of the way.

Once inside the school, I led him toward the area that was set up as a pretend hospital. The bin where we kept extra clothes was there. Wally made another attempt to swing and kick at me. "Let go of me! Let go of me!'" he shouted.

"You're really upset. I can let go when hitting stops, Wally," I said as quietly as I could and still be heard. He stopped, looking near tears now. I let go slowly and he lay down on the floor crying. I suddenly became aware of how constricted my chest felt. "I know you're upset, Wally." As I said this, I realized this was true for me too. Wally's angry outburst and attack on me had taken me by surprise; I was shaken by it. I wondered if I had intervened too quickly. Perhaps if I'd given him more time to tell me what he was feeling out there on the ramp he might not have become so upset. I wasn't sure if any of that would have made a difference, but I was sure that I was not ready to take on the next phase of problem solving with Wally. I was still too rattled and I didn't want him to mistake my startled feelings for angry ones. I reached out and lightly touched his back. He recoiled from my touch and I pulled back.

"I know you're upset. I'll give you a few minutes by yourself, Wally. I'll be right back." As I moved away, he relaxed into the soft pile of the carpet.

A break seemed like a good idea for both of us. He had a calming place there on the rug. I decided it would help me to talk to my teaching partner, Merrilee; I went back to the coatroom where she was zipping coats.

"Wow, any idea what's happening for Wally?" I whispered to her, trying to empty some of the tension out of my chest. I knelt close to her and helped Alana with her coat. Merrilee hesitated, thinking carefully about the day. I felt like I needed a hug, but I settled for the understanding look on her face as she turned to answer.

"Wally has been having a hard time with clothes," she said, "but I think he's still angry at Martha. She was blowing 'raspberries' in the coatroom when they all arrived this morning, and she sprayed spit onto Wally's baby sister. Wally was really angry. Martha slimed the baby pretty good. I think he's still angry about it." (Raspberries are loud, often wet noises made with the tongue and lips.)

"Ahhh," I sighed. Understanding now what was happening for Wally helped me prepare for the problem solving, but this new information also meant the rest of the negotiation might be tough. Wally possibly had feelings left over from this incident which he was still trying to empty out. It would not be useful to go over the spitting conflict again—I was sure Merrilee had really supported Wally when it happened—but knowing this would help me be more sympathetic. I was breathing normally now, and I felt ready to support him. I took his sweater off the peg and went back, resolved that I had to stick to the limits I had set, but feeling more prepared to do it gently, with lots of listening and acknowledging.

Wally was sitting up now. As soon as he saw me coming he reached for a box of hospital props and flipped it over, spraying stethoscopes, bandages, and pretend thermometers across the rug.

Calmly I told him, "Wally, I know you're really upset about this. If you throw things at me, I will need to stop you—I'll need to hold you again." He retreated behind a curtain hanging against the wall.

"I know you don't want to talk about this, and we need to go outside," I said.

Flinging the curtain back, Wally yelled, "I'm not putting anything on!"

"I know you really don't want to wear this sweater, so I'm going to get out some other long-sleeved shirts and you can choose something else."

I pulled out four shirts from the clothes bin and laid them out in an orderly display on the rug between us. Wally yelled to me, "I'm not wearing those!" He grabbed a shirt and tore at it. The rugged shirt seemed to be a safe target for his angry energy so I decided not to try to stop him.

"I can see you're still really frustrated about this, Wally. We need to go outside. Here are your choices. You can choose one of these or I'll choose for you," I continued.

"My mom doesn't make me wear that itchy sweater! I'm going to tell her I hate this school and never bring me here again!" Wally told me, still wrestling with the shirt.

"Well, at home, your mom and dad say what's okay and here the teachers need to decide—and we decided it's too cold to go out with nothing on your arms. I know you're really upset about your sweater, Wally. Later we could write a note to your mom about your sweater, but right now you need to choose one of these shirts."

Wally dove back under the curtain, covering everything but his legs.

"Wally, you need to choose or I'll need to choose for you. I do think you'll feel better if you choose yourself."

Wally's legs thrashed back and forth, and I began to worry about Merrilee and the other children waiting for us by the door. "We **have** to go out, Wally. It's not safe for me to leave you in here alone."

The curtain flew up and Wally grabbed a brightly batiked, long-sleeved shirt. "I want this one!" His eyebrows formed a deep furrow between his eyes.

"When I'm a grown up, I'm going to get horses and bring them here to kick down the **whole** school!" he said intensely.

Gently I took the shirt and began to put it over his head. He cooperated as I helped him get his arms in the sleeves. "You're really, really angry, so angry you feel like you want to knock things down."

He looked at me with soft, steady eyes and gently told me, "I really am."

I wasn't sure if he was agreeing with my acknowledgment of his anger or reaffirming that he would truly be bringing the horses. But I was sure that he knew I'd understood. I couldn't change how things were for him at that moment, but I could allow him to say and show, in his own age-appropriate way, how it felt for him. Then he could move on. Together we pulled the shirt straight down to his pants. He jumped up and I followed him to the door.

Outside, only moments later, Wally picked up a heavy toy and yelled to me to look. I watched and said, "Wow, Wally, you're lifting that really high!" He looked at me, smiling with pride, all other feelings left behind.

The rest of Wally's day went remarkably smoothly. He didn't ask to write a note to his mom, but as soon as she arrived to pick him up, he grabbed his sweater off the peg and told her, "I hate this itchy sweater!"

"Okay," she said quietly, gazing at me and then at him with a look of confusion. Wally went to get his artwork and I gave his mom a brief version of his problem, emphasizing how Wally had solved it. At a later conference, we discussed in more detail how the teachers were supporting Wally in working through his strong feelings. His mom explained that with a new baby sister at home, they hadn't really been listening to his anger and had been putting him in time-out. In time-out his frustration had escalated to the point where he would sometimes throw anything he could find nearby. She agreed to try more listening and acknowledging of his feelings at home.

As for the itchy sweater, we never saw it again.

◆

Conflict mediation provides a huge opportunity for adults to broaden and enrich their relation-ships with children. When emotion is raw and intense, there are enormous risks: both adults and children may do or say things they may regret later. Mistakes are inevitable, but fortunately they generate a fresh perspective.

How conflict mediation enhances adult-child relationships.

At the end of the day, as I thought back on this conflict between Wally and me, I began to understand how its intensity had pro-vided something positive for both of us. Wally had expressed very strong feelings and those feelings had been respected. Now Wally knew that he could trust me to give him understanding, time, and safety as he experienced these difficult, emotional moments.

Conflict mediation provides a huge opportunity for adults to broaden and enrich their relationships with children. When emotion is raw and intense, however, there are also enormous risks: both adults and children may do or say things they may regret later. Mistakes are inevitable, and fortunately, they can generate a fresh perspective. It is rare that I don't look back on a conflict and wish I had done something differently. I see this reflective thinking as useful—like the children, I'm always learning. Flawless use of the mediation steps is not necessary for the bond between adults and children to be strengthened. When a child and I work through a challenging set of feelings and come out on the other side having resolved a problem, it is a tremendous step forward in our relationship. Besides the new understandings and skills that we've both gained, the relationship is now grounded in a strong sense of trust.

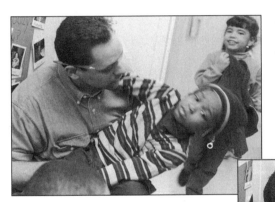

Sometimes gentle restraint is helpful. Here José gently holds a child who is trying to run from the room.

As José speaks quietly to him, acknowledging his feelings, the boy begins to calm.

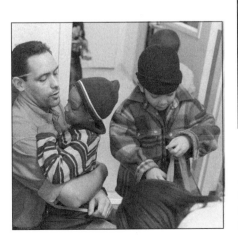

Soon the boy begins to describe what is troubling him and agrees not to try to leave before he is dressed for outside time.

When Reasoning (or Restraint) Doesn't Work

Sometimes special support strategies are needed when a child is out of control and gentle restraint is not possible. In *Meeting the Challenge: Effective Strategies for Challenging Behaviors in Early Childhood Environments* (1999) Barbara Kaiser and Judy Sklar Rasminsky describe an approach for such situations, using "Brian," a child who has become aggressive and combative, as an illustration.

Brian has thrown a chair across the room. He refuses to listen and has kicked an intervening adult in the shins. For times like this, Kaiser and Rasminsky recommend that each program prepare a special plan that describes exactly what each staff member will do when it is necessary to separate an out-of-control child from the others. In Brian's case, one of the adults is to indicate to the others that there is a major problem with Brian and that all the children should be kept safely away. Once this is done, Kaiser and Rasminsky recommend the following strategies for giving Brian the space and time he needs to calm:

"Reasoning doesn't work.*

"Because Brian is being driven by emotion, reasoning with him doesn't work. Words seem to fuel the emotion, like gas on a fire. When Brian calms down, you can use words to help him return to a more normal state. (A by-product of this approach is that he learns that he can calm himself.)

- Stay a safe distance from Brian, both for his sake and for yours, but remain close enough to show that you are attending to him.

- Distance yourself psychologically, and relax your face (even if your stomach is in knots).

- Do not confront him with your hands on your hips or make yourself big and intimidating. You will just make him feel smaller and defensive and increase the possibility that he'll lash out, especially if his reaction is based on fear. Instead of facing him head on, assume an L-stance, standing sideways, head up, body relaxed, knees slightly bent, to minimize the threat that you pose and to allow him to save face and not to feel trapped. Keep your weight on the foot closest to the child so that you can move away if necessary.

- Do not try to move him. If you do, his behavior will probably escalate. There are two exceptions to this rule. The first is when children are fighting and someone is likely to get hurt. Try hockey referee tactics—wait for a lull in the action, then step in and pull them apart. The second exception is when a child is in danger—if he's running in the street, you have to act.

- Be aware of your eye contact, which is critical when a child is in an irrational state. Although it helps some children to collect themselves, it can also ignite the situation, intensify a power struggle, or reinforce a child whose goal is to get your attention. Gaze over Brian's shoulder or at the middle of his body. This will help you to keep your face relaxed and your mind clear. When he is quieter, gradually bring your eyes to his to see if he's ready to begin interaction with you again.

---

*Reprinted with permission from the Canadian Child Care Federation, Ottawa, Ontario.

- Do not talk until he is ready to listen. Try a few short words when he is calm.
- Do not insist that the child apologize or give a reason for his challenging behavior. He doesn't know why he threw the chair, and asking him to say he's sorry gives him attention, encourages him to say words he might not mean, and suggests that it's all right to hurt someone as long as he apologizes afterwards (R. G. Slaby, et al., Early Violence Prevention: Tools for Teachers of Young Children, NAEYC, 1995).

"When he's calm, spend some private time with him. Each child needs something different, but you could help him to name his feelings ('You must have been [very]...angry') and distinguish between feelings and actions ('It's okay to feel angry,...it's not okay to throw chairs'). Talk with him about other behaviors that might have been more appropriate, and let him know that you still care about him.

"He will need your help to reintegrate into the group and to ensure that he doesn't blow up again right away. Stay with him until he feels comfortable" (pp. 29–30).

Adult strategies used in the "itchy sweater" conflict. As I thought over this conflict, I realized several strategies had been particularly helpful for Wally and me. Listening and really recognizing Wally's feelings had been most important. However, I wondered if the mediation might have gone more easily if, out on the ramp, I had done more acknowledging right away, before touching him. It was clear as we moved inside that he did not want to be held. I responded to these cues once we were safely away from the other children. Sometimes children react *very* negatively when they are touched or restrained when they are upset. Restraint does sometimes result in an escalation of their physical behavior and therefore is not always advisable. Some ideas for what to do instead of using restraint are given opposite.

Though it is usually useful for mediators to think through what could have been done differently, we aren't always able to explain why a mediation has been difficult. In Wally's case, he had had a trying morning before this incident and he was going through an adjustment to a new baby sister at home. Sometimes allowing children to do some "dumping" of their strongest feelings is necessary. We may not always know where the feelings come from, but this strategy may help the rest of the day to go better.

Another strategy that had been critical for both of us was taking a little bit of time apart before going on to problem-solve. We were both upset. Continuing while we were both so overwhelmed would have made it more difficult for Wally to negotiate and for me to be neutral and supportive of him. The 3 minutes or so that we spent separately helped us both gain some composure.

Safety is never negotiable; if children are engaging in hurtful behavior, stopping the behavior must be a clear priority. However, it is also important to talk with children about what has happened and come to an agreement about safety limits.

Asa's story: Problem solving around safety issues

Safety is never negotiable; if children are engaging in hurtful behavior, stopping the behavior must be a clear priority. However,
it is also important to talk with children about what has happened and come to an *agreement* about safety limits. Such discussions should occur before allowing children to return to play
with others. Even if children strenuously resist discussing their
unsafe behaviors, we must insist on it—it is very important that
they experience problem solving as a consistent and logical consequence to being hurtful. When a mediation is very challenging, this is not always because the details of the situation are
complex, but because complicated, resistant *feelings* are extending the process. In these instances, it is imperative to be clear
about limits and the need for problem solving.

The following story of Asa illustrates this kind of situation.
Asa had had difficulty at other times when he had been hurtful
and we had set safety limits; I therefore felt it was important to
interact in a determined and consistent way with him until he
could act safely on his own. The mediation described here was
a lengthy and challenging experience. Though its resolution was
somewhat vague, we noticed some big changes on subsequent
days.

Asa refuses to problem-solve

At work time, Asa and Ian have been building with the large,
hollow blocks. In the midst of their building, they begin to
show off by finding sillier and sillier things to do. Soon they
are running through the room, bumping into people, picking
up toys and throwing them, and calling people names as
they pass quickly by. As they run back to the hollow blocks,
I follow them.

> **Betsy:** Asa and Ian, we have a problem. Throwing toys,
> running through the room, bumping people and
> calling names—none of these are safe, Asa and
> Ian. We need to talk about this. *(Ian, who now
> finds problem solving much easier, stands still
> and listens. Asa begins to run away. I reach out
> to him.)*

Asa: Stooooop!

Betsy: I can see you're really upset, Asa. *(I gather him into my lap.)* I'm going to hold you unless you're going to stay here on your own and talk to me, Asa. Do I need to hold you or are you going to stay here with us?

Asa: What about him?

Betsy: Ian's here. Ian's staying right here. Now the problem is…*(Asa laughs loudly, waves his arms, and thrashes with his legs.)* Asa, you're not listening. You're not wanting to talk about this. *(He doesn't answer.)* Do you need to calm down for a little bit?

Asa: No.

Betsy: Until you're ready to talk this out?

Asa: No. *(He struggles to get away.)*

Betsy: No? 'Cuz you can choose a place to do that or you can stay and talk this out. But I'm going to hold you until you decide. *(He flails around loosely in my arms. My holding him seems to have no effect; in fact I wonder if it is making him more resistant. I gently let go of him and he walks off, planting himself in the corner by the door about 10 feet away.)*

Asa: I'm not going to listen!

Betsy: You're not going to listen? You're feeling too upset. You need to calm down first?

Asa: Uh-uh. *[no.]*

Betsy: Well, one or the other needs to happen, because we have a problem to sort out and if you're not ready to talk about it…

Asa: It's not just me!

Betsy: Yep, it's Ian too, but Ian is staying here. He's not running away.

Asa: I'm not running away either!

Betsy: I let go of you and you've gotten up and gone away.

Asa: I don't have to, you dumbhead! *(Asa begins to knock down blocks.)*

Betsy: I know you're really upset, but it's not okay to call

	me names. *(I move toward him as he kicks blocks.)* You know what, Asa, I need to stop you. *(I reach out to stop him from kicking blocks.)* You don't look like you're ready to talk yet.
Asa:	Do you want me to kick **you!**
Betsy:	You're feeling really angry. *(Asa begins to pull down rest mats and throw them.)*
Asa:	I'm going to throw your mat…
Betsy:	*(I hold his shoulders from behind, stopping him.)* I'm going to need to choose a place for you to calm down, Asa. I'm going to bring you away from other people. Kicking and throwing mats is not safe. This is not safe what you're doing.
Asa:	Get your hands off me! *(I hold him, as gently as I can, in an embrace from behind.)*
Betsy:	Asa, the reason I'm holding you is because we have a problem to sort out and you're feeling really upset. You don't seem ready to problem-solve. You need to stay and talk this problem out or you need to choose a place to go and calm down.
Asa:	No!
Betsy:	Well, then I'm going to choose a place for you 'cuz you still don't look ready to me. I'm going to choose a place for you to calm down unless you would like to choose a place. You're feeling really upset and you don't seem ready to talk this out with me.
Asa:	Let go!
Betsy:	I need to choose a place for you to go to calm down. *(I walk with him to the Book Area and let him go.)*
Asa:	*(Shouting)* This is the way you're going to make me calm down…by letting go of me!
Betsy:	*(Asa paces back and forth. I'm blocking the entrance to the Book Area.)* You're still really upset and we need to talk out this problem…
Asa:	If you put me in some place so I can calm down then I'm not going to calm down. I'm going to be wild, wild, wild—for all of the day!!

Betsy:	I brought you here because you did not want to choose a place. You're feeling upset and you need to calm down. You can choose a place to go to calm down—then we can talk out this problem. So would you like to choose a different place to calm down?
Asa:	No.
Betsy:	No? A place to calm down is a place that is quiet—and you can be alone until you're ready to talk things out. *(He relaxes somewhat and sits down on the cushions.)* Do you want to be alone right there?
Asa:	Fine, then I'll be alone right here.
Betsy:	I'll be back in just a few minutes and we can talk out our problem.

In this conflict, which happened near the beginning of the year, Asa put a huge amount of energy into preventing a problem-solving discussion. It seemed to me that he wanted to be in complete control of what was happening; each time I began, he made verbal and/or physical efforts to stop me from trying to mediate. Asa may have thought that at some point I would just give up and let him do what he wanted. His mother told us later that that was what often happened at home. I had hoped to give him some control over the situation by offering him the limited choices of problem solving or calming down, and then a choice of calming places. But no matter what choices I offered as I tried to share control with him, he refused to make a choice. Consequently, I gave him choices that were more and more limited, until finally I made a choice for him. It was only when he realized that I was not going to give up on the situation that he finally began to share control with me ("Fine, then I'll be alone right here"). I fervently hoped that insisting on problem solving now would help him to be more capable of problem solving in the future. I wanted him to know that I would listen to his needs and support a search for solutions, and that I would also insist on safe play.

Betsy:	*(Returning to Ian who is busy building)* Ian, it's not safe to be running through the room throw-

ing toys and bumping people. What are we going to do about this problem?

Ian: I'll stop. I won't do it anymore.

Betsy: So this problem is solved 'cuz you're going to
stop? *(He does seem completely relaxed and
ready to go back to building.)*

Ian: Yep.

Betsy: Okay, I'm going to go back and talk to Asa. *(I go
back to Asa.)* Asa, are you ready to go back to
talk with Ian? *(He doesn't respond but comes
out, goes to Blocks, and begins to move blocks
along with Ian.)* Ian, can you stop building a
minute, 'cuz it looks like Asa is ready to talk out
this problem. The problem is...

Asa: *(Giggling nervously)* No, I'm not. *(Giggles.)*

Betsy: No, you're not ready, Asa? Then I need to ask
you to be by yourself in a calming place until
you're ready, because this is a problem we need
to work out before playing and right now you
don't seem willing to talk about it yet.

Asa: I'm not willing to talk about it so go away! *(He
puts down the blocks and begins to move
away. I follow.)*

Betsy: No, I'm going to stay here. I need to talk to you.
*(We have moved toward a corner of the room,
and Ian has gone back to building.)* It won't
take very long. I've already talked it out with Ian.
I just need to talk it out with you.

Asa: I already heard it!

Betsy: Hmmm. I don't think you did.

Asa: I already know what the problem is!

Betsy: What do you think the problem is?

Asa: I already know and I'm not telling. *(He tries to
move away and I stop him by holding his shoul-
ders again. He looks like he is going to cry.)*

Betsy: *(Softly)* Asa, I know this is very hard for you, but
we haven't worked out the problem.

Asa: I already know and I'm not gonna tell.

Betsy: That's part of talking things out—we need to talk
about what the problem is. You can either tell
me or I can tell you what I think the problem is.

Asa: What is it?

Betsy: I think the problem is that sometimes when children play with other children, they start running around and other children get bumped and hurt. That's not okay. It's not safe.

Asa: I wasn't doing that.

Betsy: All those things happened. When hurting happens, I need to stop it.

Asa: I wasn't doing that.

Betsy: All those things happened and it wasn't safe.

Asa: *(Asa begins to get teary.)* I wasn't doing that! You're just making me do it! Saying these things makes me do it, when you don't say these things, then it doesn't make me do it!

Betsy: When hurting happens with you or any other children, I need to stop it.

Asa: If you're talking about it, then I'm going to do it!

Betsy: Hmmm, then I'm going to need to stop you.

Asa: I'm not stopping.

Betsy: I need to know how we're going to solve this problem so hurting doesn't happen again. How do we solve it?

Asa: How do we solve it? *(Asa's voice becomes quiet.)* There's no easy way to solve it.

Betsy: There's no easy way to solve it?

Asa: Uh-uh. No easy way. *(His head hangs down as he rubs the floor with his hand.)*

Betsy: It might not be easy, but I think there might be a way. Ian found a way to solve it. Do you want to know what Ian did to solve it? *(Asa nods.)* Well there's really two things he did. First he and I talked about being safe and he said that he wouldn't run anymore…

Asa: I wasn't even running! I wasn't!

Betsy: And then he decided that it was really more fun to build than to be running.

Asa: I know!

Betsy: So what do you want to do to solve this?

Asa: *(In a shaky voice)* I already know what I want to do but I'm not telling!

Betsy:	It's really hard for you to talk about this, Asa. *(He doesn't respond, but he looks teary and frustrated.)* You look like you're still really upset. Asa, I need to know before you can go back to play with other children that you're going to be safe.
Asa:	*(Still using a frustrated, teary voice)* I'm going to!
Betsy:	Okay, if you're ready to be safe, you can go ahead and play. *(Asa returns to Blocks. I watch from a distance. He moves too quickly and knocks over a chair. Seeing this tension, I stay nearby. He begins to play with Ian, who tells him what he's done to the building and where the "scorpions" can go. Asa begins to relax and in about 15 minutes, his anger seems to be completely gone. He is playing constructively, without trying to provoke a negative reaction from children or adults. As I see him pass by smiling, playing scorpions with several children and being careful of children around him, I speak to him.)*
Betsy:	Asa, the problem of running and hurting really seems to be solved for you now. *(He looks at me briefly, long enough to give me a sense that he knows what I'm talking about, his face relaxing into a smile. Then he continues on with his play.)*

After this incident I was exhausted and discouraged. I was concerned that Asa seemed to view adults as incapable of responding to his anger and did not believe that adults would help him find solutions ("There's no easy way to solve it," he had told me sadly). I wondered what he had gotten from the mediation. Over the next 2 weeks, I found out. During those weeks Asa was involved in several conflicts with children and adults (not always provoked by him) and there was a marked difference in his willingness to stick with a mediation and contribute to the solution. I felt like our long episode together had created an increased trust in the problem-solving process and an understanding that mediation didn't take away his control of the situation. He now seemed interested in being in control by making choices about solutions that would keep his play within safe limits. Asa had experienced my persistence, understanding that no matter how many mistaken actions took place, he could trust that I would stay with the problem until we had found a solution that worked for both of us. This intense incident, in which Asa had been very resistant to problem solving, had created a new depth in our relationship—a new respect and interest in one another.

◆

Two stories of children and animals: Challenges to personal values

In some problem-solving situations, the adult's strong values and consequent feelings can make neutrality very difficult. In such incidents it is especially important to ask "what" instead of "why" questions and also to say "I feel…" rather than blame.

The next conflict story illustrates this type of situation. Asa, the child who had refused to problem-solve in the incident just described, was a bystander in this mediation; he joined in as Ian and Mark Anthony discussed their conflict. Although Asa stated his ideas about the problem very assertively, at no time did he try to prevent problem solving from happening. This was progress for him. He not only participated willingly in the discussion but also, in the end, was the child who came up with a solution that was agreeable to everyone.

As the mediator in this incident, I found the strategy of using "I" statements to be both challenging and extremely helpful as I expressed my feelings and values.

Ian and Mark Anthony: "He doesn't want us to break worms!"

Alana and I sat on the big rock in the center of the playground, playing in miniature-sized puddles in the rock crevices. As we swished our sticks in the water, I heard Ian's voice rising. I looked over and saw Mark Anthony and Ian

> looking into a white enamel pan that once belonged in someone's kitchen. Mark Anthony was sitting on the ground by the pan and Ian stood over him. Ian cocked his head to one side as his body stiffened with tension. He began speaking louder and faster. Asa was running toward them. It was clearly an escalating situation, so I got up and walked over.
>
> "Ian, you look really upset about something," I told him.
>
> "He doesn't want us to break worms and we want to!" he answered me furiously. Asa picked up the pan.
>
> I looked quickly into it and saw five squirming earthworms. They all appeared to be whole.
>
> "You want to break the earthworms?" I asked them.
>
> "Yeah! And he won't let us!" Ian yelled, propelled backward by the intensity of his words.
>
> "I can see you're really upset about that, Ian. What's happening for you, Mark Anthony? You don't want them to break the worms?"
>
> "Uh-uh" Mark Anthony answered stiffly, not looking up from where he sat by the pan of worms.
>
> "We can!" shrieked Ian.
>
> "You're feeling really strongly about this, Ian."

Neutrality in problem solving is essential to creating trust between the children and me. I want them to know that they can tell me anything without fear of being judged. But could I discuss the breaking of earthworms neutrally? I remembered how agitated I had felt as I'd watched my father stab a fishhook into a squirming worm, the unlucky one just fetched from the coffee can by my father's favorite trout pond. I sat down between Ian and Mark Anthony as I decided to give neutrality a try.

> "Mark Anthony, can you tell Ian what upsets you about breaking the worms?" I said.
>
> Ian shouted, "We don't have to listen to him!"
>
> I looked up at Ian. "I know you're upset, Ian. I'd like you to listen. I think he might have a reason why he doesn't want you to break the worms." But Mark Anthony was silent, expressionless, staring at the worms. Asa was listening to all this as he dug in the sand nearby, the pan at his side.

"And we found 'em !" shouted Ian again.

"What happens when you break them, Ian?" I asked, trying to find out more about the problem.

"They're still alive," he told me. Then I noticed that he held a worm in his hand. We all watched as he grasped one end of the worm with one hand while the fingers of his other moved down the worm's body, pulling it until it was twice as long and stretched taut like a rubber band. Suddenly he released the worm and it snapped back to its relaxed length, unharmed. I released the breath I was holding. I turned back to Mark Anthony.

"What do you think, Mark Anthony?"

Mark Anthony didn't answer. He continued to sit silently, a stern, faraway look in his dark eyes. Mark Anthony had been finding problem solving very difficult, often getting into a conflict and then becoming blank and silent when problem solving began. He liked to be in complete control of play, and Ian and Asa were protesting this more often.

Asa looked up suddenly from his digging, "Yeah, and they grow new tails, too!"

"Yeah!" echoed Ian.

"You're both feeling really sure about that. You know, I'm feeling worried…because breaking them could hurt them," I said, feeling squeamish and not very neutral. I hoped that the "I" statement here helped to clarify that this was *my* problem.

"Yeah!" yelled Mark Anthony, suddenly animated in his agreement with me.

"Were you worried about them getting hurt, Mark Anthony?" I asked.

Mark Anthony nodded.

"They're not even living creatures!" shouted Asa.

Mark Anthony was shouting too. "Yes, they are! They're living creatures!!"

In the calmest voice I could muster, I said, "Actually they are alive, Asa, and they have a very important job to do. Do you want to know what it is?"

"Yeah," responded Asa and Ian in unison.

"Their job is to dig in the ground and loosen it so it will be easy for plants to grow."

All eyes were on me, including Mark Anthony, so I continued. "In fact their job is so important that some people grow earthworms on special farms and then sell them to people who want them as helpers in their gardens." They were quiet for a few seconds as they took this in. Everyone seemed to be breathing more easily. I hoped they were ready to move on to solutions, so I decided to restate the problem.

"So Asa and Ian, you want to break off the tails, and you feel the tails will grow back?"

"They will," Asa reassured us.

"And Mark Anthony and I are worried that the worms will be hurt. So what can we do to solve this?"

"They do grow new tails," Ian repeated, "and he can't tell us what to do." He began to walk away, worm in hand.

"Ian, I don't think this problem is solved yet."

"It is for me," he answered quietly.

Asa turned over a small rock. Finding nothing, he picked up the pan and followed Ian.

Mark Anthony and I sat quietly. I waited to see if he would react, but he didn't move. His once stern face now looked sad.

"Is this problem solved for you, Mark Anthony?"

"No," he told me quietly.

"Well, let's go talk to them again."

Mark Anthony and I walked over to the area under the pine trees where a circle of rocks lay on the pine needle floor. Ian and Asa were lifting a rock together, looking for more worms.

"Asa and Ian, Mark Anthony doesn't feel like this problem is solved."

Ian looked up at us from where he sat by the rock. "He's always telling us what to do and we don't like it!"

"You don't like him telling you what to do?" I repeated, beginning to understand the most important part of the problem for Ian. However, I was still unsure how this clarification would help solve the problem, so I decided to restate the problem and ask them again to solve it.

"So Ian, you don't want Mark Anthony to tell you what to do, and Mark Anthony is worried that the worms will be hurt. So what do you think we should do to solve this?"

Ian continued to dig in the dirt. Asa, still holding the pan, looked into it. I looked, too, still anxious about what I might see. The five worms were still there, all their parts intact. The silence seemed long. I took a deep breath and waited. Mark Anthony stood quietly and watched as Asa continued his examination of the worms. Poking them gently with one finger and talking into the pan, Asa told me, "I think he should go find his own worms and not break them if he doesn't want to."

I turned to Mark Anthony, "What do you think of that idea, Mark Anthony? Shall we do that?"

Mark Anthony nodded enthusiastically. Excited myself, I turned back to Asa and happily told him, "You figured out a way to solve this problem, Asa!" Asa looked up at me, somewhat surprised himself.

"Is this problem solved for you too, Ian?" Ian nodded as he dug.

Mark Anthony and I began our search nearby. We pushed over a large rock and Mark Anthony dug in the moist, dark earth. As I watched him, I felt moved once again by the strong feelings and questions that are at the center of children's conflicts—feelings and questions that explore the basic principles of relationships, both with worms and with each other. I was amazed by the simplicity and complexity of Asa's solution; it had accomplished both respect for Mark Anthony's needs and protection of his own.

I also realized that although the problem was now solved for the children, I still had a nagging concern for the worms, and a desire to model respect for the living things on our playground. I was worried that my information about earthworm farms might not have been enough to encourage that respect. Ian and Asa were not far away, so I called to them, "Ian and Asa, I still feel worried about the worms. I'm worried that they'll be hurt." As if surprised that I had not understood this all along, Ian responded, "We're just finding them. We're not really going to break them anyway." Ah, I thought to myself, this had been a conflict about relationships, a "who-can-tell-whom-what-to-do" conflict. The treatment of earthworms had been important, but secondary to the back-and-forth balancing of who controls the details of play.

Indeed, over the next three weeks, it became clearer that a change in the relationship among Mark Anthony, Ian, and Asa was occurring and that this change was difficult for Mark Anthony. I noticed Mark Anthony choosing to play more often by himself, while Asa and Ian were busy together. On several occasions, Mark Anthony did want to play with them, and conflicts about who was in control were again mediated by the teachers. Out of these conflicts, a new understanding was forming. It didn't happen all at once. Mark Anthony was not finding it easy to hear that he could not tell them what to do all the time. After about a month of play, some solitary and some cooperative (negotiated with adult support), the three boys came to a new place in their friendship, one of sharing ideas and control. It was a place they had begun to create in negotiations over earthworms, and because they had arrived there by mutual agreement, they could return to it over and over again.

◆

In the incident described next, I was again confronted with my own strong feelings about killing living things. I had to struggle to see the children's actions as a mistake and in the process, I made some mistakes myself. However, as we explored the situation with a problem-solving approach, the children and I learned a reassuring lesson: even though we sometimes make mistakes that we regret, there are still constructive (in this case, comforting) things we can do after mistakes are made.

Ian, Tom, and Asa: "We killed a toad."

It had been a very wet fall and the children had been finding little brown toads on the playground, hidden in the leaves or camouflaged in piles of pine needles. I never saw these tiny hiding places myself, but I often heard children shout to the others that a toad had been discovered. The captured toad then traveled about with its finder in a plastic bucket meant for beach sand or in an old soup pot. Sometimes the children made small pine needle nests and placed their toads inside.

On this day, Alexei had a toad in a large, dented metal bucket lined with pine needles. He carried it to where Asa, Ian, and Tom were stirring slushy, black mud. Alexei asked Ian, "Do you wanna come help me make a nest for my toad?"

Ian looked up from the mud. Asa held up a shovelful of thick, dripping liquid and answered, "Here, we'll give it some poison." Alexei quickly walked away, his bucket bumping his leg as he went.

A few minutes later, as Alexei, some others, and I were helping with the nest for Alexei's toad, Ian came over and told us, "Guess what we did? We killed a toad."

Despite the frustration that rushed over me, I searched for a response that would be true but not hurtful to them. "Oh, Ian, I feel really sad about that!"

He reached into Alexei's bucket, offering, "Here, I'll squish this one." I quickly reached over to stop him.

"No, it's not okay to take other people's things they've found, Ian," I said firmly.

Tom and Asa appeared, and Asa declared loudly, "I got a toad and we killed it."

I again tried to send my feelings through a "teacher sieve" of constructive response: "You know, I feel really sad about what happened to the toad. It's not okay to kill toads. I feel really **sad** for that toad."

Tom looked carefully at my face and asked, simply, "Why?" His question was such a direct recognition of my strong feelings that my teacher sieve gave way, and I answered with frustration. "Because why would you kill a toad, Tom? The toad didn't do anything to hurt you!"

I knew from many years of working with young children that "why" questions are too difficult for them, especially when they have made a mistake and they know that you are upset about it. They almost always respond as Tom and Asa were about to—they lie.

Pausing for just a few seconds, Tom became suddenly animated, "He **did** hurt me!"

"He did?" I asked. "What did he do that was hurting you, Tom?"

He made a quick, light poke at his eye, saying "He was hopping up at my eye!"

Realizing my mistake, I responded again to what had happened. "I'm going to ask you not to be near toads if they are going to get hurt. That's really not okay."

But Asa, still feeling the accusation of my "why" question, loudly echoed Tom's response. "That toad hurt me like this!" he said, jabbing at his eye. "He hopped right into my eye, like this!" he repeated, jabbing again.

Their readiness to tell me what they thought I wanted to hear made my mistake very clear. My frustration was gone and I saw their need for resolution.

"Asa, I need to know where the toad is."

"I'll give you a hint. It's down near those bushes," teased Asa.

Quietly I answered, "No hints, Asa. You need to show me where it is." He pointed toward the tire swing, and in a calm voice said, "It's right down here."

Asa led us to his bucket and I knelt by it as Ian, Tom, and a few others gathered around. I dug down through several layers of needles and mud, gingerly fingering the mixture for the toad, hoping that the toad might still be alive. As I dug, Asa added, "We put it in the poison and squished it."

I found the toad and carefully, slowly, I lifted it out, brushing off the sticky grit. I laid out a still intact, yet very dead toad in the flattened palm of my hand. The children were silent.

A few children reached out to touch it, then asked if it was dead. I looked up at them and slowly told them, "It's dead now and we need to bury it. Where can we dig a hole so the toad can be peaceful?" Not responding to this question, Ian quietly reached over and gently touched it with his finger.

Then Tom began to walk up the hill to the sand area to look for a place to dig. Ian followed. Asa headed in another direction. Ian watched as Tom picked up a shovel and began to dig. Tom had not said anything since telling me the toad had jumped at his eye. His twin sister, Athena, had followed him to the sand area, loudly telling him, "You are bad, Tom. You are bad!"

This was a label that I very much wanted to avoid. Kneeling by Tom, who was digging, I told her, "Athena, Tom made a mistake but he is not bad. I don't like toads getting killed but I do really like Tom." I watched Tom digging and told him: "I think you'll need to make the hole deeper, Tom, if the toad is going to be peaceful—if it is going to be left alone, the hole needs to be deep so that it won't get dug up."

With determination, he dug some more. Then Asa appeared. He lifted his fist close to my face and I saw two little toad eyes peering out from between his fingers. I held my breath and then slowly let it out as I noticed the eyes blink. "This is the doctor toad," Asa told me. No one spoke. Then Asa added, "He can fix him."

Moved by his wish to change what had happened, I answered, "You were hoping another toad could fix him so he would stop being dead?"

"Yeah, this one's the doctor," he answered, putting the live toad near my hand where the dead toad still lay.

The group of children that were gathered around us watched intently. For them, at this moment, anything was possible. The toad's life could begin again. The doctor toad *could* restore life. The children were open and vulnerable. An angry statement from me about their actions could have inflicted guilt and reinforced the idea that mistakes are "bad." Mistakes, however, are the essence of the teachable moment. Over the past months, I had earned their trust by telling them what was true and real. As they watched and saw that even with the doctor toad nearby, the dead toad was still not moving, I gently continued.

"I don't think this toad can fix him, Asa."

Jared, who had been watching nearby, replied, "A real doctor could."

"At a hospital," added Brigit.

"Doctors, even real doctors, can't bring dead animals or people back to life," I told them softly. There was a silence among the children as they tried to grasp this. "There are lots of things that doctors can do to help people that are sick, but they can't make dead things be alive again."

Tom looked up from the digging, "Is this deep enough?"

Brigit, laying some pine needles down in the hole, said,

"Here's a bed for him."

Quietly I said to Tom, "Would you like to lay him in the hole?" He shook his head no.

"I will," said Asa.

I laid the toad in his hand and he gently laid it in the hole. As the children took in this sad little burial, I looked at their small, subdued faces and asked, "Shall we say anything to the toad before we cover it up?"

To this, Brigit said simply, "Goodbye, toad." Alexei added, "We're sad you're dead, toad." Tom had begun to shovel the dirt into the hole. When he was finished, he got up and found a small pine branch. With Alexei's help, they stood it straight up in the fresh dirt. Tom looked very sad. Reaching out, I stroked his back gently.

Several hours later, at pick-up time, I told the parents of the children involved about the toad. Asa's mom explained that the day before she and Asa had caught a toad and had put it in a glass jar with no water. Forgetting it, they had left it in the sun for several hours and upon their return had found it dead. Asa had taken it out of the jar and put it into a bowl of water, hoping to bring it back to life. He had asked many questions about death and how things die. On this day he had found one more way.

When children kill small creatures, I get really upset. I find it takes a real effort to express my values and strong feelings with an "I" statement.

In my role as a teacher, I find that the killing of creatures on the playground especially upsets me. I have to work really hard to express my values and strong feelings with an "I" statement. In this incident I had initially succeeded at this ("I feel really sad about what happened to the toad") but was unprepared for Tom's question about why I felt sad. I should have answered, "I feel really sad when living things are hurt," but I too struggled to respond constructively to a "why" question when feelings were involved. Instead, I vented my frustration by asking Tom why he had killed the toad. Because "why" questions ask for something quite abstract—the motivation for a feeling or an action—and also make children feel blamed, they are difficult for young children (and sometimes for adults). Children frequently will respond to "why" questions with escalating emotion or by making up an answer, as happened here. My question was ineffective in helping the children resolve their feelings about the toad.

I also wish I had asked the children what they thought we should do with the toad, instead of suggesting burial myself. But teachers can make mistakes too and still go on to constructive solutions. The children did respond to my question about how the burial should happen and actively participated, each in his or her own way. Because Ian and Asa had openly said they had killed the toad, this event became an opportunity to explore questions of life and death together. All the children involved expressed their feelings and thoughts in different ways. It was simply necessary for me to stop asking why, to notice their feelings, and to give support as best I could.

In the following weeks, no harm came to any more of the playground creatures. Instead, the children spent lots of time making very large, fluffy, pine needle nests for the toads, who appeared bewildered but unharmed as they looked up at the foot-high walls surrounding them. The nests had become a poignant symbol of the children's new understanding of the fragility of life.

Interactions that involve strong feelings are among the most exasperating and rewarding of our experiences with children. During these tense, emotion-filled exchanges, our skills, values, and beliefs are challenged, and we experience a mix of emotions. For me, such experiences have sometimes evoked deep anxieties about my skills as a teacher and a parent; yet they have also stimulated profound insights. As I look back on these especially challenging conflict experiences, it's been very useful for me to notice how my own childhood conflict experiences (during which strong emotions were usually avoided) affected the changes I was trying to make in my own teaching approach. Change takes time and practice, and I'm still learning. I now see how these difficult mediations and children's inspired solutions have provided me with many opportunities to make what were once "new" strategies into my own strategies—what once felt like a costume is now comfortable clothing. Conflicts are catalysts; they help to uncover what is true and real in our beliefs and values, giving us the opportunity to confront our contradictions and fears while reflecting and then acting on what we really want in our relationships with children.

5

 **Learning to Problem-Solve: How Change Happens, One Child at a Time**

Adults are often impatient for children to learn how to work out their conflicts on their own. Sometimes it does happen that children acquire these skills very quickly, with little apparent effort, but more often children need considerable time and support to grow and change. Learning personal communication skills and acquiring an understanding of peers and appropriate social behavior is a gradual process that is different for each child. If we can see the learning of problem-solving skills as an adventurous journey and look forward to the individual differences and creative pathfinding that each child brings to it, conflicts can be enjoyable learning moments that enrich our days.

Listening for Children's Needs and Wants

Understanding and fully listening to the "needs and wants" of children is an essential part of conflict mediation. This chapter looks closely at the needs and wants of two children, Benny and Raven, both from

> "Just as a single conflict develops over time, however, so do the individual combatants; their developmental status and life histories cannot safely be ignored. Presumably individuals change systematically with age in their tendencies to initiate conflicts and to sustain them, and in their abilities to understand and react appropriately to their companions' actions. Behaviors shown while fighting and while trying to resolve disputes are at least partially the products of socialization."
>
> —Dale F. Hay (1984, p. 2)

A dispute begins between two boys over a set of bowls they are using in their "restaurant." Betsy asks each of the boys to describe what is happening and they quickly resolve the problem.

When adults hold a genuine belief that all children can grow and change, they remain sensitive to and respectful of each child's individual circumstances, learning style, and potential.

If we can see the learning of problem-solving skills as an adventurous journey focused on individual differences and creative solutions, conflicts can be enjoyable learning moments.

my classroom in Massachusetts. The stories of Benny and Raven illustrate how children's problem-solving skills develop through negotiations about their needs and wants. Although this development follows a general pattern (see chart, Chapter 4, p. 154), it happens in very individual ways.

Before turning to Benny's and Raven's stories, it is useful to consider the difference between children's *needs* and *wants,* and how this affects mediation. Children have a basic *need* for such essentials as food, sleep, safety, and loving attention. They need consistent daily routines and caring adults they can trust, and other kinds of positive experiences that sustain and enrich their lives. Parents and teachers try their very best to address these basic needs, knowing that this will promote children's healthy development. Children also have many *wants* or wishes. They may want a new toy, a bigger ice cream cone, a room of their own, or a baby sister instead of a brother. While these wants are also very important to children, they do not have the same potential impact on their physical health or emotional well-being.

As mediators, it is important for us to think carefully about whether a child is expressing a *need* or a *want.* Sometimes children have wants that seem unimportant to adults, but that actually may reflect deeper emotional needs. For example, children may tell us that they *want* a new puppy. For some this may be a passing fancy, but for a child who has just lost a sibling or a best friend, there may actually be a *need* for a new puppy, or other animal companion. A child who *wants* Mom or Dad to read more than one story before bed may also really *need* extra loving attention from a parent before settling down to sleep. Likewise, a child who has eight siblings at home may want and really *need* to have time alone in the school Block Area, whereas a child who needs a new bicycle helmet for safety may simply *want* the shiny, but less sturdy one.

Our responses as mediators during a negotiation may differ somewhat, depending on our awareness that the child's requests are based on a want or a need. Jason, who has eight siblings, may tell his classmates that he wants to play alone in the Block Area. Understanding Jason's *need* for time alone will affect how we restate the problem; keeping this in mind, we might say "So the problem is that you want to play here and Jason is saying he really wants to play here alone. What can we do to solve this problem so that he can have some time alone and at some point you all can play here, too?"

An understanding of children's needs helps us to clearly describe their requests. Knowing that Sara wants the less sturdy bicycle helmet, but needs the safer one, helps us to be sensitive to her wants while also explaining her safety needs in clear terms. By acknowledging Sara's wishes and giving reasons for the need, we can encourage her understanding and make a cooperative response more likely. We can then assist her by clarifying the limited choices remaining that will ensure her safety. "You *really* like the shiny one, Sara. It's very sparkly [pausing to allow her to respond]. These, here, are the safest ones for your head. I am going to ask you to choose from these so your head can be very safe. Which color do you like best?"

Problem Solving With Limited Choices

1. Approach calmly: Use gentle body language.

2. Acknowledge feelings: "You're feeling upset."

3. Gather information: "What is the problem?"

4. Restate the problem: "So the problem is...."

5. Give limited choices for solutions: "Your choices are to (1)____ or (2)____. Which will you do?"

6. Give follow-up support: "You solved this problem!"

Even when children's health and safety needs are an issue, as in the helmet situation, there is usually some room for negotiating. By giving children limited choices, we can help them participate in and cooperate with the solution. The negotiation will, however, be about *how,* not if, the health and safety needs will be met. For example, a child who is tired must go to bed, but there can be some limited choices about how that will happen. ("Do you want to walk upstairs or would you like a piggy back?" Or "Do you want to go up in two more minutes or three?") Likewise, a child who wants to walk without holding hands near a busy road must be kept safe, but this too can be negotiated in terms of limited choices. ("You can hold my hand or your mom's hand. Which do you want to hold so we can walk safely near the street?") A child who is protesting about departure from school can also be supported by problem solving with limited choices. ("You're really feeling sad that it's time to go. You've been having such a good time. We have a problem because the school day is over and we need to go make dinner. Your choices now are to hold my hand so we can walk together, or we could have a race to the gate. Which do you want to do?") Giving limited choices helps children share control and may prevent an escalation of the problem.

In these situations, it's important to make every effort to encourage the child to make a choice. If a child refuses to choose, it may be necessary for us to say something like this: "Because teeth do need to be cleaned before bed, a choice of who will do it does need to be made. So who's going to do it, you or me?" Pointing out "I think you will feel better if you choose what to do" gives the child another opportunity to share control. Children's need for control at these moments reflects their growth toward independence. If we can view this behavior as a positive sign of healthy development, we can often muster the patience needed for negotiation.

Humor and playfulness can also be saving strategies in many such situations. If a child yells, "No one cleans my teeth!" we can suggest, "Teddy Bear can do it or I can do it." While it is important not to make light of children's feelings, there are occasions when a touch of humor can help de-escalate a situation. If humor doesn't work and the child becomes more upset, it is necessary to acknowledge feelings and negotiate the problem in a more serious way.

All of children's wants and needs deserve our thoughtful consideration. The more we can involve children in sorting through what they need and want, the more adept they will become at doing this independently.

This chapter illustrates and reflects on the journey traveled by Benny and Raven as they used the mediation process to express their wants and needs. Their stories were chosen because learning problem solving was not quick or easy for either child. In another school, with a punitive approach to conflict, Benny and Raven might have been labeled as "difficult" children, rather

By involving children in sorting through what they need and want, even at a very early age, we help them become adept in doing this independently.

than as *children experiencing difficulties.* When negative labels are attached to children, the labels can become an expectation for behavior and little change can occur. By contrast, Benny's and Raven's stories illustrate the profound growth that can result from experience with mediation. When adults hold a genuine belief that all children can grow and change, they remain sensitive to and respectful of the child's individual circumstances, learning style, and potential.

Benny's and Raven's stories illustrate how experiences with conflict mediation can create connections—a bridge—between a child's stressful life circumstances and new skills. For both children, crossing this bridge was an inspiring and surprising journey that created strong and lasting bonds with the adults in their lives. This new learning was not the children's alone. Benny and Raven deeply touched those around them, sharing their intense desire to play and their determined creative energy with all those who mediated with them. The strategies of problem solving—and the adults who implemented them—were thoroughly tested by Benny and Raven.

Benny's Stories

Benny had started full-time family day care when he was 2 years old and had begun in our preschool program when he was 3. He was the youngest of four children; his parents had just separated. Benny was an active, curious child with dark brown eyes and an impish smile. He was often adept at getting what he wanted and needed by whatever means possible. In family day care, biting had been one strategy he had used to get what he wanted and this had frustrated and worried his parents and day care provider. After entering our school, he tried hard to be a part of the larger social scene. He was intensely interested in his peers, often expressing his desire to join children's play by hitting or pushing. Despite his aggressive responses, he was well liked by his playmates, who sought him out for his bold sense of adventure and creative imagination.

The following stories about Benny's conflicts at school trace the development of his problem-solving skills. Sometimes children experiencing challenges in their lives take to problem solving right away, quickly finding relief in the adult's accepting response to strong feelings. For other children under stress, this learning process may go more slowly; it may take extra time for them to learn new ways to express strong feelings. Benny showed a combination of these patterns. He learned to trust the problem-solving process right away; his humor, creativity, and quick thinking were an asset in the hunt for solutions. Because he was still emotionally young, however, it took him longer to learn to control his very strong emotions, and at the beginning of most mediations he continued to need a lot of support in expressing his feelings in non-hurtful, verbal ways. The adults in our classroom were both delighted and challenged by Benny. His days had no wasted or unimaginative moments; he was a child living his life with daring vibrancy.

Replacing physical aggression with verbal assertiveness

The following incident occurred several months after Benny entered the program. At the time, Benny frequently played with the large hollow blocks with two to three other children. This block-building play was full of negotiation about what would be built, how the blocks would be placed, and what roles would be played. The play was rich with opportunities for the children to learn about cooperation and communication, and Benny's ability to play with more than one other child was growing. Conflicts happened sporadically, with some days more harmonious than others. During these conflicts, Benny had been physically aggressive at times, but after these initial physical reactions, he had also come up with solutions that worked. Just before the following incident, Benny and Hyung had been working intensely on building something to ride on. Max had been trying to enter their play when this conflict occurred.

Benny hits Max, then finds a solution for everyone

Max comes to me and tells me that Benny has hit him, twice. I ask if he needs help talking to Benny. Max nods yes. I have not seen what happened between Max and Benny. We go to Blocks where Benny is building a ship with hollow blocks. As he sees us coming, he runs into an area behind a short wall of hollow blocks.

Betsy:	Benny, Max is upset. *(Benny runs around inside the structure, not looking at us, trying to find a way to get out.)* I think we better go in there and talk to him, Max. *(Benny now tries to get out of the structure.)* Benny, you know what, Max really wants to talk to you and we don't really want to chase you right now. *(I take hold of Benny, embracing him from behind and sitting on the floor with him in my lap. He doesn't resist physically.)* We just want to talk to you.
Benny:	*(Yelling)* Noooooooo!
Betsy:	You don't want to talk about this.
Benny:	*(Even louder)* NOOOOOOO!

These loud noes were an important beginning for Benny. It was plain that he was nervous about my intervention and did not want to talk about this problem. I acknowledged this by simply describing his resistance. Benny responded by fully and loudly emptying out his distress. He needed to empty out his most anxious feelings before he could go on to talking through the issues.

Betsy:	You know, we have a problem here. Max said that he was playing here and that you hit him twice.
Benny:	I did—it was just like this *(slowly moves his arm in a punching motion).*

Max:	No, he did it hard, it went...*(He hits himself hard on the arm.)*
Betsy:	*(To Max)* It felt really hard when he hit you.
Benny:	No, it was just like shhhhhh *(very slowly moving his arm in a punching motion)*.
Betsy:	*(To Benny)* You didn't feel like it was very hard.
Benny:	No.
Betsy:	It was just soft.
Benny:	Yeah.
Max:	Hard.
Betsy:	Max feels like it was hard and it hurt. Max, is there something you want to say to Benny?
Max:	Yeah.
Betsy:	What is it you want to say?
Max:	*(Softly)* Don't do that, Benny.

In discussions of "who did what" with children, adults often think their role is to make a final ruling on what is really "The Truth." It would have been easy to assume that Max was telling the truth because Benny had, in the past, hurt other children. I resisted this assumption for two reasons: First, I hadn't seen what had happened. If the adult hasn't seen what has happened, it is very important to resist making assumptions—this may be the day that the child's behavior changes. An incorrect assumption could discourage the child from trying change again.

Second, even if I had seen whether Benny had really hit Max, it would have been important for me to hear from both children, without judging; the adult's role is to stay neutral so that children can experience acceptance of their feelings while learning new ways to meet their needs and wants. By acknowledging and accept-

As we listen to children, it's often important to consider whether they are expressing wants or needs. Here Martha listens carefully as children begin to talk through the details of a dispute over a ball. She tries to simply hear out their stories, keeping the dialogue going by restating the issues.

ing both versions of the story, I could support Benny and Max in talking about what they felt. Benny knew it was not okay to hit; he had been told this many times by adults. This time, it was important for Max to tell him. Regardless of the power of the punch, Max would best learn to communicate his need for safety if he was encouraged to say "Don't do that" for himself. A neutral, accepting approach made it possible for me to remain supportive of both boys. I could support assertiveness in Max, while supporting Benny to listen to the concerns of others. And most important, this support also made it possible for Benny to honestly admit that he did hit Max.

Benny:	*(Responding to Max's "Don't do that" with a sudden yell)* AHHHHHHHHH!
Betsy:	That's making you angry, Benny, that he wants you to stop hitting him.
Benny:	Yeah.
Betsy:	So what else are you angry about, Benny?

I quickly kicked myself here for asking a question about feelings rather than saying "So, what's happening, Benny?" But Benny, having problem-solved many times before, had gotten to know the pattern of the problem-solving steps. Thankfully, he understood what I meant.

Benny:	Because I really want to play here…with nobody else.
Betsy:	Did you tell Max that before you hit him?
Benny:	Yeah, but he didn't listen.
Max:	No, I wanted to come on the ship and Benny wouldn't let me.
Benny:	Yeah, but there's no space for him and no seats! There's only two seats.

After telling about what had happened and expressing their wants and feelings, Benny and Max both seemed ready to move on to figuring out the problem. As they began to talk through the physical details of the situation, I tried to simply hear out the story. I was not in charge of solutions, but I did have an important role in keeping this dialogue going by listening carefully and restating issues.

Betsy: Only two seats. Hmmm.

Max: But that wasn't fair.

Betsy: It's not fair that there's only two seats?

Benny: Well, there has to be.

Hyung: Well, there's only one seat right now, right here. *(Everyone turns and looks at the structure as Hyung points and lifts a block.)*

Betsy: There's one seat.

Benny *(With increasing frustration in his voice, Benny turns to Hyung.)* Yeah, but you just wrecked my seat because we, but you...but we...I took yours 'cuz.... I took your seat, okay? 'Cuz my seat was right here. *(Speaking with sudden disappointment)* Now we have to make our ship all **over** again.

Betsy: Wait a minute, Benny. Is the problem that there's not enough seats for Hyung, you, and Max?

Benny: Yeah, because look it, there's one, and one's over there! *(Benny points to his structure and a block by Max.)*

Betsy: There's one seat here and how many seats are over there?

Hyung: *(Standing by the structure)* Two.

Betsy: Two seats. I count one, two, three seats and I count one, two, three people. So are there enough seats now for Max to have a seat?

Benny: Yeah!

Betsy: There are?

Max: I want to sit on a square. *(He picks up a rectangular block from the floor.)*

Benny: Okay, then you can sit on one of these two. *(He points toward the structure.)*

Betsy: Can you show him, Benny, which one he can sit on?

Benny: This one or this one. *(He touches each square.)*

Max: I don't want to sit on a square.

Betsy: Max, you just said you wanted to sit on a square.

Max: No, I didn't.

Benny: Yeah, I heard you.

Max:	I said I wanted to sit on one of **these.** (*Max holds up the small, rectangular hollow block.*)
Benny:	But I gave you one.
Max:	No, I can put this over and sit on this.
Benny:	Oh, that's what I wanted you to do. That's what you should do.

> "Along with an awareness of themselves, these children are developing abilities to assert power and status and to control the behavior of others through argument."
>
> —*C. Genishi & M. DiPaolo*
> *(1982, p. 67)*

Often conflict discussions develop digressions, like the query over Max's seat shape, that seem unconnected to the main issues. Max's request for a specific shape of seat may seem a bit "picky," coming as it did just as a resolution was at hand, but this seat discussion had an important function. Conflicts are always about balancing power and control over wants and needs. Max, by asking for a specific kind of seat, was establishing some control over the play. Once all the children felt they were again on equal footing, the building and fantasy play could resume.

Betsy:	Is this problem all figured out? It sounds like everyone has a seat, right? Can I see where you're all going to sit? Max, where are you going to sit? (*As all three children sit down, I come and kneel close by, listening to their discussion.*)
Hyung:	This is my brake.
Max:	Right here is my brake, okay?
Benny:	You can't go yet. I need a brake.
Betsy:	It looks like you've got this all figured out! (*As they busily continue to construct, no one responds. So I direct my question to Max, since he had come to me for help.*) Right, Max? Are you all set?
Max:	Yep.

The tension is gone from their voices and the movement of their bodies. Playfulness and fantasy have returned. I watch for a few moments from nearby, but see no sign of any lingering conflict. The boys play on their "ship" for another 25 minutes, until cleanup time.

◆

As Benny learned to problem-solve, expressing his strongest emotions while controlling his impulses was the biggest challenge for him, as it is for many preschoolers. When he was supported in expressing his strongest feelings, however, Benny responded verbally and did so with remarkable honesty ("I did [hit him]…") and clarity ("I want to play here…with nobody else"). Over time, as Benny experienced acceptance of his strong feelings, he learned that the feelings were okay, even though the subsequent hurtful actions were not. As Benny gained more control over his hurtful impulses and learned to express himself verbally, he also began to develop his ability to adapt and adjust to the needs and wants of others.

When adults observe children having difficulty expressing their anger or frustration in words, they can support this emerging skill by encouraging children to use a loud voice when they are particularly upset. Being verbal, however loudly, is a developmental step forward from being physical.

Observing Benny's difficulty with expressing anger or frustration in words, we decided to support this still emerging ability by encouraging him to use a loud voice when he was really upset about something. When children are trying to find a less physical way to express their feelings, it is unrealistic to expect them to state their feelings calmly and quietly. (Many adults can't manage that!) Being verbal, however loudly, was the next developmental step for Benny. During a conference with Benny's parents we explained the strategies we were encouraging. Benny's parents told us that his behavior was changing at home, too, and that a louder voice was part of the change happening there.

Each time a child becomes involved in a conflict situation, feelings and new learning from previous conflict experiences are interwoven with present needs and feelings. There is now a potential for change. Now that the child is more capable of self-control and more experienced in finding solutions and express-

The Development of "Adaptiveness" Through Child-Child Conflict Negotiations

As we've seen in the conflict stories told so far, conflict elicits a variety of interactive strategies from children. Developmentally young children who are involved in a dispute may respond to another person's demands or objections with a simple negative sound, gesture, or "no." As children mature, the strategies they use in conflict situations reflect an increasing ability to adapt or respond to the needs or demands of the other parties in a dispute. Eisenberg and Garvey (1981) studied the development of these adaptive strategies, identifying five levels of increasingly adaptive responses. The study included 108 preschool children, ages 2.10–5.7 years. The following levels of adaptiveness were documented, described here from youngest to most mature:

1. "Insistence" (p. 159) is defined as a repetition of a demand or negative response (sound, gesture, or no) that adds no new information to the interaction. For example, a child repeatedly tells another child, "Move!" after the other child has refused the same demand at least once. In my experience, this level of interaction will either escalate to a physical confrontation or will resolve with one child withdrawing. Children interacting at this level are very much in need of a mediator who can facilitate further identification of reasons, wants, and/or needs.

2. "Mitigation and aggravation" (p. 160) are defined as either submissive or aggressive responses that do not add new information, but do indicate adaptation by becoming less confrontational (mitigation) OR more demanding (aggravation). A child who adapts to the conflict by mitigating might initially insist, "Move!" When there is a negative response, the child may say, "Will you please move?" A child who adapts to a conflict by aggravating might initially insist, "Move!" When there is a negative response, the child may yell, "MOVE NOW!" Though neither kind of level 2 response adds any new ideas or reasons to the interaction, they both show an emerging ability to adapt in a limited way to the conflict.

3. "Reason" (p. 160) is defined as a level of adaptation in which the child adds explanation or reasons for the offending action or words. By giving reasons, the child demonstrates an awareness of the opposition and a willingness to try to help the opposing child understand the situation more clearly. This strategy is an important step toward a higher level of adaptation to conflict. For example, the child may initially insist, "Move!" When there is a negative response, the child may add, "I need to put my foot there for a brake."

4. "Counter" (p. 160), is seen as the next level of adaptation, in which the child refuses to give in but offers something else as a substitute for what is wanted. For example, the child who has said "Move!" and is told no, will offer an object or role (other then the one requested), such as "You could play with that truck over there" or "How 'bout you be the ticket-man." (Either of these alternatives would make it necessary for the other child to move.)

5. "Conditional" (p. 160), in which the child proposes an alternative that will happen *only* if the other child makes a concession, is the next level. For example, the child who has initially said "Move!" when opposed may add, *"If* you move, you can be the conductor's helper."
The statement is a conditional offer; the offer is contingent on the opponent's compliance with "Move." As with the "counter" strategy, the child has not given up what is wanted, but is showing an awareness of the opposing child, recognizing that that person has wants as well.

6. "Compromise" (p. 161) is defined as the highest level of adaptive response because it demonstrates not only a willingness to give information and account for the perspective of the opposing child but also a capacity for diminished egocentricity. At this level, the child offers to give up some of the original demand by proposing to share or partner in some way with the other child. For example, the child may start out by demanding "Move!" When the opposing child refuses, the child may say, "I need to put my foot there for a brake. Move over, then we can do it together."

Eisenberg and Garvey's study also looked at how frequently each kind of strategy was used and compared their effectiveness in resolving the episode. As might be expected, the highest rate of success (76.7%) occurred when compromise strategies were used. However, compromise strategies were used only 30 times out of 833 strategy tries in the 210 conflict episodes. The most frequently used strategies were insistence (336) and giving a reason (275). However, in a majority of the uses of compromise strategies, reason-giving strategies were also used, indicating an important link with this emerging capability.

In this study, the conflict interactions were unguided (there was no adult intervention). We can only speculate as to how these interactions might have changed had an adult assisted the children by mediating. However, if children acting independently are sometimes capable of adapting to the needs and wants of others by giving reasons for their demands, it becomes clearer why compromises, or even win-win solutions, happen so frequently when conflict mediation is used. I would speculate, based on these findings, that those children who respond to conflict at the very basic level of insistence will learn about giving reasons and alternatives through mediation, while those children who are already able to be adaptive to others during conflicts will quite quickly learn to adapt and collaborate at an even higher level.

ing feelings in alternative ways, he or she may respond to *this* conflict differently. This is why it is so important for mediators to remain neutral and avoid making assumptions based on children's previous behavior. When the adult remains impartial, the children can adapt their responses and try out fresh ways of reacting to conflict. In the incident in the following story, Benny did find a different way to respond. He controlled his urge to be physically assertive and instead was verbally assertive, communicating his wants clearly and giving reasons for them.

"Get off!": Benny waits for horses

At outside time Luisa and Maggie are sitting on two wooden horses. Benny and Evan come running up. Benny is holding a stick in his right hand, away from them. He tries to get on the horse in front of Luisa. She yells no, and he stands back. Sue, one of the teachers, hears Maggie yell and sees Benny with the stick. She decides to go over. Meanwhile, Evan gets on behind Maggie, who doesn't react.

Sue:	*(Gently)* What's happening here?
Benny:	I want to get on the horse. There's not a good place to be alone or wait.
Sue:	You're waiting for a turn but you don't like where you were waiting?
Benny:	Yeah, there's nowhere fun to wait.
Sue:	There's nowhere fun to wait. Hmmm. Evan, are you waiting with Benny? *(Evan is still on the horse with Maggie.)*
Evan:	Yeah.
Sue:	Do you have any ideas where you guys could wait?
Benny:	Nowhere.
Sue:	Well, maybe Evan has an idea.
Evan:	Nowhere.
Sue:	You want to wait on the horse. Maggie, what do you want to do about him being on your horse?
Maggie:	Him not be on this. I want to be by myself.
Sue:	You want to be by yourself.
Luisa:	Me, too.

Sue:	Evan, Maggie said she wants to be on a horse by herself. *(Evan gets off.)*
Evan:	But we want to go on those.
Sue:	Yeah?
Benny:	*(Shouting loudly to both girls)* Get off!
Evan:	*(Not loudly)* Get off.

At this point Sue had heard from everybody about what they wanted. Benny was beginning to get more frustrated, but he was still holding the stick without threatening with it in any way. This was a major step forward for him. Sue realized that Benny's feelings were escalating, however, and quickly acknowledged them *as he expressed them in words,* hoping to avert any physical expressions. She also patiently continued to wait for the children to come up with a solution.

Sue:	*(Responding to Benny's loud request for Luisa to get off)* Benny, you're really having trouble waiting to get a turn, huh. You **really** want to be on it right now.
Benny:	I've got a pointer and it's really sharp. *(He holds his stick up, away from the girls).*
Sue:	Hey, Evan. Do you have an idea what you can do while you're waiting? Benny says he needs to think of something fun to do, somewhere fun to wait.
Luisa:	We're going to be going pretty soon. We're going to be going pretty soon.
Maggie:	Hey, I know. How about those two could wait on that horse and we two could wait on this horse.
Sue:	So you would be with Luisa on the same horse? That would be okay? Luisa, would that be okay with you? *(Luisa nods and gets on with Maggie. Benny and Evan get on the other horse.)*
Benny:	'Cept I want to be alone on a horse.
Evan:	I want to be alone on a horse.
Sue:	You each want to be all alone on a horse. So how are we going to do this?
Luisa:	Sue, me, and Maggie are going to be going pretty soon, and they're gonna be here alone.

Sue:	So when you leave one of them will get on that horse and one on the other horse? *(She turns to Evan and Benny.)* Did you know that they're leaving in just a few minutes? So when they leave, you could each have your own horse. Would that be okay? Evan, can you ride with Benny until it's time for them to leave?
Evan:	Um *(Nods yes).*
Benny:	No way!
Sue:	You want your own horse **right now,** Benny.
Luisa:	*(Looking toward the swings, Luisa sees someone get off a swing and gets off the horse and heads toward the swing.)* Me and Maggie, we wanted to go on those [swings].
Sue:	Luisa, have you changed your mind? You're getting off the horse right now?
Luisa:	*(Walking away)* Yes.
Benny:	They were just waiting to be on the swings.
Maggie:	He [Evan] can wait on this with me.
Sue:	Oh. *(To Evan)* You know what, you were on here before with Maggie. Now she's changed her mind. You can be on here with her. *(Evan moves to get on with Maggie. Benny stands up on his horse, spreading his feet across its back.)*
Sue:	*(She looks up at him, smiling.)* Okay, Benny. You're alone on the horse. Okay? *(Benny nods happily. Maggie rides with Evan briefly, then slides off to go to an open swing.)*

Sue's patience with Benny's intense wishes helped him to stay in control. Each time Benny experienced verbal assertiveness as a satisfactory way of having his wants and needs met, he would become more and more secure with this effective strategy.

◆

Did Benny "get his way"?

When Sue discussed this conflict with me later in the day, she expressed concern that maybe she had let Benny "get his way," because he was the most demanding of the children in this dispute. She wondered, was this somehow unfair to the others? Would "getting his way" encourage selfishness in Benny? Children who get what they *want* by being physically or verbally aggressive are often described by adults as "getting their way," as if this were always a negative result. However, it is important to note that Benny did not get what he wanted (a turn) by pushing Luisa off the horse or using the stick, but by listening, waiting, and talking through the problem with the other children. He was loudly assertive about his wishes but he did wait for a mutual group decision before getting on the horse. If Sue had not assisted Benny in saying what he wanted, it is likely that the conflict would have escalated.

This prediction is consistent with research (Hay & Ross, 1982) suggesting that children who perceive themselves as losing out in a conflict are likely to become aggressive in subsequent incidents. "It was the loser of the last conflict, rather than the winner, who was more likely to initiate the next conflict" (p. 36). Adults have both an opportunity and a responsibility to help children learn how to meet their *wants* in a positive way, just as we would if the child had critical safety or health *needs*.

To better understand the rationale for Sue's approach, let's look carefully at what the phrase "get their way" might mean. Sometimes adults think negatively of children who are allowed to "get their way"—it may seem that we are rewarding selfishness. But instead of seeing these children as selfish, why not view them as *children trying to satisfy their needs and wants egocentrically or in mistaken ways?* It is important for us

Sometimes adults think negatively of children who frequently appear to "get their way." But instead of seeing these children as selfish or demanding, why not view them simply as children trying to satisfy their needs and wants egocentrically or in mistaken ways?

to accept that children will make mistakes as they learn socially acceptable ways of meeting their needs and wants. It's also important to recognize that being verbally aggressive can be a step forward from hurtful, physical behavior. If Benny had pushed Luisa off the horse and Sue had not intervened, Benny might have deduced that pushing is okay, and continued with such tactics. However, Sue did intervene before this could happen, and Benny got to be on a horse *only* by talking through the problem with everyone. Thus problem solving was a constructive, logical consequence to Benny's demands. Children are, of course, trying to "get their way"—they are trying, however egocentrically, to be heard.

Supporting assertiveness

For Benny, the horses incident was a major turning point in his move away from physical aggression to verbal assertiveness. However, we can only speculate about why Benny was less willing to engage fully in a discussion of solutions than he had been in the previous incident with Max. Perhaps this was because he did not know Maggie and Luisa as well as he knew Max; perhaps it was because it was a cross-gender conflict; perhaps he was trying to impress younger Evan with his assertiveness. Children vary in their developmental functioning on different days and with different people. It is important to resist any assumptions and continue to observe carefully, objectively documenting circumstances and progress.

Each of the four children was also able to verbally state his or her wishes, which Sue supported by listening to all the perspectives. Evan participated as a parallel player in constructive problem solving. He mimicked what Benny did and said, imitating his words and actions without feeling his feelings. He was content to do whatever Benny did. Even when Benny made a loud demand, Luisa and Maggie were still able to state what they wanted and come up with solutions that included compromises (Evan joining Maggie on the horse). Whether or not Maggie and Luisa were really just waiting for the swings from the beginning or left the horses just to leave the boys, the most important factor is that they each had a say in the outcome.

It is often useful to look at a series of conflicts before deciding whether there are patterns or gaps in children's skills. When we hear children voicing their wishes loudly, we may sometimes assume that they are dominating quieter children. However, children with mature verbal skills, like Maggie and Luisa, can often hold their own in such disputes. Children who frequently compromise or give up easily in the midst of problem solving do need extra support in speaking up for what they want. ("Maggie, what do you want to do about him being on your horse?") In giving this support, however, we must remain neutral, accepting whatever solution the children agree to. Children do not learn assertiveness by having teachers be assertive for them. Benny, Evan, Luisa, and Maggie were learning to speak up for themselves by receiving support from neutral adults who encouraged open discussion of everyone's needs and avoided imposing their own agendas on

Here the children may not decide to divide up the hoops exactly. However, the adult can best support assertiveness and fair problem solving by helping children speak up for what they want, rather than by dictating an "equal" solution.

the children's problem solving. Benny, Evan, Luisa, and Maggie all "got their way" in this dispute. In conflict mediation we call this a "win-win" solution.

Following children's leads and supporting playfulness

Playful humor can be a mediator's best friend. If the adult can follow children's leads and join in their playfulness, solutions can often come from surprising places. However, one child's

Playful humor can be a mediator's best friend. If the adult can follow children's leads and join in their playfulness, solutions can often come from surprising places.

idea of fun may be another child's flashpoint. By framing the problem discussion as part of children's fantasy play, we can sometimes help children de-escalate the tension. In the incident described in the next conflict story, Benny discovered the effect of humor in problem solving. His dinosaur character was willing to come up with a solution for Benny and Malik's problem.

Benny problem-solves with "dinosaur talk"

During work time, Benny is lumbering about on all fours, making quiet, throaty sounds. When Malik comes by, dragging the punching bag, Benny quickly pounces on it, pretending to be a ferocious animal capturing its prey. Malik immediately begins to protest.

Malik:	"Get off! Get off, Benny!" *(Benny does not respond and continues to wrestle the bag. Malik yells at him again and begins to cry.)*
Betsy:	Malik, you seem upset. What's happening?

Malik:	He won't get off! I'm using this.
Betsy:	Benny, Malik is upset. He's wanting you to get off the bag.
Benny:	Grrrr, grrr. *(He wrestles the bag.)*
Betsy:	It seems like you're some kind of ferocious animal.
Benny:	*(Quietly to Betsy)* I'm a dinosaur and I don't know how to talk.
Betsy:	*(Turning to Malik)* Malik, he says he's a dinosaur and he doesn't know how to talk. I wonder how you would tell a dinosaur to get off the bag if he doesn't know how to talk?
Benny:	*(To Betsy)* Thphhhf! *(Makes a loud "raspberry" with his cheeks and tongue)*. That's "get off" in dinosaur talk. *(Malik smiles through his tears.)*
Betsy:	Malik, dinosaurs say "get off" by going thphhhf!
Malik:	*(He smiles and even giggles a little at me as I make this sound. He hesitates for a few seconds, then loudly repeats Benny's sound.)* Thphhhf!

Benny releases the bag and lumbers away, making more quiet, throaty noises. Malik releases a laugh of relief, turns, and drags the bag off in the opposite direction. I watch them go, pleasantly surprised by this abrupt and funny conflict.

Lengthy negotiations over wants and needs are not always the most effective way to arrive at a solution. Benny simply wanted his imaginary character to be recognized. The humor of his solution softened Malik's frustration, transforming a power struggle into a playful game and creating an outcome that delighted everybody. Benny and Malik were gone so quickly, and the tension was so completely dispelled, that I sat there surprised and smiling. I wanted to tell them what creative problem solvers they were but it was clear that they hadn't needed that encouragement and follow-up support. The problem solving and subsequent solution had completely satisfied them. In this incident, Benny had been both conflict instigator *and* creative problem-solver. He had extricated himself from a potentially emotional confrontation by offering a humorous counter-proposal.

◆

Developing the ability to compromise

In the incident described next, Benny accepted a friend's mistake and suggested a creative compromise. By this time Benny had experienced problem solving for a number of months. He had come to expect sensitive listening from his teachers, as well as respect for his needs and wants. Each time Benny had been involved in a conflict, the teachers' responses had communicated their desire to neutrally support *all* the children, no matter what actions or words had taken place. Benny had participated in problem solving in many different roles, but rarely had he been the one who had gotten hurt by others, as he was in this next story.

Children respond to being hurt in many different ways. They may hurt back, cry or scream, express intense anger verbally, or withdraw and reject their playmates. Some children are able to listen and accept the circumstances of the hurting and move on. This next story offers a look at Benny's reactions during a conflict in which he was hurt by another child. It shows the growth that had occurred for Benny, not only in his ability to be forgiving, but also in his ability to compromise while deciding on a solution that worked for everyone.

◆

Benny and Ethan both want the trapeze

[This story is retold without a recording transcription.]

Merrilee, my teaching partner, and I heard screaming and crying. I saw Benny run to Merrilee, holding his chin, I also saw Ethan run and hide in the Book Area, where I found him with his head under a cushion. I followed Ethan and told him that Benny was very sad and that we needed to go talk to him. Ethan got up and willingly took the hand I offered to him. We went and sat by Benny, who was being comforted by Merrilee near the trapezes. Ethan saw Benny crying and began to cry himself. Merrilee told us, "Benny's really sad."

As Ethan turned toward me, crying, I told him gently, "You're feeling really sad, too, Ethan. I wonder what happened?" We waited as Ethan's crying quieted. Then Ethan told us that they both wanted the trapeze.

Benny quietly added, "He hit me on the chin."

I reminded Ethan that it's not okay to hit when you want something. Ethan quickly told me that he was just trying to reach the trapeze. "Ohh, so when you were reaching for it, you hit Benny's chin by accident?" Ethan nodded sadly. "You're feeling really sad about that, Ethan," I told him as I hugged him a bit tighter. "So the problem is that you both were wanting a turn on the trapeze?"

Benny nodded yes and stopped crying. He got up out of Merrilee's lap and began to swing on the trapeze. Ethan stopped crying also but stayed huddled in my lap. Merrilee left the area to answer a child's question.

I looked up at Benny on the trapeze, "I don't think this problem is solved yet, Benny." Looking at Ethan, I said, "Ethan, do you still want a turn on the trapeze?" Ethan nodded yes. I summed up the problem: "Benny, Ethan is still wanting a turn on the trapeze and Kayla is using the other one. What do you think we could do to solve this?"

Excitedly Benny told me, "I know, we could ride double!"

Ethan didn't react to this so I asked, "Do you know what that means, Ethan?" He shook his head no.

Benny then called out, "Hey Kayla, come here! Get on double with me to show Ethan!" Kayla came over and grabbed on to the trapeze bar facing Benny. Kayla looped her legs around Benny's and he pushed off. They began to giggle with delight. "See, Ethan!" Benny called out.

"Yeah!" Ethan said, jumping out of my lap. Kayla got off Benny's trapeze and Ethan took her place in front of Benny. The two boys swung, laughing, stopping, repositioning themselves, and swinging again.

"It looks like this problem is all figured out," I said. "Right, Benny?...Ethan?" Neither of them responded. They swung and laughed, uninterested in a question that had such an obvious answer.

This incident showed two changes in Benny's conflict behavior. First, although he had been hurt, he showed no anger toward Ethan. There was no argument over the details of the clash. After being physically comforted and having his feelings acknowledged, Benny quickly moved on to try to solve the

> "Seasoned negotiators could take lessons in dispute resolution from preschoolers. Usually their compromises are simple and straightforward. Occasionally the resolution results in a uniting of efforts—a true way for them to learn that a whole can equal more than the sum of its parts when people cooperate."
>
> —*Valerie Bernat (1993, p. 37)*

problem. This reflected his trust in the process of problem solving and his desire to get on with having fun. Second, in coming up with the solution, he compromised what he wanted so that Ethan could have what he wanted, too. Preschool children are egocentric and adults often don't expect such compromises. But if the solution is an interesting one (including an adventurous stunt like double trapeze-riding), children may be very willing to compromise! As for my role in this process, I knew that this idea would not have occurred to me. Their inventiveness reinforced for me the importance of supporting children's solutions. In the incident in the next and final story of Benny, he showed his growing ability to consider factors outside himself, while still asserting his own need and coming up with inventive solutions.

◆

Benny solves an adult problem

It was near the beginning of the school year, and Benny had just turned 5. It was rest time, but he had not needed a nap at home or at school since the previous spring. Because of state regulations, however, we had to require Benny to "rest" with the other children.

During recent rest times, Benny had become more and more animated—flipping about on his mat, making squeaky noises, calling out to other children. It was my day to be with the children as they rested, and I was apprehensive.

As children prepared their mats and picked out books, Benny alternately hopped about on one foot making funny noises and stretched out and rolled across the floor. He looked more like he was gearing up for a major athletic event than for a quiet rest.

Sure enough, my apprehensions came true; rest time seemed interminably long as Benny noisily crawled up and down on his mat like a bed bug, making loud, vocal squeaks. My offers of back rubs and pleas for quiet only gave us brief respites of calm before the squeaking and wiggling began anew. In no time I was exhausted and frustrated.

Finally rest time ended and children began to pack up their rest bags. I went to where Benny was working on his bag and I offered to hold it open while he stuffed his mat into it. He handed me the bag and began to roll his mat. As I pulled the bag open wide, I considered carefully how I would begin. Quietly I told him, "Benny, I have a problem that I need to talk to you about." (It was, I realized, *my* problem. Benny was being asked to do something that was no longer developmentally appropriate for him; rest time did not meet his needs or wants in any way.)

"What problem?" he asked with sincere curiosity.

"I felt really frustrated during rest time today because noise and jumping around makes it hard for the other children to rest." Benny had finished stuffing his bag. He pulled the cord tight and paused for a few seconds as he considered his answer.

"You know I shouldn't have to even do dumb rest 'cuz I'm five now."

"Ohhh...you think children who are five shouldn't have to do rest. Boy, I wish I could change the rules about rest time, but the teachers don't get to make up all the rules that we have at school." (I paused for a few seconds as I considered explaining to him about state licensing regulations, then quickly decided to keep it simple.) "You really don't like rest and I can't change the rules about rest. So what could we do to solve this? What could we do to make rest easier for you?"

Barely hesitating, Benny told me, "You could read chapter books. You know, like the *Wizard of Oz,* or those crow books."

"Oh yeah—we used to do that last year, didn't we? Like *Sammy Jay.* So you think rest would be quieter if we read chapter books?"

"A lot!" Benny told me emphatically.

"Wow—thanks for that idea, Benny! We'll try it tomorrow," I told him.

Benny took his bag to the rest mat cabinet and went off to play.

The next day I sat amid the group of resting children; I told everyone that we would be reading a "chapter" book and that since they were resting their eyes, I would not be showing pictures. I began:

"Sammy Jay..." The room grew still. A few pages into the book, I glanced around as I read. The room was calm and quiet. Some children were dropping off to sleep, some were listening. Benny lay motionless on his mat, wide awake, with a look of complete absorption on his face. He had solved my problem and his own.

This rest time story describes a clash between Benny's need (or lack of need!) and my need. An active 5-year-old is often no longer in need of a rest during the day. But my need as a teacher was to provide the required quiet rest time for everyone. We were both stuck in a situation that neither of us wanted. Understanding Benny's lack of need for rest helped me to problem-solve with him sympathetically, and the result was a cooperative "win-win" solution for us both.

◆

Like all other sets of skills that children acquire, problem solving is learned in stages (for a summary, see Chapter 4, p. 154). There are, of course, individual variations in how children pass through these stages. Some children may not ever hurt others physically. Some may struggle with expressing emotions, but easily find solutions, as Benny did. Although Benny's problem-solving journey was long and challenging, he made steady progress.

Experiencing together the challenges of resolving conflicts had created a special bond between Benny and me. Benny still visits our program occasionally, and I sometimes see him in the community. I feel instantly pleased when I catch a glimpse of him, and I delight in hearing whatever tales he has to tell. I also feel a curious and warm sense of gratitude— as one does upon seeing a beloved teacher from the past.

Raven's Stories

Raven joined our preschool program at the age of 3½ years. Her transition to school was difficult; she was experiencing challenging circumstances at home and was frequently very emotional when her parents dropped her off in the morning. Once they had left, Raven carried the resulting tension and anxiety throughout her day. Adding to her difficulties, she did not bond easily with the new adults in her life, but her compelling energy did often draw children into her play. She loved to pretend with others and commanded the lead in most of these role plays, providing ideas and giving directions. Raven's verbal skills were well developed and quick; however, she was still emotionally young and was prone to sudden impulsive reactions.

Raven's journey in learning problem-solving was more uneven than Benny's. Her problem-solving skills did not always develop in a clear sequence and were unpredictable from one day to the next. While Benny's stories are presented in chronological order (which also follows the pattern of his developmental growth) the stories of Raven's growth are told here in developmental order. As is often true when children are learning any new set of skills, many children don't demonstrate the same grasp of problem solving in every situation. Children's uneven progress in this area reminds me of my efforts to speak French during the summer I spent living with a French-speaking family. When I was rested and confident, my French was more than adequate. When I was tired or homesick, I found it very, very difficult to speak with any degree of fluency; the words spilled out sounding garbled and absurd. Sometimes I would stare red-faced or come close to tears before I could think of anything at all to say!

Likewise, as children and adults learn problem-solving strategies, some days will go better than others. New "languages" are not learned in a day. Raven's ability to use problem-solving words instead of physical responses developed sporadically. On highly emotional days, she sometimes pinched, hit, or threw heavy objects at other children. However, as she learned to problem-solve, there were days when, with adult support, she could use her new language skills to show how she felt. On other days, she had no control over her emotional impulses. Sometimes Raven's emotional responses even escalated as adults approached; she would throw herself on the floor or run away, physically showing her resistance to adult intervention. (Raven may have been expecting to be put in time-out, a no-choice strategy used at her home. It took a while for Raven to realize that this was not going to happen at school.) At these times when Raven was resistant, it was important for the adults to acknowledge her feelings, while also communicating that resistance was not going to derail the problem-solving process.

Resistance to problem solving

This first story shows Raven struggling with emotional impulses. Raven and Anita were frequent playmates. Both children had clear ideas about what they wanted, and expressed very strong emotions if their wishes were challenged.

Raven pinches Anita and responds to problem solving with a tantrum

On this day Raven and Anita had planned to play together on the trapezes. After a few minutes, Raven had another idea. She approached Sue, a teacher who was still planning with her group, and asked if Sue could go into the attic and get the cash registers. As Sue explained that this wasn't possible right then, Anita began to talk to Raven. Raven turned and pinched Anita, then ran back to the trapeze where they had been swinging together. Anita winced and held her side. I was standing across the room by the trapeze and saw this happen. Anita followed Raven to the trapeze, holding her side, but not crying or saying anything. She sat in one of the waiting chairs in front of the trapeze.

I waited to see if Anita would say anything to Raven on her own, but Anita sat looking at her sadly. I turned and calmly spoke to Raven, "Raven, please get off the trapeze and come and talk to Anita. I think there is a problem that needs to be solved."

Raven threw herself on the floor under the trapeze, making frustrated cries and kicking her legs. To acknowledge her

> frustration, I said, "I can see you're upset about something, Raven. I don't know what it is. It's not okay to be hurting Anita. That's the problem we need to solve."
>
> As Raven resisted this intervention, I calmly gave her limited choices: "Raven, your choices now are either to come over and talk·about it or to choose a place to calm down until you're ready to talk."

Even though Raven had had some experience with problem solving, she was still reacting, at least initially, with resistance. I tried to notice and respect her feelings while still letting her know that problem solving would continue, either now or after her protest. I had hoped that this would help her to let go of whatever fearful feelings she had about the situation and move on to problem solving more quickly.

> Raven answered my offer of choices by yelling, "Nooo!" and rolled around on the rug.
>
> Isaac came over and tried to use the trapeze. "Can I come on that trapeze?" he said.
>
> "Not right now, Isaac," I told him. "I'm in the middle of figuring something out with Raven and Anita."
>
> Raven had stopped screaming and was listening. The entrance of Isaac and his interest in the trapeze had gotten her attention. She sat up. Without yelling, but with some frustration, she told Anita, "Anita, I wasn't talking about painting! I was talking about something else!" Now using a calm voice, she continued, "I was talking to Sue—to look up in the attic for cash registers."
>
> I responded, "Hmmm. So the problem was that you wanted some cash registers. But what about the **hurting** of Anita?"
>
> Raven answered, "'Cuz she's...I don't remember why."

This was an important turning point in the problem-solving discussion. My description of the limited choices and Isaac's interest in the trapeze had clearly let Raven know it was time to engage in the discussion. At that point she responded openly to her mistake. My questions, rather than blaming her, sought only to gather information. This helped Raven to stay engaged in, rather than resist, problem solving.

Isaac tried to get on the trapeze again.

Raven told him firmly, "No, Isaac."

I added, "You can't use this right now, Isaac. You can go over on the chair to wait for a turn. It's Raven's turn on the trapeze right now. We're trying to solve a problem."

"Then why did you say to get off?" Isaac asked me.

I explained, "Because she's going to talk about this problem before she swings anymore." Isaac accepted this and sat down on a chair to wait. I then turned back to Raven. "So, Raven, if you're upset about something, and feeling frustrated that Sue can't go right now to get something..."

Raven quickly injected, "No, I'm not frustrated about **that**. Anita was talking about painting and I was talking [to Sue] about something else."

Raven's verbal abilities were beginning to be apparent here. She was able to clarify that the source of her frustration was Anita (not Sue, as I had thought). Adults will sometimes acknowledge children's feelings and restate problems incorrectly. An essential reason for restating problems is to enable children to correct any misunderstandings. Raven quickly corrected my perception of the problem and in the process repeated the feeling words I had just used in speaking to her ("No, I'm not frustrated about that"). She was then able to go on to clearly explain what the problem was for her.

I supported her with a quiet "Mmm-hmm," encouraging her to continue to explain.

Raven looked over at Anita, who had been quietly listening, and suddenly added, "And she bothered me!"

I restated, "So the problem was that she was bothering you while you were talking to Sue. So if someone is bothering you, Raven, what can you do?" I paused and looked at Raven and then Anita. They were both silent. "Do you want to hear my idea?" I asked. Raven nodded. "You can say 'Please don't bother me. I'm talking to Sue'— without pinching."

"Okay," Raven told me cheerfully as she began to get back on the trapeze.

"Wait a sec," I told her, "we need to see if Anita has something she wants to say. Anita, is there anything you want to say to Raven?"

> "Yeah. Stop pinching me," Anita told her clearly.
>
> "Stop pinching. You really weren't liking that," I acknowledged. "Raven, will you remember that?"
>
> "Yeah," Raven said, looking calmly at Anita.
>
> "Is this problem solved?" I asked.
>
> Both Anita and Raven nodded as they looked at each other. Raven began to swing. As she and Isaac waited for a turn, Anita moved her hand away from her side that was pinched and lifted the timer to her lap.

Raven could become easily frustrated and often expressed her emotions physically. Unfortunately, Anita happened to be nearby at one of these moments. Raven's initial reaction was to resist an intervention. I felt it was important to let her know, right away, that even though she might feel out of control, she still had an opportunity to regain control by making choices. I tried to communicate this by respecting her intense feelings and offering the choice of taking time for calming OR talking out the problem immediately.

Through this mediation and others like it, Raven's resistant reactions began to subside. As she began to explore new skills, old reactions mixed with new. In time, however, Raven did become a very confident, skilled, and proud problem solver.

◆

Intrinsic versus extrinsic motivation

We have a number of choices when young children, like Raven, lose control and hurt others. Some adults deal with this by using time-out or other punishment strategies; others may choose calming strategies or problem solving. The choices we make at such times usually reflect our beliefs about how children learn and how we should respond to the mistakes made by young learners. Continuing with Raven as an example, let's consider these choices, and what might have happened if we had taken a different approach at times when Raven impulsively hit a classmate.

When children lose control or hurt others, adults may respond with punishment, or with calming strategies followed by mediation, as Betsy does here with a child who attempted to hit a playmate.

If we had believed that punitive consequences help children learn (an *extrinsic-motivation* approach), we might have sent Raven away from play to "think about" her hurtful actions. In imposing this punishment, we would have hoped and expected that she would think about her mistakes and return knowing not to hurt others.

The difficulty with this approach is that while children may in fact learn from such experiences that adults get upset when children hurt others, *they do not learn what to do with their upset feelings instead of being aggressive.* Since children learn best when they are actively engaged, sitting in isolation is not likely to result in the learning of a new skill. The next time an intense emotion arises, they have *no other choice* but to do what they already know—to hurt as a way of expressing their emotions. No matter how clearly they might understand that hitting is not okay, they may not have the impulse control to resist hitting if they do not know another strategy.

Now let's consider the approach we actually used with Raven, one based on *intrinsic motivation.* Believing that children learn best when the motivation to learn comes from within, we try to engage children who have lost control in a problem-solving process that allows them to share control and helps them satisfy wants and needs they feel are important. In using this process with Raven, we encouraged her to be actively involved in choosing solutions to her problems and in finding alternative ways to express her needs and wants. One of the choices we can also offer children who, like Raven, are very upset, is a period of time for calming down, before problem solving begins. If a child decides to take a few minutes to calm down, problem solving should begin immediately after this break.

> "When disputes erupt about group participation, the conflictors are often directed to separate activities. Thus, teacher intervention often leads to less conflict, but likewise, less opportunity to develop conflict resolution skills…. If teacher intervention results in removal of objects or separating of participants, then positive interactions in the aftermath of conflict usually do not happen."
>
> —*Dale F. Hay, (1984, p. 41)*

A critical difference between extrinsic- and intrinsic-learning approaches is how long their effects last. The child who is controlled by an adult using extrinsic motivators such as punishment or threats is consequently dependent on the adult—the new behavior persists only when the adult is there. By contrast, new behaviors that are motivated from within the child feel good to the child. As a result, we can expect these behaviors to be repeated without the need for the adult to be present. Raven's development illustrates this. Eventually, she used problem-solving strategies independently, even offering herself as a mediator. (See pp. 35–43 for more on intrinsic versus extrinsic motivation.)

When a child's hurtful actions have no connection to the classroom

As we consider the next story of Raven, it's important to note that the challenges she experienced in learning problem solving were not simply the result of her inexperience with this new approach. Her difficulties seemed to be compounded by feelings she brought from outside the classroom. There were days when Raven arrived at school with an angry frown on her face. Right away an adult would spend time with her, acknowledging her feelings in whatever way possible in hopes of "emptying out" some of her upset feelings brought from home. Such an approach can be very helpful and reassuring to a child who is experiencing stress outside the classroom; however, there will still be times when angry feelings spill over into the child's day. In the incident described next, Franco was in the wrong place at the wrong time.

Raven pushes Franco and smiles

Raven is drifting about the classroom, unable to focus. She walks by Franco, gives him a shove, and then smiles.

Franco: *(Goes to Betsy)* Raven pushed me and then she smiled.

Betsy: *(To Franco)* Do you want help talking to her?

Franco: Yes. *(Franco and Betsy walk over to Raven together.)*

Betsy: Raven, Franco tells me that you pushed him and then you smiled. *(Raven listens, then turns to run away. I hold her.)* Raven, here's your choice. You can stay and talk this out with Franco or you will need to choose a place to calm down since pushing is not safe.

Raven: *(She shrieks, then struggles to get away as I hold her gently.)* Talk to Franco! *(She begins to hit me lightly.)*

Betsy: It's not okay to hit me but I can see that you're upset about something. Do you want to tell us what the problem is?

Raven: Nothing.

Betsy: You need to stop hitting me and listen to Franco. *(She struggles and hits me lightly again.)* Raven, you are going to need to choose a place to calm down if hitting doesn't stop. This is not okay. *(She stops.)* Franco, what do you want to say to Raven?

Franco: Don't push me.

Raven: *(In a frustrated voice, struggling and hitting me lightly again)* Okay!

Betsy: *(Still holding Raven in a gentle embrace)* Raven, this needs to stop. It is not okay to be hitting

	me. If you're going to be with us, I need to know that you are going to be safe, not hitting me or anybody else.
Raven:	*(Her body relaxes, she stops struggling, and her voice becomes calmer.)* Okay.
Betsy:	So is this problem solved for you, Franco? *(He nods and leaves for Blocks.)* How 'bout for you, Raven? How can you solve your problem?
Raven:	*(She stands up and looks around, then looks at me.)* Will you play a game with me?
Betsy:	Sure! Which one? *(Raven takes my hand and leads me to the Toy Area.)*

It was clear as this conflict ended that Raven had been in need of some attention but was mistaken in the way that she tried to get it. This is a very common mistake for young children. At this developmental stage, some children may cry, shout, scream, and become physical when they want attention. Using words to get what they want would require a self-awareness and ability to communicate that they have not yet developed. Adults often feel that children should not be given the attention they want if they have not asked appropriately. However, it is important to recognize that withholding attention for this reason is punitive and will not help children learn a more constructive way to ask for the attention they need. By pushing Franco, Raven was unconsciously asking for attention, which I felt she really did *need*. When mediation was initiated, she acted out her frustration by hitting, then soon became very aware that this was not working. The problem-solving dialogue was a logical consequence for her mistake, but Franco's solution ("Don't push me") did not meet her unspoken need. In the end, what did work for her was simply asking me to play—this was another chance to learn that verbal requests work better then physical outbursts. As Raven experienced success with this strategy and became more aware of how well it satisfied her need, she was more often able to make *conscious* requests for the attention she wanted, needed, and deserved.

◆

Verbal aggression: Name-calling—a step forward from physical aggression

As the weeks passed, Raven's expressions gradually became less physical and more verbal. She was occasionally verbally *aggressive,* and although this was sometimes hurtful and frustrating to her playmates, we saw this as progress.

Raven calls Anita a "butthead"

Raven, Anita, and Katie (all 4 years old) are at the tub table using funnels to fill water bottles. Some of the bottles have nozzles on top that squirt. As I move around the room telling children that cleanup will be in 5 minutes, I hear their angry voices by the water table and go to them.

Anita:	*(To Betsy)* She's calling me a butthead! *(Anita looks at Raven with a scowl.)*
Betsy:	She's calling you a butthead.
Katie:	*(Looking at Raven)* She's squirting me!
Betsy:	Raven, it sounds like both Katie and Anita are upset about things that are happening here.
Anita:	And she's smiling about it.
Betsy:	Hmmm, and you're smiling about it. That's making them feel even more upset, Raven. *(As I acknowledge the feelings of Anita and Katie, Anita becomes able to express her feelings even more specifically. This is important practice for Anita.)*
Anita:	*(In a loud, shrieking voice)* I'm really angry at you, Raven!!
Raven:	Shut up, poopy buttbrain!
Betsy:	It's not okay to call names, Raven. It sounds like you are angry about something too. We can talk about it. *(Raven is silent.)* What are we going to do about this problem, Raven, because they both want name-calling to stop. *(Raven begins to squirt them with the bottle.)*
Anita:	*(Screaming)* Don't!
Betsy:	*(I put my hand over Raven's hand to stop the squirting and kneel down very close to her. I speak to her in a calm but firm tone.)* Raven,

	this squirting needs to stop and both Anita and Katie have asked you to stop. They don't want to get squirted.
Raven:	I am.
Betsy:	You're what?
Raven:	I am stopping.
Betsy:	They want to know…they want to make sure squirting will stop. *(Raven nods her head indicating yes.)* You're not going to squirt anymore. And they want to know that name-calling will stop.
Raven:	No. *(Raven's calm tone indicates to me that she means to stop.)*
Betsy:	So name-calling will stop. *(I am still concerned about what Raven's upset feelings are about. I want to avoid a confusing "why" question about feelings, so I find another way to explore this. Though it doesn't succeed, it does let her know I am concerned.)* You know, sometimes when people are upset, they call people names. I'm wondering if you're upset about something, Raven. *(She shakes her head no.)* No? You're not feeling upset about anything. *(She shakes her head again. Katie whoops with excitement as her bottle overflows. Raven smiles.)*
Betsy:	Anita, is this problem all figured out now?
Raven & Anita:	*(They look at each other and respond together.)* Yeah.
Betsy:	Yeah. You both think it is. *(I pause.)* You know, one of the reasons I came over here was to tell you that it's almost cleanup time. Can you think of something we can do to make cleanup fun today?
Katie:	The timer! *(They all nod with agreement and continue to play without incident until the cleanup signal.)*

Raven's name-calling in this conflict, though hurtful and provocative, represented a step forward from physical aggression. It was not possible to find out the source of the conflict;

perhaps she was jealous of the play between Katie and Anita, perhaps someone said something I didn't hear, or possibly she was still upset about something that happened before.

In many conflicts, there are some pieces of the puzzle that are never fully explained. Impulsive reactions come from feelings that arise quickly and pass just as quickly, making them hard to account for fully. It is tempting in a mediation to feel we must get to the "why" of an incident, both for our own understanding and to make sure that the conflict doesn't recur. Certainly, if we can find out *what* happened, we will know more about *why* it happened. As explained earlier, answering "why" questions is difficult for young children. To satisfy adults pushing for an explanation, children may make up reasons. Raven did have unexplained, angry outbursts that were hard to understand, though we were aware of her general emotional needs. All I could do in this situation was to continue to be sensitive to Raven's needs while making sure that everyone was safe and had the chance to say what was upsetting them. Sometimes, this is the very best we can do. In the incident in the next story, Raven took another step forward.

◆

Raven yells at Antonio, without hurtful words or actions

Antonio and Raven have been playing in the sand table which the teachers have filled with snow. I hear them yelling at each other. As I approach, I'm delighted to see that Raven is yelling, without hurting or name-calling.

> **Raven:** You're wrecking it!
>
> **Betsy:** What is happening over here? You both sound really upset. Antonio, what is happening? (*Antonio is trying to reach something in the snow and Raven is blocking him with her hand.*)
>
> **Antonio:** I'm trying to…Move your hand, Raven! Move your hand!

Betsy:	I'm going to ask both of you to move your hands till we figure out this problem. *(They both withdraw their hands.)*
Betsy:	Tell me what the problem is.
Raven:	This is my road and he's wrecking it.
Betsy:	Aha. Antonio, she says that this is her road and that you're wrecking it. What's the problem you're having, Antonio? *(Antonio starts to show me by pulling a cup out of the road.)*
Raven:	*(Yelling)* Noooo! *(I put my hand on Antonio's to prevent the crumbling of the road.)*
Betsy:	Let's listen to what he has to say, Raven. You want to get that out of there, Antonio? *(He doesn't answer.)*
Raven:	I don't want him to wreck my road!
Betsy:	He just wants to get that out. Can he get that out? *(Raven shakes her head no.)* What do you think we could do, Raven?
Raven:	He could use this. *(She hands Antonio a cup, but he doesn't take it. Instead, he starts to reach for the one in her road. I stop him before he moves it as Raven protests again.)* Stop it!

This was an important change for Raven—she had continued to express her wants verbally while also trying to find a solution. Even when Antonio rejected her idea, she continued to use appropriate language rather than be verbally or physically hurtful.

Betsy:	Antonio, Raven said she didn't want you to wreck the road and she gave you one of these cups. So what's the problem now, Antonio? *(He doesn't answer, but steps back with a frowning face.)* Antonio, I need to know how you're going to help figure out this problem? *(He doesn't respond.)* What do you think we could do? *(He doesn't answer.)* What are you wanting to do here, Antonio?

Perhaps this last question, which focused only on him and used the most concrete language, helped Antonio to respond. He answered with a clear statement of his wishes:

Antonio: I want to play!

Betsy: You want to play. *(I glance over to the Art Area and see one of the young 3-year-olds beginning to paint her hands with the easel paint. Wondering if she'll move onto other body parts or her clothing next, I decide I'm running out of time.)*

Betsy: I have an idea about how we could solve this. Do you want to hear my idea? *(Both children nod.)* Raven, you don't want your road wrecked and Antonio, you want to play. I see a space over there where you could play, Antonio. *(I point to another section of the sand table.)*

Raven: Here. *(Raven now hands Antonio a cup and a car.)*

Antonio: *(He takes them and moves over and begins to play, making car noises.)* Errr, Errr.

Betsy: *(To Antonio)* So you're going to play there now? *(Antonio nods.)* Raven, are you okay with your road? Is this problem figured out for you? *(Raven nods and begins to talk to Antonio about the cars and the road. I leave quickly to problem-solve with the young painter who's exploring new painting surfaces. Raven and Antonio play with no further incident.)*

Later, when I told my teaching partner about Raven and Antonio's conflict, I realized how many new skills Raven had used in this mediation.

First, she did not respond physically, even though initially no adult was nearby. Second, she was not at all resistant to problem solving. Third, she quickly came up with possible solutions—offerings—for Antonio. And last and most important, Raven's feelings did not at any point escalate to intense levels that threw her out of control. This must have felt much better for her, as it did for the rest of us.

◆

Negotiations over control: An essential part of play

Many of Raven's conflicts were about control over play. Often her stated wishes—for control over materials—appeared to mask a subtler issue that was actually more important for her—control over people. Raven's relationships with the other children in the group were tenuous. Some children were fearful of her sudden impulsive reactions. However, when she was fully engaged in dramatic play, children found her imaginative pretending very appealing. Children of about the same age and with similar interests sought out Raven as a play partner. There were frequently conflicts to be mediated, but children accepted this as part of their play (often more easily than adults could have).

Understanding the ways people influence one another interests many children; the give-and-take learning that happens in relationships is critical to their success in social interactions. Children who spend more time at play in social groups do become socially adept more quickly. Sometimes the amount of conflict that happens in these play groups, however, can make adults wonder why children stay engaged in the play. When there is one conflict after another, it doesn't look like much fun! Sometimes we have to remind ourselves that *these social negotiations are one of the most important educational opportunities of the play.*

In play groups such as this one, sometimes the amount of conflict that happens can make adults wonder why children stay engaged in the play.

> "Most of the theories that address fundamental issues in cognitive and social development posit conflict as an essential impetus to change, adaptation, and development."
>
> —*C. U. Shantz (1987, p. 284)*

Shared control: A mediation outcome

In the incident in the next story, Raven became concerned when Anita tried to enter her play at the dollhouse. Raven had been playing at the dollhouse for some time before Anita's arrival; she had set up six rooms with furniture and dolls. She had begun an elaborate fantasy creation—a representation of her idea of home and family. When Anita arrived to play, Raven may have initially felt that her creation was threatened. In such situations, it is important to respect the inventiveness and time children put into their creations—whether they are on paper or in the playhouse, block area, or sandbox. We often, understandably, want children to be welcoming of other children. However, even though focused involvement in play is an ability we clearly want to encourage, we may forget that this involvement may result from the child's having control over the circumstances of play.

It is therefore important to always show respect for the ongoing play by supporting children as they say what they want and need and by giving them ample time to discuss any changes that are being considered. Once Raven was given time and choices, she became more generous with materials and enthusiastic about Anita joining her. Because she had been given control throughout the problem-solving process, *Raven herself* initiated this generous resolution.

Raven suggests a compromise solution at the dollhouse

Anita has come over to join Raven at the dollhouse (an open-sided house with four upstairs rooms and four downstairs rooms). Anita calls to me and I approach them. Anita immediately begins to describe a problem.

Anita: She's not letting me play.
Betsy: What were you wanting to do, Anita?
Anita: I'm wanting to play.

Betsy: You're wanting to play with what?

Raven: You can only play on this side, the empty side. *(Raven points to two rooms she's not using.)* Not in here, over there.

Betsy: *(Restating)* On this side?

Anita: But I won't have no people.

Betsy: You won't have any people. So you really need some people. *(Raven hands Anita a boy doll.)*

Betsy: You've got some people now.

Anita: But I need some girls and a boy.

Betsy: You want girls and boys. Hmmm.

Anita: So I can have one girl and one boy and you can have one boy and one girl.

Raven: You can have one girl. *(She hands her one.)*

Betsy: She can have one girl.

Anita: I don't want that one. *(She reaches for another one.)*

Raven: Not this one, 'cuz, only this one. *(Raven points to the girl she's given her.)*

Anita: Why?

Raven: 'Cuz. I need this one.

Anita: Why? *(Raven doesn't answer.)*

Betsy: So Anita, you have one boy and one girl now. What else do you need? *(I pause.)* And you have a side.

Anita: I need some beds.

Betsy: Hmmm. Some beds.

Anita: *(Placing a piece of cloth in the dollhouse)* This can be a bed.

Betsy: You're going to use the two rooms on that side. *(This will leave six rooms for Raven.)* You're going to do what, Raven?

Raven: Use this room.

Betsy: Oh, you're going to use that room.

Raven: *(Speaking in an excited voice, pointing to all the spaces)* Yeah! And she can use these downstairs and those downstairs, and that upstairs, I'm using this upstairs and that upstairs, and this downstairs! *(Raven has now pointed out two more rooms for Anita to use.)*

Betsy:	Aha.
Anita:	*(Sounding excited, too)* And I'm using this downstairs and this downstairs and this upstairs and this upstairs!
Raven:	Yeah!
Betsy:	So you figured this out, didn't you! *(Raven and Anita both smile at each other.)* It looks like you've got it all figured out. It'll be fun to have a next door neighbor, huh. *(Anita and Raven begin to play, describing to each other what they're doing.)*

Getting to this solution was a source of great pleasure and excitement for Raven and Anita. Note that as each of them began the journey toward a solution, each had an egocentric starting place. Raven was initially unwilling to share the dollhouse, but as she discussed the problem, her position shifted: She offered Anita two rooms almost as soon as problem solving began, and eventually offered two more. Anita was initially unwilling to accept the rooms and dolls that were offered, but as she began to see that she could get what she wanted, she became more flexible and began to find her own solutions (using cloth for beds).

Even for adults, keeping the wants of others in mind while also negotiating for one's own is challenging enough. This balancing act is even more difficult for developmentally young, egocentric children. Giving them the time and support they need to move from an egocentric to a cooperative viewpoint can prepare children to do this independently.

◆

Personal control continued to be a regular theme of Raven's disputes. The conflicts usually began with Raven's insistence on certain actions or behaviors that she wanted from her playmates. As she became more experienced in negotiation, she became skilled both at identifying her specific wishes and in offering sensitive and creative compromises that satisfied everyone.

When we see children frequently working out problems it helps if we remind ourselves that these social negotiations are one of the important educational opportunities of play.

Raven, Liza, and Anita argue over the tire swing, and Raven finds a solution

Raven and Anita are on the "teeter-totter," a tire swing that has a board through the bottom. Liza is sitting on top of the tire, holding onto the rope in the middle, and Raven and Anita are seated on the ends of the board. Raven yells at Liza to get off. Liza begins to cry quite intensely, but continues to cling to the rope. As I approach, Raven immediately begins to explain.

Raven:	We can't go wicked fast when she's on!
Betsy:	*(Putting an arm around Liza)* You can't go wicked fast when she's on? Liza, you're really upset. *(I rub her back.)* They want to go wicked fast—that's why they don't want you on.

Raven:	She can...but I don't want her to 'cuz we want to go wicked fast.
Betsy:	You think her being on here will keep you from going really fast.
Raven:	Yes!
Betsy:	*(Hugging Liza as she sobs)* You're still upset. Did you get hurt? *(As she cries, Liza shakes her head no.)* I'm wondering if your feelings got hurt. *(She nods yes)* Oooooh. *(I hug her again.)* Something happened that hurt your feelings. Raven, what happened to hurt her feelings?
Raven:	She didn't tell us. She was too sad.
Betsy:	When they said "get off," did your feelings get hurt? *(Liza nods yes.)* Yeah? Do you want to get off?
Liza:	*(Shaking her head no)* Uh-uh.
Raven:	*(In a frustrated voice)* Yes!
Betsy:	*(Raven and Anita begin to spin the tire. I stop the swing and turn to Liza.)* Are you going to be able to hold on while you're crying, 'cuz they're ready to go?
Liza:	*(Her crying subsiding)* I *(sob)* want *(sob)* to *(sob)* stay *(sob)* on!
Raven:	I don't want her to!
Betsy:	Raven, she **really** wants to stay on. *(Liza stops crying.)*
Raven:	She's too heavy!
Betsy:	This is a problem. Anita, do you have any ideas? We don't seem to be solving this.
Raven:	She can...can go on after.
Betsy:	She could go on after you spin? Hmmm. *(Speaking to Liza)* What do you think? Do you want to go on after [they spin,] Liza? *(She shakes her head no.)* No.
Raven:	*(Speaking to Liza in a gentle voice)* I'll give you a push.
Betsy:	She said she'd give you a push, Liza. Do you want to do that? Do you want to wait until after and get a push? *(Liza nods yes.)* Okay, can you get off? *(Liza nods and gets off.)*
Betsy:	Well that idea worked, Raven!

Anita:	And Raven's gonna give me a push.
Betsy:	She's going to give you a push, too!
Raven:	Yeah!
Anita:	*(As Liza gets down)* There you go, Liza, aren't you happy now? *(Liza doesn't respond.)*
Raven:	*(To Liza)* Are you happy?
Betsy:	*(To Liza)* They want to know if you're happy now. *(She nods yes. Liza and I sit on the grass nearby and watch Raven and Anita spin for a while. Then Raven gets off and Liza gets on in her place. Raven pushes Liza and Anita and they begin to spin.)*

In this conflict, Raven grasped a new concept in problem solving—offering Liza a future plan (a turn and a push) that was even more appealing than what Liza was doing. (Eisenberg and Garvey might call this a "conditional compromise" [see pp. 204–205].) This offer had two important elements: it allowed Raven to be in control of what was happening and it included a compromise. Raven had to give up some of what she wanted (to continue to swing) in order to meet Liza's wishes. As Raven pushed her friends on the swing, they engaged in a whole new level of cooperative play.

> "What children fight about during play and their degree of success in such fights are related to their understanding of peers and social rules."
>
> —*C. U. & D. W. Shantz (1985, p. 3)*

Raven—Becoming a mediator

The next two stories depict how Raven's interest in mediation took a new turn—she became the mediator. As Raven neared her fifth birthday, she began to show an interest in conflict mediations in which she herself did not have a personal investment. Children are more apt to accept other children's (rather than adults') suggestions for solutions, so Raven's contributions were welcomed and often led to successful results. Soon Raven went a step beyond this and began to attempt to mediate conflicts herself, with no adult help. This next story, of a conflict involving three new children, describes one of her first attempts.

One day I overheard Raven helping Lyba, Megan, and Tamika, all young 3-year-olds, solve a problem together.

Raven mediates with three younger children

Raven is sitting with Lyba, Megan, and Tamika. She is holding a puzzle that they all seem very interested in. Raven hands the puzzle to Tamika and then turns and excitedly calls to me.

Raven: Betsy, I solved a problem!

Betsy: What happened, Raven?

Raven: They [Lyba, Megan, and Tamika] all wanted this puzzle, but they [Lyba and Megan] just had a turn so I let...so Tamika said she could have a turn.

Betsy: So Tamika said she would have a turn, and then what is going to happen when Tamika's finished? *(Raven doesn't respond.)* It's important to work out that part of the problem. Sometimes I ask the person whose turn is first to tell the people waiting when they are finished.

Raven: *(Leaning over so she's at Tamika's level.)* When can they have a turn, Tamika?

Tamika: *(With pacifier in her mouth)* Umm.

Raven: When you're done?

Tamika: Um *(Nods yes).*

Raven: Okay.

Betsy: Well, you did solve that problem, Raven! Wow! *(Raven nods and smiles proudly.)*

This was a very exciting occasion for Raven. She loved to play the parent in her fantasy play, nurturing her "children" and solving their problems. For Raven, parents were superheroes; she was fascinated by what they could do and found satisfaction in identifying with their power. As she learned to problem-solve, she slowly found the same satisfaction and power in finding solutions to "real-life" problems with her peers. Eventually, she also found that she could be a mediator for others.

◆

Children who are experienced problem solvers sometimes enjoy mediating in other children's conflicts.

Independent problem solving

In the episode described in this last story, Raven used the steps in problem solving independently to resolve a dispute she was involved in herself.

Raven and Anita resolve a problem

I looked over to the sink, where I had heard Raven's voice. She was talking to Anita, who was a bit teary. Neither of them were looking my way. I could hear only small bits of their conversation, but it was clear from their body language that they were trying to solve a conflict that had arisen between them.

Raven leaned close to Anita, who listened quietly as a tear ran down her cheek. Raven's hand was on Anita's shoulder as Raven told her calmly, "I just wanted it..."

> I couldn't hear what the issue was, but did hear Anita respond, "Well, don't…" Raven listened patiently to Anita, and then Raven quietly explained something to her. Anita listened intently. Again, I did not hear the details.
>
> As Raven finished her explanation, I did hear her ask Anita with concern, "Are you okay?" Anita nodded yes as she wiped away her tear and looked at Raven with a small smile. They both moved on, going their separate ways.

As I watched this exchange from a distance, I quietly celebrated this moment for both Raven and Anita, as I had done when Benny had similar successes. Learning the skills of problem solving had not been an easy journey for either Raven or Benny, and although I was sure there would be other bumpy days ahead, I was confident that the skills that they had learned were theirs to keep. Recently I was lucky enough to hear about just that. I ran into Raven and her dad in the community. When I asked Raven what she likes to do now that she's in the second grade, she told me, "I like to solve problems." Her dad also described how she loves to find solutions and is very proud of her skills.

Both Benny and Raven have learned a set of communication habits which will guide them when difficulties arise. They have become capable of making positive choices on their own, choices that come from their own reckoning of what is useful, kind, and just. When I think of their earnest efforts during those preschool days and when I hear how they continue to use, enjoy, and develop these life-enhancing habits, I cheer for them.

6

Small-Group Problem Solving

It was a busy school day in October, the second month of our preschool program. The children had all moved on from their separation fears of September. Most goodbyes to parents were now quick and tearless because the children could anticipate what would happen next and felt supported during this part of the day. As they relaxed into their surroundings, they became more expressive—laughing and being silly with their new friends. In fact the whole room seemed to move faster with the excitement. Soon I heard my teaching partner, Merrilee, explaining almost exactly as I would do, "It's not safe to run. See these sharp corners on the shelf and the hard floor? I'm feeling really worried that you or your friends could get hurt. Running needs to stop."

In recent days, running through the room had become a problem. There had been a few minor bumps, and Merrilee and I were concerned. We had decided together to try to help the children understand more specifically our concern about running, but reminders were not a lasting solution—the children would listen intently and remember the warning for 5 or 10 minutes, but then something exciting would happen and the running would begin again. It was clear to us that our concerns about running needed to be communicated in a new way.

While most of this book deals with on-the-spot resolution of disputes involving two or three children, the problem-solving approach can also be applied to issues that involve the group as a whole, such as this problem of children running in the classroom. In such cases, a discussion with a small group of children can be a vehicle for generating solutions that are acceptable to everyone. This chapter describes how this small-group problem-

Merrilee listens closely during this problem-solving discussion with a small group of children. This kind of discussion can also be used at home in response to family problems and issues.

solving process works, including strategies both for planning and facilitating the discussion. This process can also be used at home to deal with family problems and issues.

There are many kinds of topics that can be addressed with small-group problem solving. These include everyday concerns, such as sharing, being a friend, playing in a way that is safe, or specific problems that arise repeatedly in the classroom or home, such as name-calling or rough superhero play. Because these are issues that usually affect everyone in the group (or family), they call for focused group attention, in addition to the mediations that may have occurred each time the issue has come up.

Once a problem is selected, an adult describes the problem and guides the small group in discussing it, and the group generates a list of possible solutions. Most of the time, small-group problem solving is initiated by adults, but once children have experienced this process, they sometimes think of problems that call for a discussion, such as frustration about one of the play

Small group problem solving allows children and adults, as partners, to make choices and share control as they enjoy the process of resolving group issues and disputes together.

areas being dominated by just one or a few children or dislike of children "shooting" at others. A primary goal of the discussion is for everyone affected by the problem to have a chance to suggest possible solutions, an opportunity best facilitated in a small group of no more than 8–10 children. Problem solving in small groups focuses everyone's attention on an issue *when the problem isn't currently happening.* Most important, it allows children and adults, *as partners,* to make choices and share control as they solve group issues and disputes.

Planning for Small-Group Problem Solving

The earlier example of our classroom's running problem is a good illustration of what events might lead to a small-group discussion. After several days of discussing, with various individual children, the problem of running in school, Merrilee and I realized that we had to do more to bring about a lasting change in the group's behavior. As we planned for the next day, we decided to do a small-group time in which we could all talk about ideas for resolving the problem. (Small-group time is a regular part of our daily routine in which the class splits into two smaller groups led by each of the teachers. See below for a description of the purpose and process of small-group time.)

Using a planning sheet

To begin planning for the discussion that would take place in each small group, we got out a planning sheet (see opposite) that is similar to the ones we've used for other small-group activities.

About Small-Group Time

The problem-solving discussions described in this chapter take place at small-group time, a regular part of the daily routine in programs using the High/Scope educational approach. In this approach, small-group time is an opportunity for children to experience a variety of materials, to explore these materials in their own way, to observe and talk with others about their discoveries, and to exchange ideas for solving problems encountered with materials. This special part of the children's daily routine provides a format that is also very effective for facilitating conversations about social issues. The following summary of the basic principles behind High/Scope small-group times is taken directly from High/Scope's preschool curriculum manual, *Educating Young Children* (Hohmann & Weikart, 2002, p. 251).

What It Is

- An adult-initiated learning experience based on children's interests and development.

- The same group of children with the same adult.

- Active learning in a supportive setting.

Why It Is Important

- Builds on children's strengths.

- Introduces children to materials and experiences they might otherwise miss.

- Provides children with regular peer contacts and interactions.

- Lets adults observe and interact daily with the same group of children.

- Enables adults to practice support strategies in a stable setting.

Where to Meet

- Gather together in a consistent place.

- Go to the relevant materials.

Small-Group Problem Solving
Planning Sheet

Materials: (Simple things for eating or handling while the discussion is happening.)

Problem to be solved:

Beginning: (Describe how materials will get to the children, and write an introductory statement that describes the problem clearly, without using children's names. If possible, illustrate the problem by using symbols or puppet role play.)

Middle: (Facilitate a discussion of the problem, then ask the children for ideas for solving the problem. Clarify and extend ideas so they are specific. Accept all ideas.)

End: (Read over the list of ideas and let the children decide on a plan of action. Note your plan here.)

[This is a reproducible page.]

As Merrilee and I began to discuss the plan and filled out the sheet, we kept in mind that this would be the first problem-solving discussion at a small-group time that year. The children had participated in a number of other small-group activities, and they had experienced problem-solving discussions as a part of many conflict mediations. The small-group discussion we were planning would be somewhat different from these mediations, we knew, but the core goal would be the same—children, with our support, would be active in finding solutions of their own making. We expected that the discussion that resulted from our plan would have similarities and differences with the problem solving that occurred at conflict times. The plan we developed and a description of the resulting discussion are given on pages 254–57.

Two important points must be considered when planning for small-group problem solving: first, the discussion is done in a small group so that it can be kept short and concrete (lengthy, abstract discussions can be difficult for young children); second, discussions focus on a general *problem* and not on specific *children* who might have been most involved with the problem. Small-group problem solving focuses on common problems and collective solutions; this distinguishes it from conflict mediation, which addresses a specific dispute between or among particular children. Another difference is that since small-group problem solving deals with problem situations that are not currently happening, the adult may need to do something to make the experience concrete (or "real") at the moment.

What follows is a set of strategies that Merrilee and I used to help us think about the most effective way to facilitate our discussion.

Strategies for small-group problem solving

Provide props or snacks to help maintain children's attention. To help occupy children's physical energy during the discussion, give them something simple to eat (carrot sticks, pretzels, raisins) or to play with (a pipe cleaner, a small piece of play dough, a piece of colored beeswax to warm in their hands,

To provide an outlet for children's physical energy, give them something to eat or to play with as they listen, think, and talk.

a cotton ball). Having something to "fiddle with" or munch on will give children something to do with their hands as they listen, think, and talk.

Keep the language of the discussion concrete and specific. There are two strategies that will assist with this: first, define the problem clearly, in concrete and neutral terms, and second, encourage children to add details to general solutions. Whether the problem-solving discussion will be taking place at school or at home, it is necessary to plan carefully how to describe the issue at hand at the opening of the discussion.

It is very important to define the problem without blaming or using the names of specific children. Plan to describe the problem positively. Rather than saying "The problem is that children aren't being nice in the classroom," use positive and specific terms: "The problem is that we need to find ways to play together so that everyone can feel safe and happy." It can also be helpful to name your own feelings using "I" statements: "I'm feeling worried that children will be hurt. We need to find ways to play safely." In addition, by illustrating the problem with symbols that children can "read," adults can assist children in gaining a clear understanding of it.

When discussing solutions, encourage the children to add specifics if their ideas are vague. For example, when children make very general suggestions such as "Everyone should be nice and share," encourage them to describe the specific *actions* needed to carry out their idea: "So, if we want everyone to be nice, let's think of what we will DO that feels nice for others" or, "If you want to share, what will that look like? What will you do while you share?"

Throughout the discussion, give children support in taking part, and express your confidence in the children and the process. After describing the problem, let children know you expect them to be successful. For example you could say, "I know that you have lots of ideas for solving problems. I want to hear what they are." Make frequent eye contact. Take time to listen to their needs, wants, and ideas. Support children by repeating their concerns about the problem and repeating their ideas for solutions. This helps them to know that you are really listening.

During the small-group discussion, make frequent eye contact, taking time to listen to children's needs, wants, and ideas. Support children by repeating their concerns and ideas, letting them know that you are really listening.

Stay focused on the problem, not people. As the discussion unfolds, children may bring up the names of specific children. Redirect the discussion back to the problem by reframing what children have said. For example, if a child says, "Sam always hurts us," this could be reframed as "You're saying that sometimes people hurt you and your friends," or you could say "We're not going to talk about people right now, just the problem of hurting."

Seek and accept a diversity of ideas. As children begin to come up with ideas, be sure to support and accept all ideas, even those that may strike you as unrealistic or possibly even funny. It is important to respect all suggestions and to help children think through how each idea might work. One of the important benefits of problem solving is that it encourages the development of cause-and-effect thinking. The more ideas the children suggest, the better the chances are that one will work.

Balance the attention given to individual children during the discussion and be sensitive to the interest level of the children. Some children will contribute more readily than others. Be sure to give every child an opportunity to contribute, without pressuring anyone to participate who doesn't want to. Some children are more verbal in groups than others. The children who are listening without talking may be learning just as much

Small-group problem solving provides rich opportunities for children to reflect on problems, engage in cause-and-effect thinking, explore feelings and needs, and plan cooperatively for change—a genuine collaboration of hearts and minds.

as those who are talking. If most of the children are not listening or contributing, this may be a sign that the discussion needs to come to an end. Do not force the children to find a solution. If you observe their reactions and end the talking when they are ready, they will have a more positive attitude toward the next small-group problem solving. If children have lost interest in the problem before finding a solution, you can give closure by saying "It seems like you're more interested in...right now. We can talk about this again another day."

Summarize the ideas given and decide on a plan of action. As the children indicate a readiness to conclude, summarize what has happened. If you have a list of possible solutions, briefly read them, and together pick an idea or ideas for the group to try first. You may also talk about what you will try next if the suggested ideas don't work. Write down your plan. If another small group is working on the same problem, discuss the suggested solutions briefly at a large-group time by telling them the solution each group picked to start with. Often it will be possible to try two ideas at once, but if this is not possible, ask the whole group to pick one. If there isn't a clear consensus, adults may need to guide children toward the suggested solution that is most likely to succeed.

During this discussion of a problem, a child describes his idea for a solution while the others listen. This give-and-take exploration is as important as the solution itself in stimulating change.

During problem-solving discussions, it is useful to keep in mind that sometimes the most valuable part of the activity is simply bringing the problem to the children for full exploration and communicating to them that their input is wanted. The discussion itself lets children know that adults are partners with children in the classroom

Families and classrooms may want to create or find an object that signals the beginning of a group discussion and helps to introduce the problem to be solved.

community or family. Often the discussion process alone is more important in bringing about a change than the actual solution the children arrive at.

In our program, "Shell Time" is the name we use for our discussions of ongoing classroom problems. The name comes from the way we open these discussions; when the children come to the small-group table, they find a large shell with a note underneath it (or taped to it) describing the problem. The shell is a signal to children of what is about to happen; it helps to focus them on the task at hand. Families and classrooms may want to try the shell, or create their own object and name for introducing this group task.

Stories of Small-Group Problem Solving

The following stories illustrate some of the benefits and outcomes of children's small-group discussions. The problems highlighted in these stories typically occur wherever there are children who are exuberant and full of physical energy, who

Small-Group Problem-Solving Plan:
Running in the Classroom

Materials: Small pretzels. Marker and paper. Shell with message taped under it.

Problem: Running in the classroom

Beginning: Put the shell in the middle of the table as children arrive. When they notice it, tell them that sometimes at small-group time we have "Shell Time"—a time when we solve problems together. Hand out pretzels and tell the children that we will talk about the problem as we eat our snack. Turn over the shell and read the attached note.

Introductory statement: "This week children have been running in our room. The teachers are feeling really worried that someone may get hurt. We want everyone to be safe. The problem that we need to figure out together is how we can help children remember to walk when they are inside. We know you have lots of ideas about how to solve problems. What do you think we can do about the problem of running?"

Middle: Follow children's leads as they begin to discuss the problem. Listen to what they say about the problem, acknowledging their feelings, and asking clarifying questions. Be flexible if children digress, allowing them time to explore these digressions and then encouraging them to refocus on the problem at hand. (If they show no interest in refocusing on the issue, follow their interests for the remainder of the group time.) As children discuss the problem, write down their ideas for solutions and ask extending questions so that their ideas include specific actions that will be different from what has already been tried.

End: Notice when children seem ready to end the discussion. Read the list of suggested solutions, discuss symbols you could draw for each one, and ask them which solution they think we should try first. Tell them that the other group is talking about the same problem and that the teachers will talk with them at large-group time about how the ideas will be used. It may be that the ideas picked by each group can be tried simultaneously or we may need to choose one together to try first. Ask the children where we might hang up our list of ideas.

see situations primarily from their point of view, who struggle to follow safety rules, and who are seeking control and power as they learn to be independent. Through small-group dialogue, the children themselves find answers to many concerns and problems, often surprising adults with their perceptions and inventiveness. Their search for solutions can be a profoundly creative process. During small-group problem solving, adults show their acceptance and respect for the wants, needs, and concerns of children. The children sense this respect, and they respond to it by working hard to resolve their dilemmas. The resulting negotiation will very likely provide the impetus for change.

This first story depicts my small group's problem-solving discussion on running in the classroom. As was normal for our small-group times, Merrilee and I planned the small-group discussion together and then conducted separate discussions with each of our groups. We were both a bit concerned about how our newest, not yet 3-year-old children would manage during this discussion. Having decided to give all the children pretzels to munch on and resolving to stay attuned to everyone's needs, we decided to just go ahead and see what happened.

Small-group discussion—
Problem: Running in the classroom

[This story is retold without a recording transcription.]

I began my small group by putting a large shell in the middle of the table and giving each child a handful of pretzels. Under the shell I had taped a note containing my introductory statement and small illustrations. I told the children what was about to happen, as we had planned, and I handed out pretzels. Craig immediately began to talk about how he had gotten some shells at the beach during the summer. For a minute or two, we discussed shells. Then I asked the children, "Would you like me to read the problem that is under the shell?"

"Yeah!" they all said at the same time.

I read the note: "This week children have been running in our room. Merrilee and I are feeling really worried that someone may get hurt. We want everyone to be safe. The

This week children have been running in our room. Merrilee and I are feeling really worried that someone may get hurt. We want everyone to be safe. The problem that we need to figure out together is how we can help children remember to walk when they are inside. We know you have lots of ideas about how to solve problems. What do you think we can do about the problem of running?

problem that we need to figure out together is how we can help children remember to walk when they are inside. We know you have lots of ideas about how to solve problems. What do you think we can do about the problem of running?"

Right away Katia responded, "I think you should tell them not to run." I explained that we had tried that, but that it had only worked for a short time—then the children had forgotten again.

Mark then said, "I think you should build fences."

I told him that I was writing down his idea, adding that walking in the room is okay. I wondered aloud whether fences might make it hard to walk in our room.

All the children appeared to be thinking about that when Juan Pablo suggested, "Make kids sit in the Book Area if they run." I wrote down his idea and asked how long they should be asked to stay there. Several children suggested different amounts of time and I wrote these down as well. We do not use time-out in our classroom, so I wondered if they were adapting an idea used at their homes.

Craig, a 5-year-old who had just begun to copy words when he made his plan at planning time, excitedly told us, "I have an idea!"

At this, I noticed everyone, including 2-year-old Indira, looking up. (She had been busy trying to fit pretzels onto her finger and then nibbling them off.)

Craig continued, "We could make a stop sign!" I wrote down his idea and asked for more details. He responded that we could make a stop sign like those he'd seen on the road. I asked how it should look and several children told me it should be red. (I heard squealing and commotion at Merrilee's table and I wondered what was happening, but I refocused on Craig.)

"What should we do with the sign once we make it, Craig?" I asked.

"We can hold it up whenever we see somebody running!" he told me, smiling.

"Yeah," I heard a few children say.

I asked the children if they would like to hear all the ideas. Then I read them. Then I asked which one we should try first. Since they were unanimous in liking the sign idea, we decided to make one a little later with cardboard and red markers.

"You really helped to figure out a new way to solve the problem of running!" I told them with genuine relief. I had a feeling that their solution would work—it was so concrete! I noticed that they were just about finished with their pretzels and I could hear Merrilee starting large-group time with a song. (We had agreed beforehand that the adult whose small group finished first would start the large-group time and that the other group would join in when ready.) I asked the children where they would like me to post their ideas. They decided to put the list on the wall right by our table. Craig asked if he could do this and I gave him the tape and the list.

As we joined the large group, Merrilee quickly told me that a bee had distracted her group. Although she had described the problem, they did not come up with any ideas for solutions because their attention had been on the bee. We agreed to tell the children in Merrilee's group about our sign idea. At the end of large-group time, I asked Craig if he wanted to tell them about the sign idea. He did this enthusiastically and then the whole group discussed when we would make the sign. Merrilee's group told our group about the bee, and I suggested children could "fly like bees" to outside time.

That afternoon the children made a stop sign with a handle. For the next few days, there was very little running, but the sign was held up anyway, as children called out "Stop!" even to those walking quickly. Each time this happened, the sign made a big impression and all those involved smiled and slowed down. In the days and weeks that followed, running was no longer an issue. Using the sign had helped, but I believe that it was primarily the problem-solving discussion and the sign-making that solved the problem. I think the group focus on the problem and the request for *their* ideas really made an impression, helping them to remember to walk inside.

◆

Introducing a problem for small-group discussion

There are many different ways to introduce a small-group problem-solving discussion. The introduction has the same purpose as the starter activity for any small-group time—to get the children's attention while communicating the purpose of the activity, in this case, to solve a problem. The adult introduces the problem to be discussed by telling a story, reading a hidden message, or some other attention-getting activity. Props, such as the shell, puppets, or pictures, are often used as a focusing device and/or a snack may be passed. In addition to, or instead of, writing the message about the problem, the teacher can use symbols and pictures to represent the problem and involve the children in "reading" or guessing this message. Whatever type of introduction is used, it is important to keep it brief and make sure the children have something simple to do with their hands while they discuss the problem.

Ruth talks to children with a puppet, getting their attention and telling them about the problem to be discussed.

The following stories illustrate some possible issues for problem-solving discussion, the variety of introductions that can be used, and strategies for guiding, extending, and concluding the discussion. During small-group discussions, the facilitator must balance two roles: keeping the group focused on solving the problem while also noticing and responding to children's changing attention levels. Staying attuned to the children's cues about their interest in finding solutions to the problem is vital to the success of each problem-solving dialogue, as well as to subsequent discussions. If the activity isn't working—children are unresponsive or uninterested—it's important to quickly summarize what has been accomplished and move on. If we want to engage children in this type of activity throughout the year, they need to have a successful experience. If this isn't happening, it will be useful to consider what might be done to improve the activity and then to try again on another day.

The next transcription is from a small-group dialogue about conflicts over sharing. The discussion was planned as a way of encouraging children to develop communication skills and a repertoire of solutions for such situations. Research has demonstrated that children can begin to learn and internalize the norms for cooperative interactive behaviors at an earlier age than many theorists have previously predicted (Eisenberg-Berg, Haake, & Bartlett, 1981). This discussion had multiple interruptions, distractions, and a brief conflict, but the children still remained fully engaged and interested in the problem, demonstrating a high level of analytical and creative thinking.

Small-group discussion—Problem: Sharing

I begin by giving children a simple snack of Goldfish crackers and telling them that today for "shell-time" we are going to look at a picture of two children with a problem. I place Goldfish crackers in front of each child, and then show them a picture of two children pulling on a garden hose. I hold it in front of each child so that they can look at it close-up.

Betsy:	I'm wondering if you can tell me what you think is happening in this picture?
Kayla:	They're pulling a boat with the hose.
Victor:	You should be careful, Willie. I put my mouth on those. *(Victor pushes away his Goldfish after eating some, so Willie begins to eat Victor's.)*
Betsy:	Oh, Willie, those need to be thrown away if he's been eating them. *(I take them and throw them in the trash. At this point a parent comes in and asks me a question. I answer quickly, then turn back to the group.)*
Betsy:	So—wait a minute, I didn't hear what you said, Kayla.

Kayla:	Maybe they were trying to pull the boat with the hose.
Betsy:	They're trying to pull the boat? Look at their faces. *(There is no boat in the picture so I hold it up for her to see closely.)*
Willie:	Mad.
Betsy:	Do you think they're feeling mad? Which one feels mad? *(Willie points to one.)*
Kayla:	Maybe they could work...try sharing it.
Betsy:	I'm going to write down "They were feeling mad." And tell me again what you thought they could do, Kayla?
Kayla:	They could share it.
Betsy:	Aha. They could share the hose.
Victor:	Don't put money in your mouth, Willie. That's what my mom always told me. *(It seems Victor is still thinking about putting things in his mouth that might have germs, so I decide to acknowledge his comment.)*
Betsy:	She did? *(I pause as Victor nods in response, then turns back to the picture.)* So how can they share this hose?
Jared:	Give it back and forth.
Betsy:	*(I write that down.)* Well that might be one idea—giving it back and forth.
Victor:	And...and...I want my turn now.
Betsy:	Okay. What do you think they should do, Victor?
Victor:	Take turns.
Betsy:	Take turns. *(I write that down.)* Isn't giving it back and forth taking turns?
Victor:	No.
Kayla:	Yes, it is!!!
Victor:	*(Sounding frustrated)* No!
Betsy:	*(Looking at Victor)* No? Well, let's see, how would that work? How would taking turns work?
Kayla:	I already know that...**it is.**
Betsy:	*(Looking at Kayla)* Maybe he has a different way of taking turns. Let's see what he says, Kayla. Maybe he'll tell us. *(Looking back to Victor)* How would your taking turns work?

Victor: The normal taking turns.

Betsy: The normal taking turns. Can you tell us what that's like?

Victor: I don't know what it's like.

Betsy: You don't know—you're not sure what that's like. Well, would that mean that one of them took a turn for a few minutes and then gave the other one a turn?

Victor: Yeah!

Betsy: Is that the kind you mean? *(Victor nods.)*

Betsy: *(Writing)* Okay. So they'd each have a few minutes. *(Picking up the picture)* When somebody tries to take something away from you, how do you feel? It looks like one of them is trying to take it *[the hose]*.

Rachael: Mad.

Betsy: It makes you feel mad? Why does it make you mad?

The blank look on Rachael's face made me realize my mistake right away. Questions about feelings are usually too abstract for young children, because they think in physical, object-related terms. As I considered ways to encourage more specific, concrete answers, however, Rachael gave an answer.

Rachael: 'Cuz he took it.

Betsy: 'Cuz he took it? Hmmm. *(She and I look closely at the picture again.)* He hasn't taken it yet. They're still pulling back and forth.

Willie: You know what? *(We all look at him.)* My hose *[at home]* has a hole in it. We can still use my hose with a hole in it. Two people can use it.

Betsy: Two people can use it 'cuz it has a hole in it?

Willie: Yeah, 'cuz then I have the sprayer. *(He lifts up his hands like he's holding it.)* And then with the hole there I put out the fire.

Betsy: So there are two places that are spraying. *(Turning back to the picture)* So if somebody tries—if this little boy right here wants this hose, what can he do? *(Something drops nearby and distracts the children.)*

Kayla:	What was that?
Betsy:	I don't know. What can the little boy do instead of pulling on the hose? *(The phone begins to ring.)* What else could he do?
Willie:	I know. He could take turns.
Betsy:	Okay. That's an idea that we thought of—that they each could have a turn for a few minutes. What if he's standing there—before he starts pulling on it—if he really wants a turn with it, what could he do?
Kayla:	Say "Could I please have that."
Betsy:	*(To Kayla)* He could ask for it, couldn't he! *(I begin to write.)* He could say…what would the words be that he'd say?
Kayla:	"Please, can I have that?"
Betsy:	*(Writing)* "Please, can I have that?" Okay. *(The answering machine goes on and the children listen to the caller leaving a message. A quick discussion follows about answering machines. It appears to me that our problem-solving discussion is over—then Victor speaks up.)*
Victor:	I have another idea!
Betsy:	You do?!
Victor:	They could quit and do something else than share.
Betsy:	*(Writing)* Ahh! They would both quit or would one quit?
Victor:	Both quit.
Betsy:	*(Evan and Kayla begin to wiggle their way up onto the table. I worry about the rest of the children trying to see the writing process that they have blocked now with their bodies.)* Can you two please sit back in your chairs so everyone can see?
Kayla:	I don't want to.
Evan:	I don't want to.
Betsy:	Well, can you move over to the side a little bit—so there's room for everyone to see? *(They move over a little. I write again.)* They would both quit, and then what would happen? Would they go do something else?

Victor: Yeah.

Betsy: *(Writing "They would both quit and both do something else.")* All right.

Victor: That was the longest word.

Betsy: That was a long sentence, wasn't it. It had a lot of words.

Willie: That was the longest.

Betsy: *(The children look at all the words.)* You thought of a lot of ideas for this problem! *(They nod.)* Are you ready to go out? *(A couple of children get up, while others finish their last few Goldfish.)*

I'm struck by two things as I look back on this discussion. One was that the children managed to continue even though there were so many interruptions—the parent's entrance, the noise, the ringing phone, the answering machine. The conversation also had digressions (discussions of Goldfish sharing, not putting money in your mouth, and a brief conflict when Kayla challenged Victor about whether his "take turns" was the same as her "sharing"). Despite all this, they came up with very constructive ideas for solutions: "They could share it." "They could give it back and forth." "Take turns." "Say 'Could I please have that?'" "They could quit and do something else than share." (This last solution was so fitting for this egocentric age.) When Kayla and Evan began to creep up on the table, I was sure, however, that it was time to end the discussion.

◆

Problem-solving discussions, like this one about sharing, do not always create obvious or immediate changes in behavior; some changes may be subtle, developing over time. Any activity that encourages children to consider and name feelings, and to think of a variety of responses to emotional situations, gives proactive support to children's social growth. Research verifies that such discussions will result in higher levels of constructive social behavior (Grossman et al., 1997). However, this type of discussion, about a hypothetical situation, is more abstract than bringing an ongoing classroom issue to the problem-solving group. To facilitate learning that is active and stimulating, adults

Merrilee uses puppets to dramatize a conflict over a toy.

Stopping the action, she asks the children what cow and duck should do to solve their problem.

Merrilee listens to their ideas for solutions, and they pick one for the puppets to try.

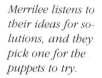

The children watch excitedly as cow and duck use their idea to solve the problem.

must take care in such instances to use a variety of discussion starters—for example, puppet disputes, pictures of conflicts, and books such as *My Name Is Not Dummy* (Crary, 1996)—to maintain children's interest and encourage a high level of creative response. Such devices keep the discussions lively, fresh, and concrete, which helps children as they construct their own perspectives on friendship and community.

The problem-solving discussion in the next story focuses on the issue of children leaving for the playground before a teacher is ready to go with them. In our program, as children dress for outside time, those who are ready must wait a few minutes for an adult to accompany them to the playground (which is located on the opposite side of the building). The children wait on the wheelchair ramp (which they call the "bridge") outside the front door. Merrilee had initiated this discussion because several children from her small group had been running off the bridge too soon, and most of the other children were following them. Although we had reminded children verbally that our rule was to wait for the adult before going to the playground, these reminders had not worked.

When general social skills are being discussed, adults can use a variety of discussion starters such as puppet disputes, photographs of conflicts, or books. Such devices keep the discussions lively and concrete, which helps children as they construct their own perspectives on friendship and community.

A Discussion-Based Violence Prevention Curriculum

"In fewer than six months, children can be rehabilitated from a tendency toward violent behavior, according to a study from the National Center for Injury Prevention and Control published in the *Journal of the American Medical Association* [as reported by the Associated Press in the *New York Times,* May, 1997, p. 1].

- The study compared aggressive behavior among 790 second- and third-graders at 12 schools in Washington state—half the students having been taught a violence prevention curriculum, the other half not.

- At a final evaluation, those who had taken the course exhibited about 30 fewer acts of aggressive behavior every day than children who did not take the course.

- Aggressive behavior—including hitting, kicking and shoving—increased in students who did not take the course.

"The training course, called Second Step, was developed in 1986 by a Seattle educator. It involves 35-minute weekly or twice-weekly sessions designed to teach empathy, problem solving, and anger management to children ranging in age from preschool through ninth grade.

"Second Step is used in about 10,000 schools in the U.S. and Canada. It is one of many programs designed to curb youth violence. Researchers involved in the evaluation said their findings are evidence that other such efforts can also work."

—National Center for Policy Analysis
(1997, May, p. 1)

Small-group discussion—Problem:
Going to the playground without a teacher

As the children finish talking about their morning activities, Merrilee tells them that today for small group she has a problem she would like help in solving. She places a large shell on the table and tells the children the problem is written on a piece of paper underneath it. She pulls the message off (it is taped to the shell) showing all the children the words on it. She begins to read.

Merrilee: *(Reading the message)* "When we are getting ready to go to the playground, the children who are all dressed wait outside the door, on the bridge. The problem is that sometimes children leave the bridge before a teacher says it's okay. What do you think we can do about this problem?"

Charlie: You could tell them to come back on the bridge.

Merrilee: Ahh, let me write down your ideas. *(She gets a marker and paper and puts them on the table.)*

Carlyn: Or you could go tell a teacher and then they would know and run after them.

Ollie: Or you could put up a note saying "No running off the bridge."

Merrilee: Or you could put up a note. (She begins to write.) Wait a minute—Charlie, your idea was…

Charlie: Tell them to come back on the bridge.

Merrilee: *(Repeats and writes)* "Tell them…"

Charlie: *(Pausing as she writes)* to come…back…onto…the bridge.

Carlyn: Or you could put up a gate so they couldn't come out.

Merrilee: *(Writing as she repeats this)* "Put up a gate."

Ollie: And the teachers only will know how to unlock it.

Merrilee: And you think only the teachers would know how to unlock it. Would you like that? To be locked on the bridge?

Several children: Uh-huh. [yes.]

Charlie: Yeah, but, even if, even if it wasn't open for me, I wouldn't go off the bridge 'cuz I was here last year.

Merrilee: Hmmm. Ollie, you had another idea.

Carlyn: Or you could tell the teacher to run after them.

Merrilee: That's part of the problem—that we have to do that. Part of the problem is that we don't want to have to run after them.

Carlyn: 'Cuz Travis thinks it's fun to run off the bridge when only a kid says it.

Merrilee: Is that why sometimes children run off the bridge—just because other children say that it's time to leave?

Carlyn: And sometimes kids run off the bridge like Sam and then we run off the bridge to get them.

David: That's why I ran off the bridge 'cuz Sam ran off the bridge.

Merrilee: So you ran off the bridge when another child ran off the bridge?

Charlie: And we were trying to catch you back down to the bridge.

Merrilee: What about…

Charlie: I had another idea too. You could put a stone wall in front of the gate, to hold the gate onto the wall.

Merrilee: *(Says and writes)* "Put a stone wall…"

Ollie: That wouldn't be good. How could we get the stone wall out of the way?

Merrilee: That's true….

Carlyn: You could step over it.

Merrilee: But if we could step over it, would it keep the people on the bridge if they wanted to get off?

Ollie: No.

Charlie: Yeah, but there would be a gate locked in front of it!

Merrilee: Hmmm. Ollie, you had an idea about a note. What was that idea about the note?

Ollie: It could say, "No walking off the bridge."

Merrilee: So we could actually hang it on the bridge. Would that help remind you?

Carlyn: But the kids couldn't read!

Merrilee: Hmmm. But you know, maybe we could write it with symbols. 'Cuz you all can read symbols, right?

Charlie: Yeah.

Merrilee: 'Cuz you read each other's when we do planning. You're able to read the planning symbols and each other's symbols, so maybe we could write a sign with symbols. Let me write that down. *(She writes.)*

Ollie: I'm looking at my symbol right now. Wanna see it? *(Ollie holds up his security blanket with his bunny symbol embroidered on it.)*

Merrilee: *(Looking up from her writing with a big smile)* Yeah. *(All the children look closely as Carlyn points to it.)*

Merrilee: The big bunny.

Ollie: Yeah.

Merrilee: *(Writing again)* So how should we say it? "Write a sign and hang it on the bridge." What do you think about that idea, Harlin? *(Harlin has been listening closely but has not said anything. He sits up, surprised, but remains silent.)*

Carlyn: I think we should just put a gate in front that could be locked and then a wall in front of it like a curve.

Ollie: Then a gate, through, in the middle, like here *(demonstrating with his hands)*.

Merrilee: Hmmm. Should I read what we have here?

Ollie: Yeah.

Merrilee: Some things that we could do. *(Reading)* We could tell them to come back onto the bridge. We could put a gate on the bridge and only the teachers could unlock it. *(Merrilee picks up the paper so everyone can see it and points to the words as she reads.)* We could put a stone wall. Or write a sign and hang it on the bridge.

Carlyn: *(Rather loudly)* I think we should do all those things! That's what I think we should do!

Ollie: We should do one each day.

Merrilee: Oh! We could do one each day and see which one works the best?

Several children: Yeah!

The children and Merrilee talk briefly again about the ideas and decide to make a sign to be hung up by the bridge. Then the children become interested in the shell, and they pass it around for a few minutes. Soon it is time to get ready for outside time.

At small-group time the next day, Merrilee brought a piece of cardboard and some markers to the table. The children knew right away what she had in mind and they discussed what the sign should be. They decided that one side would be in red with the word *STOP*, the other, green with the word *GO*, and they began to make the sign before outside time. The sign was hung by the door with the *STOP* side facing out and all the children wait-

"Shooting" play can quickly become a problem in the classroom as the "guns" and accompanying noises may annoy or frighten some of the children.

ed and watched as a teacher turned it over to *GO* before leaving. In fact, from the day the sign was hung (midwinter) until the end of that school year, no one left the bridge too soon again. (It is interesting to note that the idea of the sign was similar to the solution for running in the classroom. However, this was a different group of children 2 years later!)

◆

The discussion described in the next story took place early in this same year. The children were not yet fully adjusted to school, and many of them had been bringing security objects—dolls, blankets, or stuffed animals—to school. Others tried to help themselves feel powerful and safe by creating their own versions of security objects—they made guns. In the struggle to feel in control and secure, children were turning to the power symbols that they saw in their home, neighborhood, or community, as well as those they saw on television.

Children used all kinds of materials in their gun-making, and the process was often surprisingly inventive and involved. Elijah made a gun using a long paper-towel tube, two smaller tubes, and tape. He spent a lot of time cutting the tubes to the size he wanted and more time getting it all taped together securely. Other children became interested and made their own guns out of tubes, Legos, or snap blocks.

But once they had finished this creative process, "shooting" (pointing with the toys and making gun sounds) quickly became a classroom problem. The children with the "guns" shot randomly in the classroom. These guns and the accompanying noises frightened some of the children; others were merely annoyed.

The adults had responded to each situation with conflict mediation, and during these discussions the children with the guns were frequently told by other children that they didn't like to be shot at. But the shooting problem would subside only briefly before it recurred somewhere else in the room or on a subsequent day. Teachers Merrilee and Sue decided it was time to focus the attention of all the children on the shooting issue and decided to plan a small-group problem-solving session. They planned to introduce the problem with a puppet play, using the Fuzzy Bear and Jumper Rabbit puppets to act out the shooting. As the puppet play progressed, they planned to ask the children what they thought Bear and Rabbit should do. Here's how the children's discussion unfolded.

Small-group discussion— Problem: Shooting in the classroom

As the children came to the small-group table, Merrilee told them that they would be helping Fuzzy Bear and Jumper Rabbit solve a problem together. She gave each child a snack and began the puppet play with Fuzzy Bear and Rabbit starting to build with blocks. Then Fuzzy Bear began to "shoot" at Rabbit, using a block as a gun. As Rabbit began to cry, two children, Tamika and Rico, immediately began to complain that they didn't like shooting.

"What do you think Rabbit should do?" Merrilee asked.

Tamika said, "He should say 'Don't shoot me!'"

Merrilee told Rabbit what Tamika had said. Then she had Rabbit repeat this to Bear, and Bear stopped shooting. Now that Bear and Rabbit had solved their problem, they said thank you and goodbye and Merrilee whisked them under the table.

Then Merrilee thanked the children for helping solve Bear and Rabbit's problem and asked what they thought about the shooting that had been happening at school. The children responded immediately with comments like "There should be no fighting."

"Cause it makes me feel scared," Owen said.

"You could really get hurt and get bleeded," Tamika added.

"No shooting 'cause that's scary too," Rico told the group.

Merrilee then asked, "What do you think we should do about shooting here at school?"

Some children suggested that it could be okay for children to make guns in the Art Area or with Legos or Bristle Blocks, but not with big blocks. "Those could bump somebody and hurt them."

Rico repeated his idea that there would be no shooting with the guns.

"But guns really do shoot," Andrew pointed out to everyone.

"You can ask somebody if they want to be shooted," Reese suggested.

"You could shoot at those animals in the Block Area," someone else suggested.

Merrilee wrote down all of these ideas. After a few more minutes of talking, it was clear that no one liked the shooting (including those who had been doing it), but two children were unsure—"We want some guns," they told her.

Noticing that they were running out of time, Merrilee told them that she had a suggestion about how to put all their ideas together and asked if they would like to hear it. They nodded yes and she asked them if they would agree to try the following rule: "Guns are okay to make. You can carry them in your pocket or belt, or put them in your cubby, but no shooting."

The children said yes, they wanted to try it. Merrilee brought closure to the session by acknowledging that they had thought of a lot of ideas for the problem of shooting. She restated the new rule and told them that they would see how it worked. Merrilee spoke to Sue and found her group had come up with a similar solution.

Merrilee and Sue noticed some reduction in the shooting over the next few days. Four boys, however, made objects that looked like the guns they had made before, but now they were calling them "cameras." When they used the cameras to shoot at other children, the children protested, and Merrilee and Sue reminded the shooters about the new rule against shooting. The boys claimed again that these toys were only cameras. The children who had protested appeared to accept this explanation; they either ignored the camera play or played along with it (throwing an arm around a friend and smiling for the "camera").

The adults, however, were concerned that the new rule had forced the boys into a lie, as well as some new, secretive behaviors—whispering to each other and hiding things they'd made from the adults. Although there was a change in the amount of shooting and the children had stopped making shooting noises, the adults felt discouraged, not wanting the children to become skilled at deception. They decided to continue to observe for another week and then hold another small-group discussion if difficulties still remained.

The four boys continued to use "cameras" for a few more days. However, the children they shot at made little response, and so the adults did not intervene. By the following week, there was no interest in camera construction or in shooting. It is likely that the discussion had affected the children in different ways and resulted in a resolution for different reasons. The children interested in shooting may have been affected by the clear message that another group of children did not like their shooting because it was "scary." And, the children who had expressed this dislike may have been satisfied by being heard as well as by participating in a solution. Consequently, their *reaction* to shooting changed. It appeared that the four boys had lost interest in shooting, perhaps due to the lack of reaction. Occasionally someone made a "gun" and put it in a pocket or cubby, exactly as described in the group's solution.

◆

Like the discussion of shooting, the next story reflects the issues that can arise when children are exposed to violent TV or movie characters. In this instance, the need for small-group problem solving stemmed from children's fascination with characters from the *Power Rangers* program. At the time of this story, Power Rangers were at the height of their popularity. Many children were leaping and kicking their way through the day, and some children were getting hurt. In my years as a preschool teacher, I had seen many superheroes come and go, but the children's reactions to Power Rangers were more intense and confused than any I could remember. Although children's interest in these characters had resulted in some worthwhile talks about "being powerful," the play mainly involved potentially hurtful actions. When we mediated during Power Ranger–related conflicts, the resulting discussions often consisted of vague and angry arguments about who was good and bad, whether the characters were "real," and what they did (similar to what occurred during the following problem-solving discussion). The resolutions usually involved the children stopping their kicking, but interest in being "powerful" remained high.

To encourage more reflection about these issues, my teaching partner and I decided that I would facilitate a small-group discussion *only* with those involved in Power Ranger play; I hoped this would be an exploration of more positive actions that are "powerful." This was the very first small-group problem solving for this group of children and for me. While we later added the technique of using a shell with a message to introduce the issue (the reader will notice how this would have helped!), here I began by giving out pretzels and simply explaining what it was we were about to do.

Small-group discussion—
Problem: Being safe while being "powerful"

Betsy: *(Making eye contact with all the children)* There's going to be a new kind of small-group time today. It's for all of us to do together.

Rachael: *(Enthusiastically)* Then we'll have to do it too. *(I nod yes to her, and pass out small pretzels as I continue.)*

Betsy: It's a time to talk about how to solve problems, and how to solve problems so everybody can feel happy and safe when we're here at school.

Children: *(Excitedly, all together)* Yeah! Yeah!

Betsy: *(Surprised and pleased by their enthusiasm, I acknowledge them.)* You like to feel happy and safe, don't you? *(They nod and munch their pretzels.)* So, I might have a problem and I want you to help me solve it. Or, you might have something that's a problem and you want some help from all of us to solve it. Today I have a problem. This is a problem that I have seen at school sometimes. And the problem is that what I see sometimes is that children try to be powerful....

Rachael: *(Injecting)* What does that mean?

Betsy: *(Even though I have not finished explaining the problem, I decide to see where an explanation of the word "powerful" might lead.)* What does that mean? Does anyone know what it means to be powerful?

A few children: No.

Victor: *(He is dressed up in a cape and hat.)* Power Rangers. They're pretending to be Power Rangers or Ninjas.

Travis: Or to hurt somebody.

Rachael: They're trying to hurt the bad guys.

Betsy: But I'm not talking about Power Rangers. I'm just talking about ways that sometimes children try to be powerful and other people get their bodies hurt or their feelings hurt. So the problem I'm trying to figure out is how we can be powerful and have people feel happy and safe. *(This last sentence, finally, is how I had wanted to introduce the problem.)*

Rachael: Okay.

Betsy: So I thought maybe you could help me...

Victor: *(Injecting excitedly)* I know. You could pretend to be Power Rangers and Ninjas.

Betsy: The Power Rangers that I've seen usually try to hurt people.

Rachel: Real ones?

Betsy: No, the ones that I've seen children play. Usually they end up hurting somebody.

Victor: The Power Rangers that we play don't hurt.

Betsy:	The Power Rangers don't hurt? What do they do, Victor, instead of hurting?
Jarad:	They kill the bad guys.
Betsy:	Isn't killing a way of hurting people, Jarad? *(Several children nod and say yes.)*
Victor:	No. You know what they really do?
Travis:	They kill the monsters.
Victor:	No. They put the bad guys in jail.
Several children:	*(Disagreeing emphatically)* No, no! Uh-uh.
Victor:	*(Loudly)* Yes!

Here the children had returned to the ongoing argument about what Power Rangers actually do. Knowing that this discussion had not in the past yielded any clarification or new ideas for the children, I decided to insist on staying with the problem as I had introduced it. Since my explanation of the problem had been interrupted twice, I tried again.

Betsy:	You know what? *(The children quiet and refocus, listening.)* I don't want to talk about Power Rangers. I want to talk about ways that we can be powerful by doing things that can make people feel happy and safe. And I'm going to give you an idea. There was something that I saw today that was very powerful that made somebody feel happy. And you know what it was?
Victor and Rachael:	What?
Betsy:	Willie saw that Hannah was really sad today.
Rachael:	Because she didn't get a ride [in the wheelbarrow] 'cuz Libby wanted to have all the rides.
Betsy:	She didn't get a ride, so what did Willie do?
Willie:	Hug.
Betsy:	*(Smiling at him)* You gave Hannah a hug.
Rachael:	And I gave her her Teddy.
Betsy:	You gave her her Teddy! Ohhh, so one of the things you can do to be powerful is you can

	help people feel better when they're sad by giving them hugs or giving them things that make them feel better. *(I begin to write down their ideas on a big piece of paper in the middle of the table.)*
Kayla:	When I'm sad, somebody can give me my bunny.
Betsy:	Yeah! Just like that. So you can give hugs or something they like.
Kayla:	Write my bunny.
Betsy:	Yep. *(Writing and reading aloud)* "Something they like, like a bunny."
Kayla:	His name is Winnie, Winnie.
Betsy:	*(Points to the writing)* There's the word "bunny," right there. Can you think of other ways that people are powerful when they help people feel better and safe and happy?
Kayla:	How 'bout get dressed?
Betsy:	Oh, you can help people get dressed. So when you help someone get dressed, maybe you know how to tie shoes?
Rachael:	I do.
Betsy:	So if you needed help tying shoes, Rachael can help you. She can be very powerful 'cause she can help you to tie your shoes.
Kayla:	I don't know how to tie shoes.
Betsy:	But I bet there is something you do know how to do.
Kayla:	What? I know how to put my clothes on.
Betsy:	So do you know how to put on your coat? *(Kayla nods yes.)*
Betsy:	So if someone needed help putting on their coat, they could ask Kayla *(I write this down.)*
Willie:	*(Holding up his fingers with pretzels stuck on each one)* I know how to make knots.
Betsy:	You know how to make knots! So that's something really powerful that you know how to do.
Victor:	I do, too.
Jarad:	Me, too.
Rachael:	I know how to make bows.

Betsy: *(Noticing how excited they are feeling about naming skills that they can share, I acknowledge each of them, nodding, smiling, and listening. Eben, who is sitting next to me, has been occupied with his pretzels, but now he reaches over and begins to twirl his fingers in my hair. I turn and put my arm around him.)* So let's think of other things people know how to do to make people feel happy and safe. What is something Eben knows how to do? *(No one answers. Eben, at 2 years, 9 months, is the youngest child in the classroom. I remember what I saw him do earlier.)* You know Eben knows how to make collections. He knows how to get a bowl, right, Eben? *(He nods, smiles, and straightens up proudly in his seat.)* And he puts lots of things in it. You did that today, didn't you? *(Eben nods enthusiastically, curls bouncing around on his head.)* So that's something Eben knows how to do. So we'll write that down. He knows how to make collections, so if you need a collection, Eben can help you to do it.

Rachael: I know how to tie shoes.

Victor: I know how to play.

Betsy: Tell me more about that, Victor. What kinds of things do you know how to play that other children can learn?

Victor: I know how to play Power Rangers

Betsy: Yeah, is there something else? What else do you play?

Victor: I can play Superman.

Betsy: *(I realize that Victor is still stuck on his TV version of powerful, so I decide to see if a suggestion might help. His cape and hat remind me of his ever-present fantasy attire.)* You know what I notice about you, Victor? I notice that you really know how to dress up.

Victor: Yeah.

Betsy: You do, don't you? You know how to put on costumes.

Victor: Yeah!

Betsy: You're usually dressed up when you're here at school. Victor, if somebody needed help dressing up, could that be something you could help them with?

Victor: Yeah! *(I write this down.)*

Rachael: I know how to trace people. *(I look at her and nod.)*

Betsy: Let's see, Jarad. We didn't find out something from you that you know how to do.

Jarad: I know how to draw a forest.

Betsy: You know how to draw a forest! So if anybody wants to know how to draw a forest, they can ask you! *(Jarad nods proudly.)* So Travis, how about you?

Travis: Make 'em laugh.

Betsy: How would you do that?

Victor: You could make funny faces. *(Several children make faces at each other and laugh.)*

Betsy: *(Laughing with them)* That's a lot of funny faces. Do you have another idea, Travis?

Travis: Tell jokes.

Betsy: You would tell jokes! *(I write this down. Eben pulls my arm and makes a funny face.)* Is that your funny face, Eben?

Victor: You could do funny tricks.

Betsy: You could do funny tricks and that would help make them laugh?

Victor: Yeah!

By this time, I was nothing short of amazed at the variety of ideas they had generated. Rather than imitating or giving similar ideas, all of the children, except for Eben and Victor, had individually thought of contributions that were unique to their interests.

Betsy: *(Looking at them giggling with each other)* You know what I see? I see that there are a lot of ways to be powerful that help make people feel happy and safe. Would you like me to read this?

All the children:	Yeah! *(I begin to read all of their ideas. As I near the end, Victor interrupts me.)*
Victor:	*(Pointing to the paper)* One last sign.
Betsy:	One last sign?
Victor:	Yeah, there's space there and I'm going to fill it up.
Betsy:	*(Trying to grasp what he means)* Let me finish reading…or is there one more thing you want me to write?
Victor:	Be powerful by protecting things.

By making this suggestion, Victor demonstrated that he now understood the positive twist we had given to the idea of being powerful. As I acknowledged his idea, I asked him for more details, just to be sure his idea really would be safe.

Betsy:	Be powerful by protecting things! How would you protect someone in a way that was safe?
Victor:	Watch it.
Betsy:	Watch something someone made so it wouldn't get knocked over? *(Victor nods and I write this in the space left at the bottom.)*
Betsy:	I'm going to finish reading this. *(I read the last two things on the list.)* You thought of a lot of ways to be powerful and to help each other. We need to stop now. Shall we hang this up and try all of these?
Children:	Yeah!
Rachael:	Hang it right there! *(She points to the wall behind us.)*
Betsy:	Maybe you will even think of some new ones to add. Next week we'll talk about this again and see how it's working.

Though I have now done many small-group problem-solving sessions, I still look back on this as a truly remarkable discussion. I was amazed at the length of the children's attention spans, as well as the extent and diversity of their ideas. The ages of the children ranged from not quite 3 years (Eben) to nearly 5 (Rachael). Eben, the youngest, did not speak, and even though he did make one quick exploration under the table, for the most

During the "power play" discussion, children began to define being powerful in terms of their individual strengths rather than in TV terms. They became aware of other kinds of power, such as using a special skill to help out a classmate.

part he enjoyed his pretzels and listened to the conversation. All of the other children were fully engaged in the discussion and sincerely interested in one another's ideas. I was so delighted at the end when Victor, clearly a major superhero fan, began to fully understand that this conversation was about real people being powerful. Without any prodding from me, he had offered to fill up the last space on the paper with an independent contribution ("one last sign...be powerful by protecting things"). To me, this showed both his unwavering interest in the discussion and a change in his thinking.

In the days that followed, the children thought of other ideas for our list, adding new skills they were willing to share. The "power play" in the classroom became less and less hurtful, and there was more recognition by the children of the helpful things that they did for each other. They had redefined, on their own terms, the sources of their individual and very real power. They had set aside, at least for now, the definitions given to them by violent and disturbing television characters.

◆

Joyce balances the attention given to individual children during this spontan-ious discussion of a problem. Giving each person a chance to contribute ideas is just as important when families use this discussion process.

Family problem-solving discussion

During a training workshop for early childhood teachers, a par-ticipant came to me as the day ended. She looked very uncom-fortable as she told me that she had recently begun to spank her son. She quickly added that she was feeling terrible about it and wanted to know if I had any suggestions. Often training partici-pants ask me about individual children they find challenging, both at school and at home. I emphasized to this teacher, as I do with all participants, that since I don't know the child or the situation well, it's most useful for me to listen and describe strategies only, encouraging each participant to decide how they will implement the strategies.

The participant described her problem: her 2½-year-old son, Trevor, was having a very difficult time during the evenings when she was trying to feed and put his new baby sister to bed. Each evening as she rocked the baby, Trevor would run up and down the hall or engage in other loud, disruptive play activities. She was becoming increasingly frustrated and angry with Trevor, and unsure of what else to do, she had spanked him. She and I discussed again the strategies we had covered in the training, and she decided to try problem solving with Trevor when the problem was not happening. (We discussed how this was similar to small-group problem solving for a recurring problem in a classroom.) We also talked about the importance of encouraging Trevor to come up with ideas on his own.

Several days later, during training, she told a story something like this to the whole group:

Family discussion—
Problem: Being quiet for baby sister's bedtime

A few days ago, Trevor and I found some quiet time during the baby's morning nap and I told Trevor that I had a problem that we needed to work out together. I explained to Trevor that when I rocked his baby sister to sleep, there was a lot of noise and it was hard for the baby to go to sleep. I explained that the baby needed quiet in order to go to sleep and that the faster the baby went to sleep the sooner we would be able to spend time together. I also acknowledged how hard it was for Trevor to have to be quiet while he played on his own for a while.

I asked if he wanted to make a list of all the things that he could do during this "quiet" time. Trevor got very excited about the list and we got out paper and a crayon. He thought of nine things he could do, including tiptoeing up and down the hall, doing a puzzle, and getting out his dinosaurs. I wrote down all his ideas and drew a little picture so he could "read" each one.

That evening, before I went to put the baby to bed, we hung up the list together. I asked Trevor which activity on the list he would like to do first. Trevor picked "playing with my dinosaurs on the living room rug." As I rocked the baby, I listened and waited, but there was only the occasional quiet noise of toys rattling. Soon the baby was asleep and I joined Trevor. Immediately he pointed to three things on the list that he had done while he waited. I gave him a hug and told him, "Wow, Trevor, you really solved this problem!" He grinned from ear to ear.

As the teacher finished her story, the group applauded. I watched as *she* grinned from ear to ear.

Solving problems in this way with young children can dramatically alter how parents and children relate to one another. Trevor's mother had been headed down a punitive path that might eventually have had a very alienating effect on her relationship with Trevor. As she told her story, we all could sense her relief, and even more important, her newfound respect for her child's ability to find creative solutions.

◆

Making a poem from children's ideas

This last story speaks for itself.

Spontaneous small-group discussion—
Problem: What does peace mean?

One day during snack time a spontaneous problem-solving conversation began about words and their definitions. It began with the children's conversation about the word *war* and what it meant. The children quickly offered definitions: "It's when people kill each other." "It's a lot of fighting." "It's people shooting." "People get dead in war."

There seemed to be considerable awareness of what war was, and I became curious to know if they understood the word *peace* as clearly. In anticipation of their possible responses, I took paper and a marker from a nearby shelf, and asked, "So what is *peace?*"

Three 4-year-old boys were very interested in the question. Their answers came slowly, thoughtfully, their inspiration extending from one boy to the next as their ideas became a spontaneous poem. On the opposite page is the poem they created, while munching on carrot sticks.

Although at first the boys' words did not come as quickly as the words that defined war, as they talked they became more and more thoughtful and pleased with their vision of peace. As they finished with the last contribution to the list, it reminded all of us that it was in fact time to go outside. I thought this was the end of the discussion. I hung the list near our table and we went out. As the boys were running to the playground, one of them shouted, "Let's find a

Peace ......

is not shooting

is quiet

is not killing anything

is not throwing litter

is eating healthy stuff

is being silly

is not breaking glass

is not walking in the house
   with muddy boots

is not stealing money

is not pulling somebody's
   hair out

is giving someone a present

is giving someone something
   to eat if they are homeless

is playing peaceful and sharing
   toys and something real tasty

is playing outside together

RYAN EZRATHAD

peaceful place!" They found a shallow dip in the yard, a little grassy crater that fit all three of them cozily. They lay on their backs in this little hollow, watching the clouds float by. "This is peace," I heard one of them say.

Small-group problem solving provides rich opportunities for children to reflect on problems, engage in cause-and-effect thinking, explore feelings and needs, and plan collaboratively for change.

These sessions can be planned by a teacher around a classroom problem or a universal social issue, or they can happen spontaneously as concerns arise through play and conversation. These problem-solving dialogues, whether planned or spontaneous, are important for two reasons. First, the solutions that children choose themselves are the ones that are most likely to be successful and to create real growth and change. Second, the problem-solving session provides a unique learning opportunity—a genuine collaboration of hearts and minds.

As a teacher and a parent, I thoroughly enjoy this type of problem solving. Without the stronger emotions of a conflict-in-progress, those involved can relax into the thoughtful give-and-take of finding a solution that works for everyone. Children can be surprisingly insightful during these discussions, offering solutions that reflect their unique thinking and generous natures. Each time I facilitate a small-group problem-solving session, my respect and belief in the abilities of young children is reaffirmed.

7

Preventing Conflicts and Creating Emotionally Healthy Environments

The most carefully planned, supportive classrooms, centers, and homes have conflict despite our best efforts to avoid disputes among children. All of us have days when we wish conflict could be banished, even though we know that this is neither possible nor useful. Fortunately, there are many ways we can reduce the amount and intensity of conflict in settings for young children. Many factors—ranging from separation difficulties to daily routines to adult-child interaction strategies—can influence the level of conflict in classroom or homes, and an approach to prevention that considers these factors can bring about many improvements.

The purpose of adult support and conflict prevention strategies, other than the obvious goal of keeping conflict to a minimum, is to create a positive, vibrantly healthy, social and emotional environment. In such an environment, children not only have fewer conflicts, their sense of self flourishes. As we consider all the elements of creating environments for young learners, it is most important to remember this: *Children learn best when they can trust caregivers to respond to their developmental wants and needs, when their attempts at autonomy and initiative are encouraged, and when their natural capacities for empathy and self-confidence are nurtured.*

In this chapter we will explore how to create such an emotionally balanced climate in which all children feel valued, safe, and encouraged. To set a positive "tone" for a group of children,

Reducing the number and intensity of conflicts is part of an overall process of creating emotionally healthy and happy environments in classrooms and homes. Many factors contribute to a positive balance of activities and interactions.

many factors require careful consideration; a group of children can be unsettled by just one or two factors. For example, every child absorbs an adult's loud, scolding voice, not just the one it is directed at. Likewise, a daily routine that is unpredictable creates an "out-of-control" feeling for both children and adults. On the other hand, a change in even one factor can lead to improvements in the climate; adults who try to offer more choices have found that this alone can have an enormous impact in reducing conflicts. Working with children is a complicated process requiring purposeful planning and careful attention to detail. Ultimately the adult who enjoys being with children, relishing their unique view of the world, will find this to be a rewarding and successful process.

The rest of this chapter discusses basic strategies adults can use to provide an emotionally balanced climate with a minimum of conflict. The strategies are organized in five categories: child development, adult-child interaction, learning environment and daily routine, home-to-school transitions, and assessment. They are summarized in the checklist given opposite.

Preventing Conflicts and Creating an Emotionally Healthy Environment: A Strategies Checklist

Child Development Strategies

✔ Keep in mind the young child's unique developmental perspective.

✔ Encourage children to be active learners throughout the day, supporting their feelings and choices; avoid the use of praise or evaluation.

Adult-Child Interaction Strategies

✔ Be fully available to and respectful of children.

✔ Establish a safe community for children and include them in deciding guidelines for the classroom.

✔ Mediate conflicts as they occur, focusing on actions, rather than people, when stopping hurtful or destructive behavior.

Learning Environment and Daily Routine Strategies

✔ Plan a learning environment that includes a variety of areas and materials.

✔ Establish and maintain a consistent daily routine.

✔ Help children anticipate and enjoy the transitions in the daily routine.

✔ Plan strategies for making cleanup time fun and interesting for children.

Home-to-School Transition Strategies

✔ Plan an "orientation" period for each entering child.

✔ Plan strategies for parent departure times.

Assessment Strategies

✔ Record observations of children on a regular basis.

✔ Examine your reasons for choosing to work with children.

Child Development Strategies

✔ Keep in mind the young child's unique developmental perspective.

Young children between the ages of 1½ to 8 years have many unique characteristics that affect how they think and feel about their world and how they interact with others (Hohmann & Weikart, 2002). Understanding and accepting these characteristics is essential for adults who seek to create an early childhood setting in which children feel supported. Chapter 1 introduced some of these developmental characteristics, relating them to the problem-solving steps. Here, each characteristic is discussed in relation to teaching strategies for preventing conflicts and creating a more positive environment.

Egocentrism. Children learn by constructing their own knowledge of the world in a process that begins with individual thoughts, feelings, experiences, and questions. Because young children are egocentric, they see the world from this very individual point of view. Only with experience do children come to know that other viewpoints exist. Thus, adult questions like "How do you think that makes her feel?" are not useful. When children are asked to explain or understand the feelings of others, and they fail to as a result of their developmental immaturity, resentment or anger may escalate, causing conflict. Questions like "How can you make him happy?" are particularly inappropriate because they force the child to be responsible for both the feelings and perspective of another child. Such questions put the child in the impossible position of trying to change another person's feelings.

Teaching practices that take children's self-centered thinking into account contribute to a more positive climate, for example, *naming* feelings rather than asking questions about them ("You are feeling upset" rather than "How are you feeling?"); providing multiple copies of favorite toys, so children can play cooperatively and with fewer conflicts; and creating many "helper" jobs so that children can be important every day. While adults cannot directly teach children to be less egocentric, they can facilitate discussions during play that will enable children to describe their ideas clearly and to hear the viewpoints of others. "Egocentrism of thought during the preoperational period diminishes slowly through the child's dealing with the thoughts of peers that conflict with his own thinking" (Wadsworth, 1978, p. 19). Such experiences result in a maturing appreciation of others that eventually leads to a reduction in the number of conflicts.

Concrete thinking: judging by appearances. Young children base their understanding of the world on easily observed physical characteristics. They believe that one person is older than another because he is taller, that the moon is alive because it moves and appears to follow them, and that one group of objects has more than another because it is spread out over a larger area. Because of children's tendency to judge by appearances, we can avoid unnecessary conflict by taking care to hand out very equal-*looking* quantities of materials or snacks. Similarly, if we are aware of the possibility that some children may be very frightened by some kinds of realistic fantasy props, we can help them understand the make-believe purposes of costumes, masks, and puppets. For example, we can often avoid emotional upsets by having children watch as people put on costumes or scary make-up.

We can reduce the number of conflicts through practices that take children's self-centered thinking into account, for example, providing multiple copies of favorite toys.

Because children derive much of their understanding of the world from obvious physical cues, visual messages are very effective ways to communicate expectations and routines. In one preschool, this sign signifies that a child has set aside an unfinished personal project, and that others are not to touch it.

In addition, because children tend to make judgments based on how things look, visual messages are often very effective ways to communicate with them about expectations or routines. For example, a series of pictures or photos may be used to depict a child's bedtime ritual, the classroom daily routine, special events that will occur in the classroom, or a safety limit for the playground. A photo of one child on the slide ladder can illustrate a "one child at a time" limit; a simple piece of tape on the floor can clarify a boundary; a large "X" over the symbol for a classroom area or an "X" taped to the on/off switch of the television or computer can remind children that these objects are "off limits" for the moment. Such visual cues reduce the number of adult verbal reminders and help children predict what will happen next, reducing difficulties during transitions from one activity to the next.

José gives a child time to say what he is feeling and thinking (pausing 5–10 seconds to wait for his response). This will encourage the child to ask for the book, rather than try to take it.

Limited verbal skills. Since young children or children with developmental delays are still acquiring a substantial part of their vocabulary, the words for expressing needs and wants and the words of problem solving may be very new to them. If we give children time to say what they feel and think (pausing 5 to 10 seconds to wait for their responses), this will encourage them to use language, rather then physical responses, to handle problems. Creating opportunities for children to hear the words of problem solving during stories, songs, and puppet plays encourages them to use problem-solving words to resolve difficulties before they esca-

Problem Solving With Toddlers or Children With Developmental Delays

Toddlers' language skills are even less developed than preschoolers', so to problem-solve, they need extra response time and other kinds of language support. When working with toddlers and young children with language delays, adults usually find it necessary to provide a lot of the language of problem solving. This can be done by asking questions that the child can answer with yes, a no, or a nod of the head. For example, we might say: "I can see that you're both very mad. Do you both want the truck?" (Look for yes or no response.) Or: "You both want a turn. What can we do?" (Wait for child to point or indicate an idea.)

Very young children can come up with ideas for solutions at this point if we are patient. Their solutions are often surprisingly simple. For example, in a dispute between toddlers over a toy truck, a child may answer the adult's request for ideas by simply getting another truck or handing over the one he has. However, if we have allowed ample time (20–30 seconds) for a response and the children have still not come up with a workable idea, we can ask, "I have an idea. Do you want to hear my idea?" (Wait for yes or no.) "We could use the timer. Shall we do that?" (Wait for yes or no.) Our patience and support help the children stay engaged with the problem-solving process and insure that they have control over the solution.

Very young children or children with special needs can begin problem solving as soon as they understand some language and can indicate yes and no. Children who have learned the skills of problem solving early will be very capable of dealing with the increased social activities and the resulting problems that usually occur by the time children reach 3 or 4 years.

late. When problem-solving language is familiar to children, this also helps them reach solutions more quickly. The following stories illustrate the growing problem-solving awareness and capabilities of a 15-month-old boy who was used to having his feelings and problems identified and acknowledged. Initially, he used very limited language himself, though it was clear he understood the concepts. The last story describes how, as a 3-year-old, he intervened in a conflict between his mother and brother as an independent problem solver.

Grandma wants to vacuum: Tom wants his blocks

Young Tom, aged 15 months, was playing on Grandma Brennie's living room rug with a special set of small blocks she kept for him. Eventually he became distracted, got up, and began to play outside in the garden with his Auntie Rachael. Grandma Brennie, who was vacuuming, entered the living room. Seeing that Tom was busy outside, she picked up the blocks and put them away in the cupboard so that she could vacuum the rug.

A little while later, Tom and Rachael returned to the living room. When Tom saw that the blocks were gone, he burst into tears.

Rachael reached out to him with a gentle stroking of his back and named his feelings, "You're feeling very sad, Tom." Tom continued to cry. "You're feeling very, very sad."

Beginning to calm, Tom told Rachael, "Block."

Rachael acknowledged his feelings and the problem. "You're feeling sad because you wanted to play with the blocks some more." Tom nodded as a big tear dropped off his chin. Rachael restated the problem for him, "So the problem is, you wanted to play with the blocks some more and Grandma Brennie didn't know you wanted to use them some more, and she wanted to vacuum." Tom was completely calm now and listening. "What do you think we can do, Tom?"

Tom was quiet and Rachael waited. Then he looked up and told her softly, "Hug." Rachael opened up her arms and so did Tom, and they enjoyed a long, lovely hug together.

◆

Tom doesn't want to ride in the stroller

Young Tom, now aged 18 months, was preparing to go to the store with Kerrie, his mother. He went to the closet and got his coat. Kerrie helped him to put it on. When she got out the stroller, Tom immediately began to cry and yell, "No stroller, no stroller!"

It was a long way to the store. Kerrie did not have time to let Tom walk, and he was too heavy to carry that distance. Kerrie got down on one knee and acknowledged Tom's feelings: "You're feeling really upset, Tom." She paused as he calmed down. "You're really don't want to go in the stroller," she continued. Tom shook his head no and ran to the door. "You really don't want to go in the stroller," she acknowledged again.

Tom stopped crying. "We have a problem, Tom. We don't have time for you to walk and I can't carry you that far," Kerrie said. Noticing that Tom was listening, Kerrie continued, "So the problem is, you don't want to go in the stroller, and I need to push you in the stroller today. What can we do?"

Tom repeated, "No." He pointed to the stroller.

Kerrie asked Tom, "I have an idea. Do you want to hear my idea?" Tom nodded. Gently Kerrie told him, "My idea is that you can get in the stroller yourself or I can put you in the stroller. Which would you like to do?"

Tom answered, "Me," and climbed in the stroller.

Tom becomes an independent problem solver

Almost 2 years had gone by and Tom, now almost 3 years old, had a younger brother, Jack, who was 16 months old. Kerrie had consistently responded to Tom and Jack's conflicts with problem solving, which had worked well for all of them. One morning Kerrie, Tom, and young Jack were preparing to go to the store. After helping Tom and Jack with their coats, Kerrie got out the stroller. Jack began to cry and yell, "No, no!"

Feeling anxious to get to the store quickly and a bit exasperated by Jack, Kerrie wasn't ready to problem-solve. She decided to take a few deep breaths and get her own coat from the closet first. As she walked down the hall, she heard Tom talking to Jack by the front door.

"Now Jack," Tom began, sounding very grown up, "we have a problem. You have to ride in the stroller because we have to hurry. You can get in the stroller yourself or Mom can put you in. Which one, Jack?" Jack climbed into the stroller himself.

Problem-solving skills learned at a very early age, even when verbal skills are still quite limited, can become a natural response to conflict. Very young children respond to conflicts with surprisingly simple, generous solutions. As they get older and their conflicts and disputes become more complicated, this problem-solving response grows with the challenge and children develop increasingly sophisticated communication skills. One of

Conflicts are fewer when children are encouraged to fully express their feelings and ideas. That's why listening carefully to children, as Merrilee does here, is one of the most effective ways to reduce the frequency and intensity of conflicts.

the most effective ways to reduce the frequency and intensity of conflicts is to encourage the development of children's speaking abilities and vocabulary.

Physical expressiveness. Young children may show excitement by jumping up and down, express sadness by crying or withdrawing, or communicate anger by hitting or grabbing.

These non-verbal expressions are developmentally normal—they are often the only ways children know to express feelings. Children's physical expressiveness provides a rich opportunity for adults to connect with and positively enrich children's emotional lives. Adults can respond to physical outbursts by naming feelings and providing limits, as well as by giving children alternative ways to express feelings physically. For example, for a child who is angry and hitting someone, we can support the child by saying "Hitting people needs to stop. You're feeling really angry. Please use gentle hands on people; you can hit the pillow." It is appropriate to suggest positive alternative expressions for feelings. For a child showing anger by throwing blocks we could say, "Throwing blocks needs to stop. You're feeling very frustrated. Blocks stay in hands for building; you can throw the ball (soft bear, pillow)." (For more on describing limits positively, see 307–308.) Shorter versions of these support statements may be used for younger children or children with language delays. When children are supported emotionally in these ways, children's positive sense of self and readiness for learning new social skills are enhanced.

On the other hand, when adults react to these physical mistakes with blaming or punishment, children's self-esteem may be adversely affected, and conflicts may actually increase. (Children who have a poor sense of self are more likely to provoke conflicts.) A lacrosse coach (my husband actually) once told me that it is good coaching technique to leave players on the field right after they've made a mistake. This way, they can immediately correct themselves, and consequently will remember the *correction* rather than the mistake. Such corrections are especially effective because of their *physicality* (as contrasted with verbal harangues from the coach on the side-lines). Likewise, when children express feelings physically, we can discourage their hurtful actions while also moving immediately to help them find new ways of expressing feelings with words and positive actions. This kind of quick response keeps children physically "in the moment," reaching them at their developmental level. Learning that is so tangibly connected to the physical details of the situation hastens the development of new expressive skills, resulting in fewer aggressive outbursts.

Exploration of independence and control. Doing things independently is of great interest to young children. This is a very healthy and important need that provides the motivation to learn new skills. As children explore their independence, they become aware of their newfound abilities and the resulting reactions of others. Making choices and decisions can be frustrating as well as interesting to children; sometimes the child wants to have all the control and make all the choices at once. Young

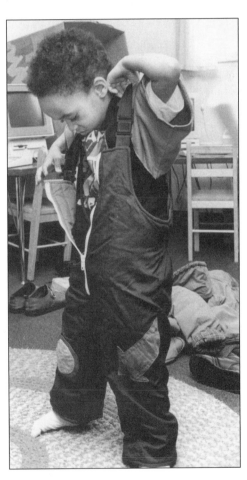

Encouraging children to do tasks for themselves, even under challenging circumstances, helps to minimize frustration and hastens the growth of new skills.

children are both egocentric and interested in control, a combination that can result in exasperating conflicts in which children are in conflict with themselves as well as with others. For example, 2-year-old Piyali wants to go out to play in the snow and is struggling with her snowsuit. When offered help by her dad, she runs off with the suit, yelling, "Me do it!" Encouraging children to do tasks for themselves, even under challenging circumstances, helps to minimize frustration and hastens the growth of new skills. If possible, Piyali's Dad could allow lots of time for Piyali to continue on her own, or if he knows they must get dressed quickly, he could say, "Piyali, I know you'd really like to put on the snowsuit yourself. It is time for us to go so we're going to do it together. You help me put in your legs and arms and then you zip yourself." Children's struggles for independence can result in new learning when adults share control with children, encouraging and accepting the emerging abilities of this developmental stage. This lessens children's frustration and enhances their self-confidence, reducing the likelihood that they will become involved in conflicts.

One-thing-at-a-time thinking. Young children can focus on only one or two attributes or ideas at one time. We can help prevent confusion (and reduce related conflicts) by taking care not to overwhelm or frustrate children with too many activities or materials or too much information (for example, saying "Will all the children wearing blue on their clothes and who have brown hair stand up and walk to the bathroom"). When handing out materials to a group of children, it is helpful to give out just a few items or sets at first. Children can explore these without being distracted or overwhelmed; other materials can be added as they are ready. This avoids competition for materials and worry over who has what and how much. When giving instructions, it is likewise useful for us to keep them short and simple to avoid problems, or when limits are discussed, to talk about those limits by naming the action first: A simple direction like "Spitting needs to stop" (versus "You need to stop that spitting") names the offending action right up front and avoids aggravating the situation with a blaming or demanding tone. Giving children just the information that they can handle and act on easily can stimulate a quicker response, possibly defusing the situation before it becomes a conflict.

Empathy. The ability to empathize (understand how another feels) begins when children are very young and develops slowly over the early childhood years. Some infants notice and respond to the obvious, physically expressed emotions of others. "Developmental psychologists have found that infants feel sympathetic distress even before they fully realize that they exist apart from other people" (Goleman, 1995, p. 98).

Though preschoolers may be *aware* of the feelings of others, it is often challenging for them to *understand* such feelings because they still tend to see things from an egocentric viewpoint. Consequently, if we acknowledge and support children's awareness and expression of feelings, we can have an enormous impact on the development of empathy. "Empathy builds on self-awareness; the more open we are to our own emotions, the more skilled we will be in reading feelings" (Goleman, 1995, p. 96). By acknowledging children's feelings, we support children's awareness of their own feelings and needs, and, by extension, their awareness of and empathy for the feelings of others. As children learn to read the body language cues of other children and adults, and learn how to respond to them constructively, they will strengthen their developing empathic skills. This, in turn will reduce conflict.

An awareness of the developmental characteristics and strategies described here can assist us in understanding the unique perspective of young children. We must *always* keep this perspective in mind as we play and mediate with them.

Comforting and naming feelings at a very early age, as this dad is doing, helps to develop awareness of feelings as well as the ability to empathize.

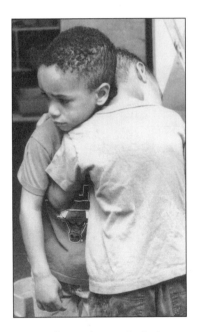

Having learned empathy by having his own feelings noticed and named frequently by adults, this boy comforts an upset friend.

✔ Encourage children to be active learners throughout the day, supporting their feelings and choices; avoid the use of praise or evaluation.

Programs are likely to have fewer disputes when they are committed to promoting learning through playful, warm relationships with adults and through experiences that offer children lots of choices for active play. Children will be less prone to conflict if they are encouraged to enjoy themselves and if they can exercise some control over their day. In such conditions, children tend to choose play activities that express their personal interests and are appropriate for their skill levels, and they usually become very engaged in their play. As a result, they are likely to be successful in what they are doing and be self-motivated to learn new skills and further extend their interests.

To develop as active, intrinsically motivated learners, children need an organized setting with a wide variety of materials, and consistent support from adults. As children work with the materials and interact with one another, we can act as their play partners, enhancing the active learning process by encouraging, rather than praising, their ideas and efforts. By responding to the details of children's work with an interest in what children are actually doing, rather than in the end products of these activities, we can help children stay focused and encourage them

Children who often receive affection from adults in the setting are likely to openly and easily show affection to others. These warm relationships create a climate that promotes learning.

to learn concepts and skills necessary to carry out their goals. This nonevaluative adult approach also helps to reduce competition among children over who does the "best" drawing or who is being "good." Instead of making comparisons, we can accept every child's work, recognizing that children are at varying developmental levels and approaching mistakes as catalysts for new learning. When we share control with children by reducing our authority in

When their choices are supported by adults, children are motivated to expand their skills.

this way, children learn to value their own work, rather than becoming dependent on the opinions and evaluations of others. This non-judgmental, control-sharing approach contrasts with adult-directed learning approaches in which praise, reward, and/or punishment are used as reinforcers and in which drills or rote instruction are common learning activities. Such approaches may promote passivity, aggression, and competition among children (Kohn, 1993).

In an active learning approach, adults offer choices during all parts of the daily routine. When choices are limited, at times like lunch, rest, or transitions (as in the next story), we can still share control with children by communicating clearly the reasons for giving limited choices. For example, if it is time to end a small-group activity and a child is resistant to finishing, we can do some quick problem solving with him or her, giving choices about how to finish and allowing the child time to adjust to the necessity for a transition. Notice how Michelle did this in the following episode, preventing a potential conflict from escalating.

It's outside time, but Andrea is still busy indoors

It was time for the children to go outside but Andrea was still working intently with her materials from small-group time.

"Andrea, I can see that you are still really busy, but it's outside time. So how 'bout if we think together of a place where we can put these things for tomorrow, so you can use them during work time?" Michelle said to her.

Andrea shook her head slowly and continued wrapping a stick with tape. Watching Andrea closely, Michelle gently suggested, "Would you like them in the same place where the tape is kept at this school? Since you're using tape with them?" Andrea nodded yes. "Okay, well, then we can make a spot."

"I said yes!" Andrea added enthusiastically.

Michelle said, "Look over at the shelf. Tell me, do you want them to be put on the top, the middle, or the bottom shelf?"

Andrea looked up at the shelf. "Where the tape is," she said.

"Okay, here's a box." Michelle gave Andrea a box and Andrea collected all the extra sticks and pine boughs left over from the small-group time and put them inside the box. She set the box by the tape. She then took the stick she'd been working on and went to get ready for outside time.

When children are having difficulty with a transition, giving them some choices, however limited, about what will happen next communicates respect for their needs, as Michelle did with Andrea. Even in the most difficult or potentially hurtful situations, when it may appear there are no choices, adults can support children's need for control by giving at least two very limited choices. Gently telling a child "Hitting needs to stop or I will need to stop the hitting" can make it possible for the child to CHOOSE a new behavior independently. If the child is unresponsive, it can help to add "If a choice isn't made, I will choose for you. I think you'll feel better if you make a choice yourself."

◆

Adult-Child Interaction Strategies

✔ Be fully available to and respectful of children.

In supportive environments, adults make every effort to be "fully present" for children, demonstrating respect for children; listening with interest to their concerns, feelings, and ideas; and offering themselves as partners in children's play and learning. Adults who are attentive in all communications (i.e., adults are not trying to do other things *and* listen to children) send a message that each child is valued. Children who do not receive such attention are more likely to be involved in conflict situations. Lack of attention, blaming, and punishment can communicate that children are not seen as important, decreasing their self-esteem and the likelihood of angry expressions. When adults refer to children as "bullies" or "bossy," children will fulfill these labels. During problem solving, giving our full attention to each child's point of view, without labeling or making assumptions, can help children view themselves more positively, and increase their cooperative interactions with others.

Communicating interest through body language. There are many ways we can physically show children that we are fully present. These steps can also assist us in actually *being* fully present. A first step is to show our desire to really hear from children by getting down at the child's level, making eye contact, and using a gentle tone of voice. This not only helps the child know we are listening but will also help us to be completely attentive.

Dealing with competing demands on our attention. A second step that helps us focus our attention is deciding where our attention should go. In a busy day with children, adults have a multitude of jobs and distractions. It is challenging to fully attend to all the communications, both verbal and nonverbal, from children. Often adults have to perform communications "triage," setting priorities for their interactions with children. Obviously, attending to children who are potentially unsafe, hurtful to others, or upset is a first priority. Adults need to move quickly and calmly to those situations. Children who have immediate physical care needs are another clear priority. But beyond these obvious choices, how do we decide where our attention should go? In considering this, it can be helpful to review what we know about each child and what we see happening right now. Who is playing independently and who is wandering by themselves? Do we often spend time with certain children? Why? Can those children who are often needful of our attention be included when we join other children whom we spend less time with? Are there children whom we avoid? It can be helpful to identify why, and then consider how to change this pattern. Another strategy is to check our written observations of children. These notes may help us set some priorities. Such questions are important to consider over and over throughout the year; children need to be valued and supported all the time by their caregivers, and they need this to happen in different ways, at different times.

At times when we feel pulled in many directions, taking a problem-solving approach and engaging children in our dilemma can help to prevent conflicts. As children converge on us with many needs, we can try telling them "Wow, I have a problem! Joey wants me to look at his painting, and Forest

In the midst of a busy classroom, this adult makes herself fully available to the children.

wants me to do a puzzle, and I was thinking about spending time with Chris, who has been reading by himself for a long time. I wonder if you have ideas of how I should solve this?" It can be very useful for children to see things from our perspective. Without expressing resentment or blaming, this kind of description lets them know about the complications we face. Also, by posing our question as a statement ("I wonder if you have ideas . . . ") we are gently inviting—not demanding—their participation in resolving the dilemma. Engaging children in this broad social view of the classroom (or family experience) can help them understand the needs and wants of others.

When children are encouraged to help with decisions like this, it is possible that one of the children may offer a suggestion like "How 'bout if you look at Joey's painting, then let's ask Chris if he will do a puzzle with us!" Such creative suggestions may not arise the very first time we ask for ideas, but if we frequently solicit and use children's ideas, they will come to trust that we are genuinely interested. When children's concerns, feelings, and ideas are fully heard and valued, they become more articulate and increasingly able to act on their wants and needs independently.

Respecting children's physical autonomy. Respecting children's ideas and feelings must also include respect for their physical autonomy. It is important for adults to avoid grasping children suddenly, without warning or explanation. If circumstances require us to hold a child who is threatening others, it is important that we give reasons for our actions. For example, if a child is about to hit another child, the teacher may quickly take hold of her arm, saying "Janie, you're feeling so angry that you want to hit. Hitting people hurts. Here's a pillow to hit." When this kind of necessary physical restraint is done respectfully and an alternative physical expression has been suggested, children will be more responsive to our intervention. However, when adults suddenly and physically stop children or pick them up without warning or explanation, children may become resentful, and "out of control" behavior may be the result. Children's angry or resentful feelings about adults' unexplained physical interventions may spill over into children's interactions with peers, contributing to hurtful actions. By contrast, respectful behavior modeled by adults promotes children's learning of respectful behavior.

✔ Establish a safe community for children and include them in deciding guidelines for the classroom.

Keeping children safe is one of the most important roles of the classroom teacher. A sense of safety is a critical component of children's ability to learn. Children need to be safe, both physically and emotionally, to function at their highest potential. For a safe classroom or home, adults can first agree on a set of guidelines that includes the safe use of space and materials (what materials can be moved from area to area, where can children use water, etc.), supervision patterns, and a commitment to a consistent interaction approach. (See opposite for a list of basic guidelines for supportive adult-child interaction. See Hohmann & Weikart, 2002, pp. 43–67, for a full discussion of effective adult support strategies and Tompkins, 1991/1996, for a discussion of praise versus encouragement strategies.)

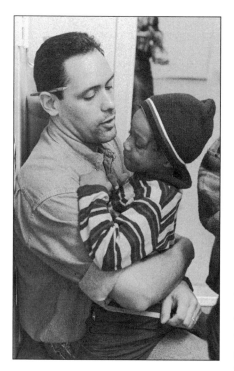

A sense of safety based on supportive relationships is a critical component of children's ability to learn. Children need to feel safe, both physically and emotionally, to function at their highest potential.

As adults maintain physical safety and set limits, they can help children *understand* safe behavior in the classroom or home by stating expectations positively and concretely. Children can better grasp what we want or need them to do if we state this specifically, rather than focusing on what we *don't* want. Young children, and especially toddlers, can be very confused by negative limit setting. Because most toddlers are told limits so often *and* because they can only hold one or two things in mind at a time, limit-setting language needs to be very clear.

Guidelines for Adult-Child Interaction

Consistent adult support for children is an essential feature of emotionally healthy environments in which conflicts are kept to a minimum. The following guidelines for supportive adult-child interaction are taken from the *High/Scope Program Quality Assessment (PQA)—Preschool Version* (High/Scope, 1998, pp. 24–35).

III-A. Children's basic physical needs are met.

III-B. Children's separation from home and daily entry into the program is handled with sensitivity and respect.

III-C. Adults create a warm and caring atmosphere for children.

III-D. Adults use a variety of strategies to encourage and support child language and communication.

III-E. Adults use a variety of strategies to support and include children whose primary language is not English in classroom communication.

III-F. Adults participate as partners in children's play.

III-G. Adults encourage children's initiatives throughout the day.

III-H. Adults provide opportunities for children to explore and use materials at their own developmental level and pace.

III-I. Adults acknowledge individual children's accomplishments.

III-J. Adults encourage children to interact and turn to one another for assistance throughout the day.

III-K. Children have opportunities to solve problems and act independently.

III-L. Children participate in resolving conflicts.

Children learn safe behavior most effectively when limits are presented *one at a time* and there are opportunities to actively experience the need or reason for the limit. Consequently, it is not effective to verbally tell children a list of limits while they sit in a large group. A *single* safety guideline may be introduced using a puppet or a story. After a month or so of school, when children know the safety guidelines, adults can facilitate problem-solving discussions in small groups (as discussed in Chapter 6) to address any current safety issue. This inclusion of the children in deciding on how safety problems should be solved helps to ensure their cooperation with the solution.

When choosing safety guidelines for the classroom or home, it is best to keep them simple, use language children can understand, and avoid making lists of "don'ts." The guidelines for children might be as simple as this: *Be safe with yourself, with others, and with our classroom toys.* However, rules like "We're all

Limiting Setting With Positives: Say What You *Do* Want

Negative limit setting	Positive limit setting
"No throwing the toys!"	"Toys need to stay in your **hands.**"
"You shouldn't get mud on your pants."	"Mud needs to stay on the **ground.**"
"No running in the classroom."	"**Walking** in the classroom keeps everyone safe."
"Whining is driving me crazy."	"I understand you better when you speak **clearly.**"
"You are being very bossy."	"All the children want a chance to **make choices** about...."
"You are making a mess."	"The paint needs to stay **on the paper.**"
"You shouldn't put that in your mouth."	"Toys are for touching with **hands.**"
"Don't throw your food."	"Food stays clean on the **plate.** Are you finished?"

friends" are not effective with preschoolers. Children have their own definition of who is a friend; a friend is whomever they are playing with at the moment. As tempted as we may be, we cannot legislate friendship (see pp. 107 & 124 for more discussion of this issue).

✔ **Mediate conflicts as they occur, focusing on actions, rather than people, when stopping hurtful or destructive behavior.**

When conflict resolution strategies become the norm for responding to disputes, this has a stabilizing effect on everyone in the classroom or home. For adults, knowing they have a set of tools for a variety of challenging situations reduces the worries and stresses of working with children of any age. Parents feel relief from the burden of having to be the one with solutions for sibling difficulties. Teachers take solace in knowing that the whole class can talk through classroom problems. Since supporting children's solutions is a straightforward process that relies on adults remaining neutral, adults who use this approach can avoid the pitfalls inherent in deciding who's "right." By focusing on mistaken actions, rather than people, and on alternative ways

1. As a dispute erupts in the classroom, José moves quickly and calmly to support both children.

2. As he begins to hear from both children about what happened, he focuses on the actions that occurred without blaming children for any mistakes they may have made.

3. Feelings and tensions subside as children see that José will not be deciding who's "right."

4. With José's support, the children begin to resolve the details of this dispute. They are also building a repertoire of new skills, reducing their future need for adult involvement. ◆

to approach problems, adults can help children build a repertoire of new skills for solving conflicts independently, reducing their future needs for adult involvement.

For children, the presence of adults who approach conflict confidently has a profound calming effect. Children who are involved in conflicts, as well as those merely listening nearby to negotiations, will find the adults' calm and neutral approach to be a reassuring change from loud, accusing voices. Such voices can send a disturbing message—"There is a scary adult in the room"—to every child listening. As children come to trust that adults will consistently respond to conflicts supportively and with a real effort to understand rather than punish the disputants, the number of conflicts will lessen. Those conflicts that do occur will not escalate as far. Children will begin to think of conflict in a different way; rather than signifying "badness" or failure, conflict will be experienced as an opportunity to talk things through, a way to find common ground and successful solutions. In fact, many conflicts will not even be perceived as such, since children will begin to respond to difficulties by thinking of lots of ideas to solve them.

This positive perception of conflict is illustrated in the next two stories, which depict children who have had many experi-

Children who experience a mediation approach learn to trust that adults will respond to conflicts by supporting their feelings and making a real effort to understand rather than punish mistakes.

ences with mediation. The first story reports an incident in which Alex, Hakeem, Reese, and Leroy built a "slide" with the large hollow blocks. After the four boys played with the slide for a while, Hakeem and Alex began to talk about making something else—a "ship"—but Reese and Leroy said they didn't want to take the slide apart. This scenario could have gone very differently if the children had not previously experienced mediation. Although there was no grabbing or yelling, the children *were* in the middle of a conflict—they disagreed about how the blocks were to be used. However, no mediation was required; instead the boys became involved in a very animated discussion about "ideas," alternately sharing and listening, bouncing one idea off another. Reese and Leroy even jumped up and down with pride as they shared their ideas. Demonstrating their grasp of the art of negotiation, the boys not only listened but also showed appreciation for the ideas of the others. ("That's a good idea!" Leroy said. Alex told Reese "I couldn't think of that idea.") The boys then began to talk about what to do. The boys also showed they were patient listeners; they appeared to take no special notice of Hakeem's extended stutter, waiting calmly each time he spoke.

As these almost-5-year-old boys talked, they climbed on and off the "slide," moving around each other with excitement. As they spoke, they looked back and forth to one another, checking for reactions to ideas.

Alex, Hakeem, Reese, and Leroy: "Wanna hear my idea!"

Alex: Hakeem just came up with an idea and we don't know if it'll work. Can we just make a little port back here where the end is?

Hakeem: Yeah, climbing up this part *(points to slide end)*, we want to attach a little ship—he and me. *(Reese and Leroy continue to climb around on the blocks. Hakeem and Alex wait, watching them closely for a response.)* We can take off the slide and make a ship.

Alex: I got it. We'll take off that slide, okay? And then we'll put another block on for the other side.

Hakeem: No, no, remember we wanted a ship?! 'Member, 'member, we wanted a ship.

Alex: Oh yeah.

Reese: We should make the slide part of the ship! *(Excitedly clapping his hands)* Make it so they both look the same!

Hakeem: But we don't want a ship that looks just like this!

Leroy: I know! We could make part of the ship a slide and part of the ship not a slide!

Hakeem: Oh Alex, how 'bout if…

Alex: I got an idea…

Leroy: Wait just a second. I'll tell you my idea….What if we make one slide one part and no slide the other part?

Alex: Well, want me to tell you my idea?

Leroy: Okay.

Alex: We could trade a little with the blocks.

Leroy: Okay! That's a good idea!

Reese: Wanna hear my idea?

Hakeem: We could trade a couple of blocks so me and Alex both have our little ships.

Reese: *(Jumping up and swinging his arms excitedly)* Wull, I got an idea! Wanna hear my idea?

Hakeem: Yeah.

Reese: Mine's even better. We could both have the same amount.

Hakeem: I couldn't come up with that. *(Reese smiles. Another child flies into the room and the boys all turn and watch him for a moment.)*

Betsy: *(Noticing from nearby that this has distracted them from their discussion, I decide to ask a question to help refocus them on their solution.)* So Reese, your idea is to count the blocks and each have some of the blocks? *(He nods.)* So how would you know how many each person would get?

Reese:	We'll count both ships, and if both have seven we'll leave it like that. If both have ten we'll leave it like that.
Betsy:	Oh, so you would both need to have the same amount.
Reese:	Yeah.
Leroy:	Yeah, if both have one block we'll leave it like that!

The children, now including the child who has just "flown" in, begin to reassemble the blocks into two structures. Their "conflict" has been resolved with an enthusiastic exchange of ideas.

◆

The argument described in the next story occurred as Jason and Nicolas were playing with the marble-chutes construction set. They each had built separate constructions, but discovered as they put their marbles through the chutes that Jason's marble did not come out at the bottom because his final piece was a "spacer" with no exit holes.

Both children were experienced builders, having used the chutes many times. Jason had been spending a lot of time on various construction projects and his spatial language had become quite sophisticated. After the boys found a solution to their problem, Jason told Sue, his teacher, in very specific detail, how he and Nicolas figured out what to do. He began by declaring "Sue, I solved a problem." This way of identifying the situation and his admission that they had had a "little bit of an argument" revealed his *awareness* that they had solved the dispute rather than aggravated it. As a teacher, these are the moments I live for.

"We got into a little bit of an argument": Jason solves the problem

Jason:	Hey, Sue, I just solved a problem!
Sue:	What was the problem?
Jason:	*(Pointing to the spacer and then back and forth to his and Nicolas's marble tracks)* We had no

more of these [tracks with exit holes] and the marble went down there…but there was a spacer there [which the marble doesn't roll out of]. I thought it was going to go down to here …I thought it was going to go on this part down to there—but instead I just put a spacer there and it made the marble go down to there. So I just…we just…Nicholas and I got into a **little** bit of an argument. And then I said, "Well, I know a idea" and then I just took this one off here [a piece with a track with an exit hole] and put in [replaced it with] a spacer and so the marble can go down here.

Sue: Oh, so now you have one where you need it.

Jason: Yeah!

Sue: You didn't need it over there.

Jason: No.

Sue: A good solution.

Jason: Even though spacers are not strong.

Sue: It makes it a little tippier, doesn't it?

Jason: Before I just went down here, but I just said, "Do you want it to go on the yellow one?" and he said yes so I turned it around.

Sue: You've done that so much that you knew how to get it to the bottom.

Jason: Yup!

◆

Conflicts occur as a result of children's mistaken actions and/or disputes, not as a result of "bad, misbehaving" children. Children make mistakes because they are still learning social skills, consequently responding physically or hurtfully to problems. If we consistently respond to children's mistakes and disagreements with a problem-solving, non-punitive approach, these occasions become an opportunity for new growth and eventually, *independent* problem solving, as seen in the ship and marble chutes stories. Thus mediation is not only an approach for responding to problems but also for *preventing* them.

Learning Environment and Daily Routine Strategies

✔ Plan a learning environment that includes a variety of areas and materials.

Well-organized environments that offer young children lots of choices for different types of active play meet children's learning needs and contribute to a positive climate in which conflicts are reduced. Children learn best when supported by adults as they interact with others and a wide variety of materials. It is the "action" itself that assists children as they construct their own understanding of the world. Consequently, it is imperative that

Guidelines for Organizing Space and Materials

A carefully planned physical setting is essential for creating a supportive emotional climate and reducing the number and intensity of conflicts. The following guidelines for planning the learning environment are taken from the *High/Scope Program Quality Assessment (PQA)—Preschool Version* (High/Scope, 1998, pp. 1–9).

I-A. The classroom provides a safe and healthy environment for children.

I-B. The space is divided into interest areas (for example, building or block area, house area, art area, toy area, book area, sand and water area) that address basic aspects of children's play and development.

I-C. The location of the interest areas is carefully planned to provide for adequate space in each area, easy access between areas, and compatible activities in adjacent areas.

I-D. An outdoor play area (at or near the program site) has adequate space, equipment, and materials to support various types of play. [Note: Where extreme weather conditions or safety considerations prevent the regular use of outdoor play space, a large and open indoor space, such as a gymnasium, may be used as a substitute.]

I-E. Classroom materials are systematically arranged, labeled, and accessible to children.

I-F. Classroom materials are varied, manipulative, open-ended, and authentic and appeal to multiple senses (sight, hearing, touch, smell, taste).

I-G. Materials are plentiful.

I-H. Materials reflect human diversity and the positive aspects of children's homes and community cultures.

I-I. Child-initiated work (work designed and created by children) is on display. [Note: This item does not refer to designated areas of the room where information is posted for teachers and parents.]

adults create environments that encourage active play in order for real learning to take place and to prevent the conflicts that occur when children are frustrated or bored. Some general guidelines for organizing the physical setting are presented on the previous page.

Evaluating the play spaces. To prevent conflict, it is important for adults to evaluate the arrangement of the setting frequently to see whether the materials or their arrangement are contributing to children's disputes. For example, it is often necessary to provide multiple copies of popular materials and/or to add space to popular play areas to provide room for active, cooperative play. When adults attempt to avoid conflicts over space by setting limits for the number of children in play areas, children often engage in exclusion behaviors ("There are already five in here. You have to get out!"). Instead, we can plan for ample space and if conflicts arise over the use of a space, encourage children to negotiate solutions (such as taking turns in the space, sharing the space, or other creative ideas).

Environments that are inviting, warm, and comfortable, with soft, calming spaces, color, and light, send a message to children that this is a safe, happy place to be. Such a feeling lays the foundation for the emotional stability needed by both children and adults.

Power-play materials. Inclusion of materials that give children a sense of power or strength enable children to express their interest in control and independence in constructive ways. As discussed earlier, young children are experimenting with the concept of control as they separate from their parents and become more independent. As a result, they find powerful and intrusive objects and characters very interesting and reassuring. Adults can support children in expressing this interest by providing power-related materials: capes, scarves, headdresses, and colorful, shiny fabric scraps for making fantasy character costumes; large, heavy materials and structures, such as blocks and climbers, that give children a sense of power and strength; paper towel tubes, dowels, or long blocks to serve as pretend wands; and other fantasy character props, such as toy

By encouraging children to incorporate a variety of materials in their fantasy play about powerful characters, adults help children move beyond repetitive physical expressions that can often lead to conflict. Flashlights have much of the same appeal as the weapons children make, but they have a wider variety of creative possibilities.

Inclusion of materials that give children a sense of power or strength enables children to express their interest in control and independence in constructive ways.

Young children are experimenting with the concept of control as they separate from their parents. As a result, they find it interesting and reassuring to role-play powerful characters.

"Feeling very fearful at times, young children want to identify with characters that can always 'beat the bad guys.' And, as children develop a sense of what it is to be male and female, they become very attached to 'exaggerated symbols' of masculinity and femininity."

—Elizabeth Austin (1992, p. 1)

dinosaurs and wild animals. Such objects not only satisfy children's need to explore power-related themes but also assist them when they feel fearful as they exercise their newly found independence. By encouraging children to incorporate such materials in their fantasy play about powerful characters, adults help children move beyond repetitive physical expressions that can often lead to conflict.

✔ Establish and maintain a consistent daily routine.

A consistent routine provides a predictable structure for the day that allows for a varied range of activities. This helps children feel secure and in control. The consistency of the routine is very important as a conflict prevention factor because the routine is the child's clock. When children are familiar with the routine, they know what to expect and experience less confusion and frustration as they move from activity to activity. The daily routine components, however, are only of value if each activity period supports active learning experiences for children. The routine should provide a balanced range of engaging experiences, including times for solitary and collaborative play, small- and large-group experiences, and child-initiated as well as adult-initiated activities. Within a predictable structure, the experiences provided should be flexible enough to meet the varied needs of children. (Guidelines for effective preschool routines are summarized opposite.)

✔ Help children anticipate and enjoy the transitions in the daily routine.

Conflicts are common at transition points in the daily routine for many reasons. Children often feel frustrated at having to stop doing something they are enjoying, and adults are sometimes too busy to give individual children the support they need to move on to the next activity. Transitions are also difficult be-

Guidelines for Organizing the Daily Routine

A consistent, well-planned routine supports children's emotional, cognitive, and physical development and helps to prevent conflict. The following guidelines for organizing the daily routine are taken from the *High/Scope Program Quality Assessment (PQA)—Preschool Version* (High/Scope, 1998, pp. 11–22).

II-A.   Adults establish a consistent daily routine. Children are aware of the routine.

II-B.   The parts of the daily routine include the following: time for children to plan; time for children to carry out their plans; time for children to recall and discuss their activities; time for children to engage in small-group activities; time for children to engage in large-group activities; snack or meal time; cleanup time; transition times; and outside time.

II-C.   An appropriate amount of time is allotted for each part of the daily routine.

II-D.   The program has a set time during which children make plans and indicate their plans to adults.

II-E.   The program has a set time (e.g., work time, choice time, center time, free play) during which children initiate activities and carry out their intentions.

II-F.   The program has a set time during which children remember and review their activities and share with adults and peers what they have done.

II-G.   The program has a set time for small-group activities that reflect and extend children's interests and development.

II-H.   The program has a set time for large-group activities that reflect and extend children's interests and development.

II-I.   During transition times, children have reasonable choices about activities and timing as they move from one activity to the next.

II-J.   The program has a set cleanup time with reasonable expectations and choices for children.

II-K.   The program has a set snack or meal time that encourages social interaction.

II-L.   The program has a set outside time during which children engage in a variety of physical activities. [Note: Where extreme weather conditions or safety considerations prevent the regular use of outdoor play space, a large and open indoor space, such as a gymnasium, may be used as a substitute.]

cause children experience time differently than adults do. Since they do not use clocks and formal time units to organize their day, they are often taken by surprise when it is time to move on to the next part of the day. To avoid confusion and disruption, it is important for adults to plan strategies to help the children learn the routine as well as activities that will make transitions easier and more fun.

Preparing for a transition is a three-step process: first, the adult plans activities or materials to support the children during the transition. Second, the adult gives children a verbal warning

The consistency of the routine is very important as a conflict prevention factor because the daily routine is the child's clock. When children are familiar with the routine, they know what to expect and experience less confusion and frustration.

When children are engaged in enjoyable activities as they clean up or make transitions from one activity to the next, few difficulties occur.

that the transition is near, perhaps including a description of what will happen during the transition. This gives children time to adjust before the transition is under way. For example, near the end of large-group time we may hand out small pieces of clay and tell children they can play with it while they wait to have their turn to use the bathroom, or, right before outside time, we may explain that everyone will be moving like their favorite animals from their small-group tables to the coat racks. Third, the adult gives a signal or verbal go-ahead indicating the transition is beginning. By using this three-step preparation, we can enable children to predict and look forward to the next activity. This helps to avoid confusion and prevent conflicts.

The next section looks carefully at a particularly important daily routine component, cleanup time. The principles already presented for facilitating smooth transitions are just as applicable at cleanup; however, this particular activity period is discussed in more depth due to its complexity, expectations, and length, and the strong reactions it may elicit from both children and adults. Cleanup goes best if it is seen as a regular component of the daily routine, with its own time slot, rather being seen only as a transition from one part of the routine to another.

✔ Plan strategies for making cleanup time fun and interesting for children.

Cleanup time is another turning point in the day that can often be an occasion for conflict. This time can be very stressful for both adults and children—for different reasons. Adults often have high expectations, hoping that the classroom will be thoroughly cleaned by willing and cooperative children. And yet there is often no plan for how this will happen.

Children understandably have difficulty with cleanup because it is often not as much fun as the other activities of the day. And because young children are focused on the "here and now," they do not understand why cleanup is necessary. After they've been enthusiastically supported in becoming engaged in play, it may be baffling to them that adults are now trying to get them to stop playing. Children also find it difficult to clean up in a way that satisfies adults.

Children happily join in at cleanup time when there are choices and fun ways to get the job done.

Like some transitions, cleanup time can be a chaotic, noisy event that includes lots of movement that may not necessarily be purposeful. When children are not sure what to do, are not having fun, and are not experiencing success or support, conflicts are likely to occur.

Considering children's difficulties with this part of the routine, it is useful to set some realistic goals for cleanup time. If we want children to engage in this activity every day, with enthusiasm, then the most important goal is to make cleanup time FUN—yes, fun! A second goal is to create a high probability that children will be successful at cleaning up. We can do this by *not* expecting children to clean to adult standards. Instead, we can adjust our expectations to fit children's capabilities. Third, we need to give children choices. By using a variety of cleanup strategies, we can encourage children to decide where to clean, what materials they will put away, and who they will clean with. Finally, if we find ways for children to have fun, make many choices, and experience success at cleanup time, then children are likely to learn how to be skilled and cooperative cleaners who actually *enjoy* cleaning up. During cleanup, there are many opportunities for children not only to understand the "use and return" process but also to engage in logical, mathematical, and collaborative experiences. These cleanup goals, and some specific strategies for accomplishing them, are listed opposite.

Making Cleanup Time Fun

Cleanup Goals

1. Make cleanup fun for everyone.
2. Create a high probability of success—expect a child's standard of "clean" not an adult's.
3. Give children choices about what, how, and/or where to clean.
4. If we've met the first three goals, children are likely to acquire the motivation and skills they need to clean up effectively. Let's look at some strategies adults can use to accomplish these goals.

Cleanup Strategies

With sticky notes:

1. Put symbols for each play area (for example, a picture of a paintbrush for the art area, a block for the block area) on the notes, making duplicates depending on how many children will be needed in each area. Line the "tickets" up on a wall and ask the children to pick a "cleanup ticket" for an area.
2. Put each child's personal symbol on a note and ask them to stick it in the area where they will clean.

3. Ask children how many things they will put away and write the number on the sticky note.
4. Ask children to form a team of three or four and give each team member a "pass" with their team symbol (index cards with stickers). Then ask them to choose an area they will clean together.

With a basket:

1. Put play area symbols on index cards and place several of each in the basket (include only the areas that need cleaning). Ask children to draw a "magic card" or a "ticket" and to go to that area to clean.
2. Tape a square of different colored construction paper by the sign for each play area, then place corresponding colored squares in a basket (decide how many cleaners are needed in each area and put in that many squares of each color). Ask children to draw a "mystery" color, find where the corresponding color is posted, and clean in that area.
3. Place playing cards (or any other cards that can be matched in pairs) in the basket and ask children to draw a card. Have them find a similar card held by another child in order to form a "team" for cleaning together.
4. Place an item from each area in a basket and have teams draw out an item and clean the area in which that item belongs.

With paper bags:

1. Give each child an "oops" bag and ask them to find the lost pieces of a particular toy set that, "oops," are out of place.

(continued on next page)

Making Cleanup Time Fun (cont.)

2. Put one item from each area in a bag and have teams draw out an item and clean the area it came from.

3. Give each child a bag with an area symbol on it and ask them to look for items that belong in that area.

With music:

1. Clean up to loud, rhythmic music. After a few minutes, turn the music off and call "freeze." Repeat.

2. Put on parade-style music. Children parade briefly, then the music stops and they clean wherever they are.

3. Play music fast, and have everyone clean up fast. Play music slowly, clean up slowly.

4. Clean up to dance music.

With fantasy:

1. Children pretend to be an animal and clean up.

2. Children line up as a snake or a train (one adult with each group). The snake/train moves through the room and cleans up an area together.

3. Children pretend to be "detectives." Hand out cardboard magnifying glasses and ask the children to "inspect" the room and clean up.

With games:

1. Children choose areas to clean. When they are done they ring a buzzer (or some other loud noise-maker). Everyone gets to ring it (no competition).

2. Set a timer and encourage children to try to beat it.

3. Hide your eyes and count to 25 as children clean up. Children finish cleaning before you get to 25.

4. The children "trick the teacher" by cleaning up (with the support of the other teacher) before the teacher being tricked realizes it.

Have fun and they will clean!!!

Home-to-School Transition Strategies

✔ Plan an "orientation" period for each entering child.

In the early days of adjustment to a new setting, children just separated from their parents may be feeling frightened, confused, excited, angry, or all of these feelings at once. The upset feelings of one child can have a ripple effect, unsettling everyone around that child and increasing the likelihood of conflicts. This section on orientation activities and the section that follows on parent departure times describe some things adults can do to ease this transition period for children. By helping individual children adjust to separation from loved ones, adults can lighten the separation tensions felt by all the children in the group. This in turn contributes to a more positive climate.

Planning an orientation period at the beginning of the school year is one important step programs can take to promote children's adjustment to the program. Orientation activities may include home visits, an open house, short days, and efforts to prepare each child's "place" at school. Each of these activities can be adapted for children entering the program later in the year. Guidelines for planning orientation activities are given next.

Orientation activities help to build trust between the child and new adults at school.

Home visits. Making a home visit before school begins (or before a new child enters an ongoing program) can make an enormous difference in the child's transition from home to school. When the teachers visit the child and family on their "home turf," this communicates to the child that the family accepts and trusts the adults at the school or center, and this encourages the child to develop a trusting relationship with these new adults. During home visits, the teachers may talk with favorite relatives, meet family pets, or play with the child using his or her favorite objects or toys. These shared experiences form important connections that the teacher and child can recall together in the days ahead. This can be especially helpful if children are struggling with missing their parents at school.

Home visits also provide an opportunity for teachers and parents to get to know each other better. The visit can help teachers communicate their desire to form a partnership with the parents in the education of the child. Often parents are more willing to ask questions or offer information about their child in the safety of their home.

It's helpful to allow 30–60 minutes for the visit. There may be tasks that teachers hope to accomplish during the visit, such as bringing an item from the classroom for the child to play with or talking about something the child can look forward to seeing or doing at school. Teachers may also want to have the child choose a personal symbol or picture that can be used together with his or her name for identification in the classroom. Even if teachers have plans for the visit, they should not feel bound to stick to them rigidly. It is important to remain open to cues from the parent or child and let the visit unfold accordingly.

On a home visit, a teacher gets to know a child's pet.

Each home visit is different and time should be allowed for responding to the individual needs of the child and parents. However, the primary focus will be on the child. If two teachers can make the visit together, one can focus on the parents and one on the child.

A sample letter to inform parents about the home visit is provided in the Appendix, p. 390.

Open house. An open house can be another event in the orientation period. This is a unique opportunity for a child to be with family, friends, and/or neighbors at "my new school." This event can be scheduled for the week before school begins. The open house is an informal, drop-in occasion lasting 1 or 2 hours. Its purpose is for children to spend time in the center with familiar adults. During the open house, the center staff focuses on encouraging children and families to feel comfortable in the new setting. Children arrive with their significant adults, put on a name tag, and move about the classroom as they wish. During the event there are opportunities for children and adults to meet other families as well as to converse informally with teachers. It is best to keep this occasion very casual, avoiding paperwork or presentations. This is a time for classroom adults to follow the interests and needs of the children as they get to know this new

An open house is an opportunity for a child to spend time with family members or friends at "my new school."

community of friends. It is helpful to schedule the open house after the home visit, so that the children have already gotten acquainted with the teachers.

Short days. It can be very helpful for new children to have their first day of school be brief and limited to a smaller group of new children. For example, some programs start the first week of the school year with half of the children coming for alternate blocks of time. These short sessions might last only one or two hours, insuring a successful experience for children who may be staying away from home for the first time.

The short day may include one or two of the usual components of the daily routine. During the session, teachers respond flexibly to children's needs; for example, if some children are resistant to sitting in a group or eating snack together, the teachers can help them find an alternative. Small- or large-group times can be very new and scary parts of the routine for some young children. Allowing them to observe these activities from a distance so they can see they are fun and non-threatening will help them to eventually join in on their own. It can also be helpful to have one or two short days for any new child starting later in the year, when school is in full session. A slow transition may be a bit bothersome to implement, both for teachers and parents, but the resulting smooth adjustment for the child is well worth the investment of time.

Preparing each child's "place" at school. If possible, have children choose personal symbols (to identify their work and belongings at school) at the home visit or open house. This will make it possible for adults to prepare a "place" in the classroom for each child. This may include labeling a coatroom hook and cubby with the child's name and symbol, as well as posting the child's family pictures on a family display or bulletin board. Children gain a sense of belonging when they see their personal spaces are "ready and waiting" for them.

Teachers may also plan the groupings for small-group activities in advance so that children right away begin to form a sense of membership in a smaller group of children within the large group. The groups are kept consistent for at least half of the school year, if not the whole year. If possible, teachers should avoid assigning seats for the small groups. Seating flexibility makes it easier for children to form new friendships.

As the year progresses, teachers can encourage children's sense of ownership of the classroom space by asking them for suggestions when changes are made in the room's arrangement or materials. This encourages children to feel the space is theirs to care for and enjoy and helps to avert unsettling feelings stemming from an unanticipated change in the environment.

✔ Plan strategies for parent departure times.

Separation anxiety, a healthy developmental milestone. When parents drop off their child at the preschool or day care center, both parent and child can experience a range of strong reactions. To develop effective ways of working with children and parents at this time, teachers need to understand separation anxiety.

Separation anxiety is a universal and understandable emotional reaction that often occurs when parents leave their children in another adult's care. Separation anxiety may occur even when the child is familiar with the caregiver or setting. For ex-

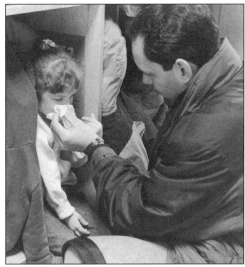

As children separate from their parents they may be feeling anxious, confused, and frightened...

ample, it may appear in a long-time student who is experiencing stress at home, such as the birth of a new sibling. Separation anxiety can happen for a child at any point during the year because it is the experience of being separated from parents, not just the change in the environment or caregiver, which is frightening for some children.

Separation anxiety is not only distressing for the child experiencing it but also can be upsetting for adults and create tension for the group of children as a whole. Chil-

...or happy and excited.

dren who miss their parents (especially if they have not received sufficient support from adults) may act out their feelings impulsively and hurtfully, at unpredictable times. Other children naturally react to these outbursts, creating an emotional "domino effect" in which the stability of the whole group may quickly unravel. The contagious effects of separation anxiety are often apparent at the beginning of the school year (or any time when more than one child is new to the program). At these times many teachers notice general discontent or an increase in conflicts in the classroom. When adults plan effective ways to ease children's feelings about separation, children will feel more comfortable and secure, and conflicts will decline.

Responding to separation anxiety. Separation anxiety occurs in varying degrees and can require different types of adult responses. Though it is an inevitable part of becoming independent, the experience of separating from a parent can be very challenging for some children and easy for others. Some children may feel only a heightened sense of excitement and a brief moment of worry as a parent leaves. Others may experience anxiety so severe that they become extremely upset or even ill. All the teachers or caregivers in the center must be prepared for a range of reactions. Here are some suggestions that will help teachers support each child at departure times, lessening the potential impact of children's unmet needs.

- **Reassuring greetings.** Greetings may seem like an obvious ritual, but being welcomed in a conscious, sincere way sets a positive tone for a child's day. One effective greeting ritual is to have one teacher or caregiver stay at the door to say

1. This child happily says goodbye to her mom as part of her routine of arriving at school.

2. After her hug, she puts her photo up on the "Who is here today?" board.

3. Then she joins her friends at the breakfast table, completing a predictable and reassuring transition into the day. ◆

hello to arriving children and their parents, leaving the other available to be with the rest of the children. It is important for the teacher who is welcoming children to adjust the greeting to the needs of the individual child, getting on the child's level and responding in a way that suits him or her. A boisterous, physical welcome can be very disturbing to a child who communicates quietly but a delight to a child who likes lively, loud play. A greeting that is responsive to the needs and cultural experience of the child communicates immediately that the center is a safe, caring place.

- **Predictable routines.** When children follow a predictable routine at arrival time, this is reassuring because they know exactly what they will do next. For example, right after being greeted, children know they will hang up their coats and go to the breakfast table, where another teacher is offering cereal and milk and talking with children about their plans. Or, the routine may be to go to the book area where the other teacher is reading stories and exploring books with children, while the first teacher continues to greet children as they come in. Parents may be encouraged to stay to read for a few minutes with their child in the book area.

- **Responding to extreme anxiety.** If a child's separation anxiety is severe, it is important for one of the teachers or caregivers to be fully available to the child. That teacher can acknowledge the child's feelings with warmth, sincerity, and patience, taking care to avoid rushing through this process. If the child is able to fully express his or her sadness or anger (which may be done with loud crying and/or angry or sad words) and these feelings and words are completely accepted by the receiving adult, the child can let go of the strong feelings and regain emotional balance.

  When the child has calmed and is ready to move on with the day, he or she may want to participate in classroom activities with the company of the supporting adult. Or, the child may find it comforting to stay close to a new friend or to be in a particular area of the room where he or she feels secure. Adults can support whichever of these options most helps the child. It may also be helpful for the child to bring in a special doll, a stuffed animal, an item belonging to the parent, or a family photo.

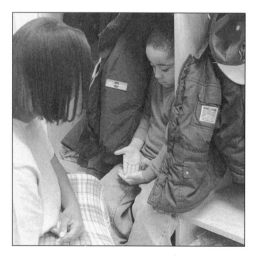 

Joyce comforts a child as he arrives. "You're feeling very sad," she says gently to him. As the child begins to calm, Joyce tells him what is for breakfast and they decide to go together to the table. This support helps him move on from his sad feelings so that they do not carry into his day, resulting in tension and possible conflict.

Preparing parents. To ease transitions for children, it's also important to prepare *parents* for the possibility that their child may express sadness or anger when they leave. Often the child's difficulties are prolonged by a parent who is unprepared and undone by the intensity of the child's reaction. Providing parents in advance with information about this step in becoming independent can make it easier for them to accept and respond to the child's strong emotions. (See the Appendix, pp. 391–93, for a sample parent letter and handout on separation issues and strategies. These are designed to be sent to parents at the beginning of the school year.) Providing information that helps parents understand and respond to children's distress helps to reduce the likelihood that children's unresolved feelings will provoke conflicts and interfere with relationships or learning in the classroom.

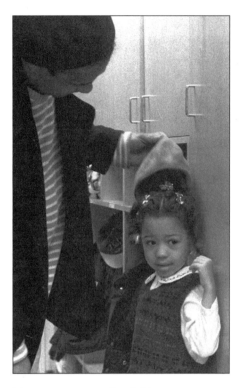

To ease transitions for children, it is important to prepare parents for the possibility that their child may be ambivalent about school.

The following separation story describes Joel, a child whose way of arriving at the program may seem atypical since a parent is not involved. However, the incident illustrates support strategies that adults can apply to a wide range of departure situations.

Joel arrives at preschool

Joel, a preschooler who had been coming to the program for just a few weeks, had been experiencing difficulties at home. He frequently arrived at the classroom door looking pained and dejected. One day Joel was brought in by his older brother, who pulled Joel toward the school door by his jacket and walked quickly away without saying goodbye. Joel stood still with a very sad face. Joyce, one of Joel's teachers, immediately went to him. She got down on one knee, put an arm around him, and spoke softly to him. Joel moved to his cubby and sat with his head down. Joyce followed him and acknowledged his feelings, quietly and sympathetically saying "You're feeling very sad, Joel." Joel continued to hang his head, occasionally glancing up to look at Joyce. After a few minutes, he slowly took off his coat and hung it up. Then Joyce took his hand and they walked together to the breakfast table. Joel sat very still there, watching the other children eat.

José, the other classroom teacher, walked over and said hello to Joel, gently touching Joel's head and lightly rubbing his back. Joel then breathed in deeply and released a huge sigh. He slowly reached for the plate of waffles and began his breakfast.

Joel's separation ritual, begun without support from a family member, was different than most of the other children's, but his arrival at a place that helped him to feel safe and secure was now complete. The warm and patient way teachers had welcomed Joel to the center would help reduce the potential for conflicts during his day. Although Joel often experienced anger and sadness at school, the trust he felt in his teachers' support would help him express those feelings without becoming hurtful.

◆

Assessment Strategies

✔ Record observations of children on a regular basis.

Establishing a note-taking system for recording daily observations of children's actions is essential to creating an environment that is supportive of every child. Daily observations, recorded in the form of brief, objective notes on children's actions and language, enable us to respond to the individual needs and wants of children. The observations give us information that is helpful in planning for materials, activities, interactions, and changes in the environment that will extend and support children's individual interests and growth. Such careful use of child observations enables us to challenge and fully satisfy each child's learning

Recording careful notes on observations of children's play assists adults in creating new challenges that fully satisfy each child's learning needs.

needs. The observations can assist us in creating a balance of cognitive and emotional experiences with activities and interactions that provoke children's critical thinking while maintaining a strong sense of self. By sharing these observations with parents, we can encourage a dialogue about the child's well-being at home and at school and provide a foundation for discussing any concerns that the parents or caregivers may need to problem-solve together.

✔ Examine your reasons for choosing to work with children.

As adults who have chosen to work with young children, it is important for us to periodically examine our thoughts and feelings about this choice. Some questions to guide this self-examination: What draws me to work with children? Do I enjoy the

Warm acceptance of and participation with children provides a foundation for positive relationships and stimulates children's growth as caring, respectful, and resourceful individuals.

challenges of early childhood? Do I relish knowing the individual differences between children, accepting them for who they are at this moment in time? If I could choose again, would this be the age group I would work with? The adult who answers no to any of these questions may be a negative presence in the classroom.

It can also be useful for us to closely examine the beliefs we may have about how children learn. To use an approach that welcomes problems as an opportunity for learning, we must feel comfortable sharing control with children. Sharing control means being willing to support the child in exercising the fullest capacities available to him or her at a given time, while encouraging the child to learn from mistakes made along the way. Those of us who fully accept and enjoy the intuitive, not logical, nature and abilities of the young child will communicate this in our own teaching practice; this acceptance and enjoyment provide the very foundation for positive interactions and an emotionally healthy environment.

As teachers and parents, we must anticipate and accept that there will always be conflict—it is a healthy, normal outcome of people working and playing together. There are, however, many ways to reduce the number and intensity of conflicts in a classroom, center or home. The ultimate goal of adult support and conflict prevention strategies is to provide a healthy social and emotional environment for learning. The most important factor in such environments is the safety and acceptance children feel as they explore and grow. In a climate of safety and acceptance, children develop and change, not by being told how to behave, but by being allowed to make mistakes and to actively learn from these mistakes. Young children, who see things from an egocentric viewpoint, need time and many social experiences to learn how to express their own needs, wants, and feelings while respecting those of others. While accepting conflict as inevitable, supportive adults also take steps to create positive environments in which conflict is kept to a minimum. Such environments stimulate children's development as caring, respectful, emotionally healthy individuals.

Mediation in Elementary Schools

I watched children as they ran, yelled, and chased each other on a busy elementary school playground. There were about 80 children at play, and I was waiting to observe a conflict. I waited and waited, but no conflicts happened. So I began to focus on just watching, curious to see why they were having such a good time.

I saw ball games—lots of different kinds, organized (well, not really very organized) by small groups of children. The kindergarten games looked more like chasing games. The older children near the goals were playing a variation of soccer—mostly they were trying to kick the ball into the net. Other children were playing kick ball, still others, dodge ball. Some games had no rules or boundaries that I could figure out; the balls and groups of children overlapped in ways that only they could understand. Children yelled to each other energetically, sometimes arguing briefly and then continuing to play. Suddenly, a soccer ball rolled quickly by me. A young boy, apparently in first or second grade, was running after it. As he neared where I stood, he shouted, "Oh, the mediator has it!" As I looked to see what he meant, I spotted a tall, thin boy, about 10 or 11 years old, wearing a bright orange banner across his chest. As he

To imagine for one brief moment the broad implications globally of children moving into the challenges of adult life with mediation skills is to imagine a world in greater harmony with itself.

picked up the ball, his banner flapped loosely in the breeze, held only by a button that read "Conflict Manager." Apparently he was better known to the children as "the mediator." He tossed the ball to the younger boy.

I realized then that this was part of what I'd come to see—small children who know what a mediator is. I had not yet seen the mediator in action, but I realized that every child on this busy playground, and all those inside, already knew the job of "peer mediator."

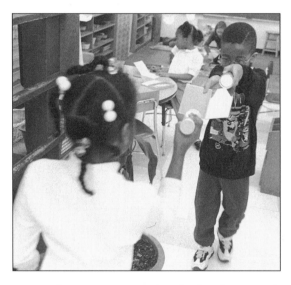

Peer mediation is one part of a school-wide approach to conflicts and violence prevention in many elementary schools. Children know that if they have a conflict with another student that a peer mediator may be assigned to help them sort out their difficulties.

To me this seems profound—a world in which children encounter mediators every day and accept them into the normal rhythm of their lives. These children all know that if they have a dispute with someone on the playground, either a peer mediator will notice and come over, or an adult supervisor will signal the need for a mediation. In these mediations, each disputant has the opportunity to describe what happened and how he or she feels about this, without interruption or judgment. Subsequently the children discuss how they might resolve the problem, ultimately agreeing on a solution. The peer mediator remains impartial throughout, facilitating the discussion by restating thoughts and feelings and verifying the final agreement. Usually, all this happens without direct adult involvement.

The intention of this chapter is to give the reader a glimpse of what is possible if mediation support continues past the early childhood years. Though most of the children in the stories told here did not have mediation experiences during their youngest years, it is clear from the stories that they have adapted to it quickly, their skills in problem solving growing along with the social demands of this age group. To imagine for one brief moment the broad implications globally of children moving into the challenges of adult life with these skills is to imagine a world in greater harmony with itself.

There are many variations in the mediation practices used in elementary schools, depending on the age of the students, the specific program used, and the school's overall approach to curriculum. The stories and strategies described here are from two schools in Massachusetts. These examples illustrate two of many models for implementing a school-wide mediation approach. In both these schools, small groups of students are trained without their teachers. In models used in other parts of the U.S. and in some programs in the U.K., an entire classroom may be trained along with the teacher, creating an ever-widening circle of children and adults who become knowledgeable mediators. Training the classroom teachers along with the children, though not always possible, is certainly the ideal.

These fourth graders role-play a dispute as the two mediators-in-training approach to begin the mediation dialogue. Children of this age are very responsive to their peers, both in practice and real situations.

In some peer mediation models, an entire classroom is trained along with the teacher. In this role-play session students congratulate each other on finding a solution to their dispute.

In many elementary schools, peer mediation is just one element of a school-wide conflict resolution and violence prevention program. Often these programs also include a resident adult mediator who responds to child-child as well as adult-child

Elementary students learn mediation skills with Cate, a trainer from The Mediation &
Training Collaborative of Greenfield, Massachusetts. The outdoor camp setting creates an
informal atmosphere.

conflicts throughout the day. A third element of many programs
is a classroom curriculum of discussing social issues and strategies for responding positively to problems. This chapter looks at
these three elements of current approaches to conflict prevention and mediation in the elementary school. From my perspective as an observer in these schools, rather than as teacher or
trainer, I want to share how mediation is used at this developmental level to assist children in solving problems and developing constructive social skills.

In the programs spotlighted in this chapter, the basic goals
of mediation with school-age children are the same as those for
younger children discussed in earlier chapters: children are encouraged to solve their own problems by talking out issues, and
to listen to and respect the ideas and feelings of others. Despite
these similar goals, some of the peer mediation steps and questions used at the schools observed vary from those in the six-

step process for young children described in this book, and these differences seem appropriate for mediation facilitated by children (see pp. 352 & 360 for more discussion of differences).

Though mediation strategies and steps may vary depending on the specific program used and the ages of the children served, all these approaches grow from a common premise: children are capable, with mediation support, of expressing strong feelings in positive ways and of finding successful solutions. Mediation practices that grow from these beliefs promote communication skills and lead children to a deeper understanding of the wants and needs of peers as well as of the adults in their lives.

About Peer Mediation

In the school observed in the opening example, there are 31 peer mediators for 260 children. The mediators are elected at the end of third grade and then serve as mediators through their fourth-, fifth-, and sixth-grade years. At the end of each year, the fifth- and sixth-grade mediators role-play a mediation for the third graders and present information about the mediator's role. This job is enthusiastically sought after by both girls and boys. Each candidate submits an essay describing personal characteristics they feel will help them become successful mediators. The third graders listen to the essays and elect those they feel are best qualified. This process makes it possible for all children, not just the academic stars or those considered to be "well-behaved" by adults, to be in the pool of candidates. After the selection process, the third graders attend a summer training program (usually a day camp) in preparation for their new role as they enter fourth grade. Some considerations for selecting mediators recommended by the Colorado School Mediation Project (2001, February 28) are presented on page 346. Considering children's enthusiasm for this program, it would be best if funding would allow all those who are interested to be trained.

Peer mediators usually work in pairs, a new mediator with an older, more experienced one. When I met some of the mediators, they told me proudly how many mediations they'd done that year—often as many as 20. They described how much they

Conflict Resolution Steps

The peer mediation steps used in the elementary schools described in this chapter are based on these steps from the Colorado School Mediation Project (1995, p. 11).

4 Steps to Conflict Management*

1) Entry: Getting Commitment to Mediate

- Introduce yourselves: *"Hi, my name is…and my name is…and we are conflict mediators. Would you like us to help you solve your problem, try to talk it out yourselves, or go to an adult?"*
- Ask for their names: *"Could you tell us your names?"*
- Move them to a separate place: *"Can you come with us over here?"*
- Establish ground rules**: *"We have some ground rules we need you to agree on. Will you agree to…*

  1. Try to solve the problem
  2. No put downs
  3. Do not interrupt
  4. Be honest in describing your point of view."

- Confidentiality. *"We agree to keep this confidential and not talk to other students about what is said here."*

2) Each Side Tells What Happened

- Ask one person what happened. *"Can you tell me what happened…?"*
- Ask them how they feel: *"How do you feel?"*
- Restate what they said: *"So, it sounds like …and you feel…"* (Repeat steps a, b, c with the other person)

3) Clarifying Needs/Goals

- Ask them what they need: *"What are your needs?"*
- Restate and reframe what they said: *"So what you need is…"* (Repeat steps a & b with the other person)

4) Reaching an Agreement

- Ask them if they have any solutions: *"Do you have any solutions where you both will be happy?"* or *"What ideas do **you** have to solve this problem?"*
- Ask for ideas from the other person: *"What ideas do you have to solve this problem?"*
- Evaluate options to see which ones works best: *"Which solution will work best?"*
- Write up their agreement.
- Congratulate both of them for solving the problem.
- Ask them: *"Would you tell your friends this conflict has been resolved?"*

---

*Reprinted with permission from the Colorado School Mediation Project, Boulder.

**In the peer mediations described in this chapter, some additional ground rules for the mediators' own conduct are part of this agreement: "We won't tell you what to do," "We won't judge what is right or wrong."

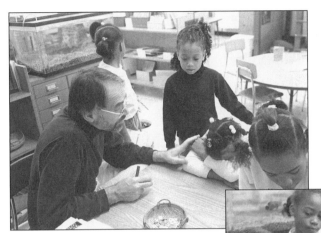

*At the heart of
the preschool
and elementary
approaches is
a common
premise:…*

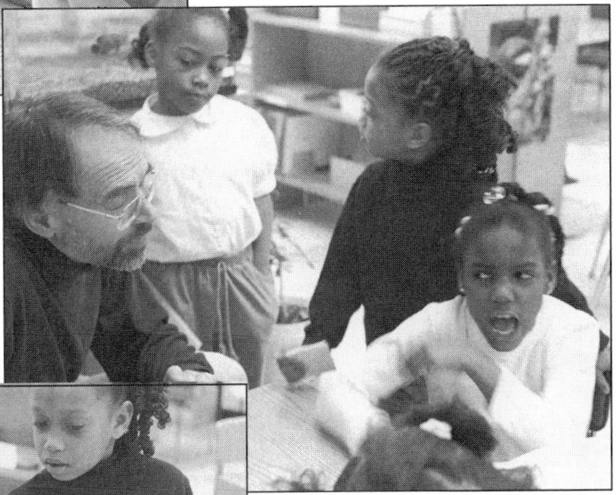

*…children are
capable of expressing
strong feelings in
positive ways.*

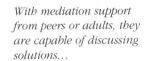

*With mediation support
from peers or adults, they
are capable of discussing
solutions…*

*…and resolv-
ing their dif-
ferences.*

liked mediating and how disappointed they were on days when they left the playground without getting a chance to mediate. They added that even when they were "off-duty," children still asked for their help. They also told me about the other bonuses and responsibilities enjoyed by the mediators: going to the mediation training camp in the summer, which the children say is great fun; attending a more advanced summer mediation camp in middle school; attending other special mediation parties and meetings; and getting to lead lines of children in from recess.

At the summer training camp, the children learn about the steps of mediation through role plays, cooperative games, and other activities led by the adults and the fifth- and sixth-grade mediators. The new mediators also learn about the duties that they will have at recess and breakfast. Time is spent helping everyone understand the philosophy, purpose, and expectations of the mediation process. Mediators are also told about the expectations for keeping up with schoolwork; they sometimes miss

Selecting Peer Mediators

"There are a variety of ways to select students to be peer mediators. Two critical considerations in choosing students are,

- choosing a wide spectrum of students to be involved and not just the "good" students;
- keeping it a voluntary process. Schools have found that some students can be encouraged to be peer mediators, but these students must recognize it is their choice, not someone else's.

Some methods of choosing students include:

- random selection of students who have volunteered
- staff selection of positive and negative leaders from the school
- student and staff nomination (from each 4th and 5th grade class) and staff selection
- peer mediation nomination at the end of the semester for next year
- interviews with interested candidates

Remember that students need to know the benefits of being involved. They too need to 'buy-in' to the process." (*Colorado School Mediation Project, 2001, Feb. 28*)

Student Comments on the Results of Their School's Conflict Resolution Program*

"No one argues or fights anymore. Our teachers don't have all of those problems to deal with."

"It made me feel like I was expressing my feelings without violence."

"If I got in a fight after school, I'd use problem solving."

"It helped or convinced me you do not have to use violence. But just talk."

"One time I got in a fight with the kid in back and we solved it by talking instead of fighting."

"One time Jenny told me my jacket was a piece of junk and we talked instead of fighted."

"I haven't been in a fight for some time."

"It helped me a lot because I don't fight anymore."

"There's not much fighting on the playground anymore."

"At home it helps to not get in a lot of trouble and to not get in fights with Tina."

"Well, if I was not a problem solver, I would be more violent in solving problems."

(Greenwald, 1987, July, p. 4)

---

*Reprinted with permission from the Colorado School Mediation Project, Boulder.

class time when they are involved in a mediation, and they are expected to make up any missed work. They also must maintain passing grades in order to remain in the program. The adult mediation coordinator monitors any academic or social concerns of the peer mediators, supporting them to find solutions so that they may keep an active status in the program. Besides attending the summer camp, the mediators meet monthly for skill-building and recreational activities that support their development as role models in the school community.

Examples of Peer Mediation

Observing a peer-mediated conflict: Responding to line scuffles

On the day spent observing ball games, as described in the chapter opening, patient waiting on the playground finally led to my chance to observe a conflict. Scuffles in lines are a daily occurrence in schools and sorting them out can be a time-consuming and frustrating drain on teacher energy. To lessen the frequency of such incidents, adults need to have more responses prepared than the typical one of just saying "STOP!" At this school, the adoption of peer mediation for these incidents has started a process of meaningful learning. The children each describe what happened from their point of view, an intricate storytelling that requires careful and honest attention to details. These negotiations and the solutions children reach, however obvious, are slowly creating change. According to the school principal, playground conflicts of all sorts were numerous before peer mediation was established. Over my 5 days of observing playground lines, the following incident was the only line scuffle I observed. This experience confirmed the informal reports of the principal and teachers that the peer mediation program had sharply reduced the number of conflicts. It also verified for me that young children still learning mediation skills can independently facilitate productive discussions.

"Sean pushed me!"

About 60 children lined up in three lines, ready to go inside after recess. They stood waiting for a couple of minutes as the last of the children ran to the end of the line. Noticing a scuffle beginning in the fourth-grade line, the two mediators, Andy and Rory, moved calmly toward the children. "Do you need a mediation?" Andy, a tall fifth-grader, asked. One of the boys began to tell what happened. "Wait 'til the mediation. Wait," Andy told him firmly. A teacher suggested they go to the library for the mediation (this was the only adult participation).

Andy and Rory headed off with the two disputants, Sean and Miguel. Rory, looking apprehensive, followed Andy. In the library, the four boys sat at a large table. Andy put the mediation clipboard on the table.

"Do you both want a mediation?" Andy asked, looking to each of them. They nodded. He slid the clipboard along the table to Rory and pointed to the next step.

Rory read self-consciously, "'We won't tell you what to do, we won't judge who is right or wrong, we'll keep it private. Do not interrupt, no name-calling or put-downs, agree to solve the problem.'"

Andy asked the two boys, "Do you agree to those rules?"

"Yep," said Sean. Miguel nodded.

"We're not going to put down no one," Sean added.

Andy continued, "Okay, Miguel, what happened?"

"Sean pushed me...in the back."

"How do you feel...that he pushed you?" Andy asked.

"I wasn't pushing him," Sean injected.

"Sean, no interrupting," Andy reminded him. "So how do you feel, Miguel?"

"Not good," Miguel answered.

"So Sean, what happened?" Andy asked.

"Well, Tyrone...," Sean began.

"Leave Tyrone out of it...what happened between you two?" Andy asked.

"Well, I can tell you that somebody was pushing me and it seemed like I was pushing Miguel but somebody was pushing my back so it looked like I was pushing Miguel," Sean explained.

"I saw you pushing Miguel," Andy told him. (Andy had briefly stepped out of his neutral role here but quickly regained his impartiality.)

"Well that's not quite how it happened," Sean said.

"How do you feel?" Andy asked.

"Well, I don't feel good because the other people on that line...I don't feel good because the other people on the line made it look like I was pushing Miguel," Sean said.

Andy pointed to a line on the clipboard for Rory to read.

He read haltingly, "What is something...you can do...now...to resolve the problem?"

There was a silence. Andy prodded them, "Guys, you got to think of something before we can go back to class." More silence. "Do you know? Keep thinking, guys. You've got to think of something before we go back to class."

Sean began to drum on the table with his fingers. Andy wove the string from his pencil around his fingers. Sean had begun to lightly bang his head with his hand as he thought.

"Sean, don't hit yourself," Andy gently told him.

"I know," Sean said. "Say 'sorry'?"

"That's what a lot of people say, but it has to be something more than that," Andy answered.

Miguel quietly suggested, "Well, we could stop pushing and try to get along."

"Try to get along…that's a good one," Andy said.

"Well, I didn't *mean* to push him," Sean repeated urgently.

"Yeah 'cuz there were other people pushing him," Miguel, one of the ones who had been pushed, now said in support.

Sean explained further that there had been another boy and girl involved in the pushing. Andy decided to get them. Caitlin and Tyrone came back with Andy and sat down opposite Sean and Miguel, with the mediators in the middle.

Calmly Andy said to Caitlin and Tyrone, "Sean and Miguel say that you were involved in this pushing incident. Is that right?" They both nodded yes. "What happened?" Andy asked.

Tyrone explained that he and Sean had disagreed about Tyrone cutting in line. Caitlin described how she had tripped and accidentally pushed Sean. Sean then had pushed Miguel, she said. Miguel further explained that he had turned and pushed Sean with the ball he had in his hand.

Sean continued, "So that made it look like I pushed Miguel…but I was trying to move back [to the end of the line]. I left out a little detail at the beginning."

"Well you can't leave out anything," Andy reminded him. "It all has to be one hundred percent the truth."

"Okay," Sean said quietly. "Well, I was trying to tell the truth…I just left out a little detail…'cuz they just reminded me about what I did."

Sean restated what had happened, with all the details that each person had included, this time adding that after Miguel pushed him with the ball, "I whacked it out of his hands."

Andy told them impatiently, "That's…you can't do anything like that. That's really against school rules. You guys, what can we do to make this problem right?"

"I don't really know," Caitlin said.

"Not pushing in line, " Miguel suggested.

Tyrone started discussing the details of the pushing again. Sean then interrupted him.

Andy reminded Sean of the rule against interrupting: "Sean, you can't interrupt. Do you want to stay at the table?"

"Yep," he answered.

Andy tried again to encourage a solution: "Well, we're going to try to solve this on our own. You guys have to think of something before we go back to class."

Caitlin started repeating what she had already told them.

Andy asked, "Can you guys think of anything..." Caitlin started explaining her part again as Andy continued, "anything to solve the problem?"

All four children began to explain about how Jack was there and he saw the whole thing.

Andy reacted to this: "All right guys, we need to think of something. We're not getting Jack." The foursome didn't respond. Andy restated the solution Miguel had suggested earlier ("not pushing in line"). "Well, can you guys just get along in class now?" They nodded. "Do you guys agree to stop pushing each other?"

"Yeah," Caitlin quickly answered.

The others nodded. On the agreement form Andy wrote "Stop pushing." He dated it and each of the six children signed it. Sean sighed with relief as he watched the signing. He began to zoom his finger up and down the table, then asked Miguel to race his finger. Miguel imitated him. "You guys, stop," Andy quietly told them. The last person signed and Andy told them all, "There you go. You all can go back to class."

◆

How productive was the "pushing" discussion?

Since the agreed-upon solution was "stop pushing," readers might ask whether this discussion was sufficiently productive. It is necessary to look beyond the stated solution to see what children can learn when mediations are conducted independently of adults. First, it is important for all children who are being treated unfairly or aggressively to know that they can talk about it with their peers. Open and honest communication builds trust. Second, talking through these situations on their own is critical to children's emerging abilities. As they do this, each child experiences respect for his or her point of view while also meeting the requirement for respecting others by listening without interruption.

Readers may also wonder about the differences in how feelings are addressed in elementary versus early childhood mediations. In the elementary steps used in the examples here (these steps are typical of peer mediation approaches used with school-aged children throughout the U.S. and U.K.), questions are first asked about what happened and then about what each child is feeling. By contrast, in the six-step early childhood process described elsewhere in this book, acknowledging feelings takes place first, and asking questions about feelings is not recommended. In addition, as I observed the unfolding of the elementary mediations, I noticed another difference. In the process of adult mediation with younger children, problem solving occurs immediately or as soon as all involved are calm enough to participate. However, the elementary peer mediation process begins when a conflict occurs and the need for mediation is identified; at that point, a time and place is chosen for the discussion. This means that there is a brief delay before mediation actually begins. During this pause, some calming inevitably happens, perhaps because children receive some comforting (e.g., an arm around a shoulder) or simply because they know that the dispute is about to be fully heard. In any case, children arrive at the mediation calmer. As I observed each disputant tell his or her part in these episodes, I noticed that some of the emotions of the situation returned. At this point the mediator's question "How do you feel?" was very timely, encouraging each child to try to name that feeling just as the emotion was rising once again. Each of the children in the following story was very willing and able to do this, evidence that they had taken a critical step forward in emotional growth. (See p. 360 for more on the role of discussing feelings in this process.)

Children experience two key concerns as they negotiate conflicts: concern about attaining what they want or need and concern about their relationship with the other disputant (Johnson, Johnson, Dudley, Ward, & Magnuson, 1995, winter). With these concerns as powerful motivating factors and with practice, this type of discussion becomes a communication *habit.* New mediators, like Rory, may at first simply go through the words and motions of mediating, acting out a scripted role that may not feel comfortable. Likewise, the children involved in the dispute may initially give perfunctory descriptions of their feelings such as "not good" or "bad." However, it is typical both for the mediators and the children involved in disputes to use increasingly sophisticated patterns of communication as they gain experience with problem solving. More articulate and detailed descriptions of feelings and events eventually become the norm.

The communication process: The essence of peer mediation

The next story depicts a typical dispute that occurred during a ball game. The three boys involved, Asa, Archie, and Max, were in different second-grade classes, but they often played together on the playground. Asa and Archie were in class together, and it was clear that there was a strong friendship between them. Inclusion of a third person (in this case, Max) in play with an established pair of friends is a classic early childhood dilemma. During mediation, Asa and Archie became aware of the impact of putting Max on an opposing team. Though mediators Andy and Rory did not elicit a clear resolution of this "teaming up" problem, they did facilitate an awareness of it and this was an important beginning.

The essence of peer mediation is the opening of a dialogue where before there was only anger, frustration, hurt, or confusion. This dialogue is facilitated by a sequence of communication steps, in which the peer mediators encourage the children in-

> "Cognitive developmental theory posits that conflicts resulting from intellectual maturation spur revisions in understanding of the self and relationships (Piaget 1932/1965). Conflict is the mechanism by which children and adolescents acquire new cognitive structures, developing new perspectives and stagelike shifts in patterns of reasoning which result in changes in behavior toward parents and peers. The new behavior patterns create new conflicts, as roles and normative expectations are renegotiated. Negotiation is thus viewed as requiring advanced stages of reasoning and being the most cognitively sophisticated conflict resolution strategy (Selman, 1981, Smetana, 1989, Youniss, 1980)."
>
> —*D. W. Johnson & R. Johnson, (1997, p. 5)*

Peer mediators meet with two fourth graders who want help settling a conflict. The mediators go over the opening agreements and then ask the students what happened.

Each student describes what happened from his or her viewpoint. As agreed, there is no interruption from the other student.

As the students agree on a solution, the mediators congratulate them on their accomplishment.

volved to articulate feelings, needs, and wants as they listen and collaborate in order to find a solution. Often, participating in this sequence is at least as important as the final solution. For example, in the incident in the next story, the communication skills of Andy, one of the mediators, showed important growth. According to the adult mediation coordinator, Andy had, in the past, often acted more like a "sheriff" than a mediator, more "tough guy" than sensitive listener. As this mediation unfolded, it became clear that he, as peer mediator, was also a learner in this process.

A ball game: Archie and Asa "team up" without Max

As the children lined up to go inside, three boys were arguing. One was crying. Andy and his mediation partner, Rory, went over.

"Do you want a mediation?" Andy asked.

The three boys nodded. Andy put his arm around Max, the crying child. "Let's go inside." They followed the lines of children finishing recess and heading for the classrooms. The boys went to the library and sat down at a large table.

"Do you want help with the mediation?" Rory asked.

"Uh-huh," Two of the boys answered. Max, who had stopped crying, nodded his head yes.

"Okay," said Andy. "Can I read the rules?" Rory passed him the rules and Andy read, "'We won't tell you what to do, we won't judge who is right or wrong, we'll keep it private. Do not interrupt, no name-calling or put-downs, agree to solve the problem.' Do you agree to those rules?" The three boys nodded yes as Andy said each of their names and made eye contact with each.

"What happened?" Rory asked.

Max began, "I was kicking the ball, and then you [he looked at Archie] had the ball and I told you to pass and then he [Asa] said "You already had enough ball."

"Oooh...And then you said something you shouldn't have said?" Andy asked.

"Yeah," answered Max.

"How do you feel, Max?" Andy asked.

"Bad," Max told him, still teary.

"Bad," Andy repeated. "Asa, what happened?"

"He was saying *shut up* and stuff…and like saying *stupid* to us," Asa related.

"How do you feel?" Andy asked.

"Bad," Asa told him.

"What happened, Archie?" Rory asked.

"He was saying *shut up* to us and he was like poking us with the ball. And he was saying to Sallie about the base. And he was like saying *shut up* to us…like that," Archie explained.

"And how do you feel?" Andy asked.

"Sad," Archie answered.

"Sad," Andy repeated. "Well, what can you guys do to solve the problem?" There was silence. "Can you guys think of anything?" More silence. Andy and Rory waited. Max sniffled a little. "Max, stop crying, okay?" Andy gently told him as he reached out and touched Max on the arm. "Stop crying, buddy. Do you want a tissue?" Max nodded. Andy asked the playground supervisor who was walking by if she would get some tissues. She returned quickly with a small stack and Max blew his nose. "Okay, can you guys think of anything?" Andy asked again.

"I have something—" Asa said quietly, "stop being mean."

"Are you guys friends?" Andy asked. "I mean all friends get in trouble, but do you guys normally get along?"

"Sometimes," Asa answered, "sometimes we have some arguments."

"I have something," Archie volunteered.

"Yeah?" Andy asked.

"That we stop saying those bad words…like *shut up* and stuff," Archie said.

"Do you agree with that, Max?" Max nodded.

"I have another solution…if we stop saying 'You've had enough balls' and play like we're a team," Asa suggested.

"Do you agree with that, Archie?" Andy asked.

Archie nodded and explained further, "Most of the time when we don't get along it's when we play soccer. I don't know why. It's either that or kick ball."

"So you guys don't get along when you play sports?"

"Yeah," they all said softly.

Asa clarified. "Not when we're not on the same team. But if we're on the same team, we...like...get along."

"If you're on the same team you get along?" Andy asked.

"Yeah," Asa answered, "most of the time."

"So you guys agree to get along and be friends? And stop saying words like that?" All three boys nodded yes. Andy filled out the mediation agreement, stating that they would "get along and will stop saying bad words." All five of the boys signed it.

"Do you need more tissues, Max? Do you want to take them back to class in case you need them?" Max shook his head no. Andy looked to the others. "Is everything solved? You guys are going to be friends?" (They nodded.)

"Yup!" the boys responded cheerfully.

"I know you're all really nice guys," Andy added as the boys left the table and headed for their classrooms.

As the boys left, I wondered what changes would result from this discussion. Asking children to "get along" may have been general, but the discussion itself had contained important details and a potential for building new awareness. Perhaps the boys would remember that being on opposite teams had not worked, and next time they would include Max on their team. The origin of the "get along" idea had been a suggestion by one of the disputants, as had "Stop being mean." Since these solutions had been their ideas, it was likely that they would act on them.

Besides these solutions, other aspects of the boys' discussion held promise for creating new ways of communicating. Andy's sensitive response to Max's tears had been a touching model for acknowledging the feelings of others. Having feelings acknowledged is especially important for boys, who are often conditioned to hide their feelings. "Thrust into competition with their peers, some boys invest so much energy into keeping up their emotional guard and disguising their deepest and most vulnerable feelings, they often have little or no energy left to apply themselves to their schoolwork. . . ." (Pollack, 1998, p. 15). Andy had shown tenderness and kindness even in the midst of an initial discomfort with feelings ("Stop crying, buddy"). He had followed this first reaction with a gentle touch and an offer of tissue. Such modeling by an older boy hopefully had a significant impact on the younger ones who were watching, and especially on Max, whose feelings had been described.

It also seems very important that the boys, having experienced sad or frustrated feelings, had an opportunity to talk about those emotions and to move on to an agreement, due in part to the honest expression of those feelings. All too often, children have quick, frustrated exchanges during play and the experience hardens into a conclusion like "We don't like him, let's not play with him anymore." Instead, the boys had been honest about what happened and how it felt, emerging with a positive experience and a strong likelihood that they would play sports again together another day.

◆

Frequently children's angry exchanges during play can lead to conclusions like "We don't like her" or "Let's not play with him." Mediation, however, allows for honest expressions and successful solutions that strengthen and enrich relationships.

Research on the Effects of Peer Mediation

In a 1998-99 study by the University of Florida, three socioeconomically and racially diverse middle schools participated in a study of the effects of peer mediation and conflict resolution. Each school had implemented a 3-year conflict resolution curriculum and peer mediation training protocol. Over the 3-year period, 85 peer mediators mediated a total of 195 conflicts. The findings have interesting parallels in the pushing in line (p. 348) and ball games (p. 355) conflicts described in this chapter. Following is a summary of the findings, based on survey and/or interview data gathered from peer mediators, a matched control group, disputants, parents, and teachers.

"Descriptive Data

1. Sixth graders constituted the majority (64%) of disputants. We hypothesized that these students might have been more recently exposed to mediation in elementary school and more open to seeking help.

2. The issue in 84% of referred conflicts was verbal harassment; disputants mentioned gossip (36%) and physical aggression (19%) frequently also.

3. In over 95% of referred conflicts, disputants reached an agreement, usually consisting of avoiding each other (44%) or stopping the behavior (39%).

   Note: Mediation is voluntary, and students or adults may make referrals.

"Survey data

1. Disputants reported high levels of (a) satisfaction with the mediation process and (b) adherence to the agreement reached after at least one week following mediation.

2. Mediators reported generalization of skills to "informal" conflict situations and expressed high levels of satisfaction with the mediation process.

3. Parents of peer mediators reported mediation as a positive experience for their child and indicated skills were generalized to the home environment.

4. Mediators' ratings of teacher communication dropped following training (vs. those of a matched group). We hypothesized that training sensitized mediators to optimal communication skills, thereby raising their evaluation criteria.

"Extant Data

At one of the middle schools, the number of student disciplinary incidents declined markedly following early and effective implementation of the CR/PM program. Incident data for the other two schools showed a less marked but possible trend toward a decline over time following program implementation." (Conflict Resolution/Peer Mediation project, University of Florida, 2000, March 15)

These data support the informal reporting from the visit to a Massachusetts elementary school described in this chapter: the content of the disputes was similar, the teachers and students reported high satisfaction with the process, and the students also reported a generalization of their skills to "off-duty" situations. The principal also reported that the incidence of conflicts had declined markedly since the implementation of the program.

In the peer mediation process, feelings are recognized in a different way than in the six-step process described in the other chapters. Step 2 in that process *(acknowledge children's feelings)* is intended to support calming (as well as awareness of feelings). Since incidents in elementary schools that involve very emotionally expressive or explosive children would be facilitated by an adult, not a peer mediator, the children in peer mediations have usually calmed before the mediation begins. Even more important, in an elementary program that encourages awareness of feelings through mediation and other curriculum activities, children benefit from the chance to name their feelings themselves. Also, it is more appropriate for the peer mediators *not* to try to name feelings for the disputants, since the social and language skills they would need to do this are still emerging. As noted earlier, the feelings discussion in the peer mediation steps comes *after* discussion of what happened. Describing the incident first seems to help children become more aware of how they were feeling and thus better prepared for the mediator's question about feelings. From my observations, this sequence seems to work well for this age group, with the principle of the importance of feelings still receiving central attention.

The stories of peer mediation just presented are dramatic examples of the positive impact this process can have on children's developing social skills. Research over the past 20 years has helped us to understand the early indicators of aggressive, antisocial behavior. Some of these are specific skill deficits: in empathy, impulse control, problem-solving skills, anger management, and assertiveness (Committee for Children, 1992a, 1992b). Lilian Katz and Diane McClellan, in their checklist summarizing components of the social development of young children (1993), illuminate some key social attributes that need to be supported at an early age: "Shows the capacity to empathize, has positive relationships with one or two peers..., usually...expresses wishes and preferences clearly..., asserts own rights and needs appropriately..., expresses frustrations and anger effectively and without harming others or property..., negotiates and compromises with others appropriately..., accepts and enjoys peers and adults of ethnic groups other than his or her own" (p. 2). Without at least minimal social competence, McClellan and Katz state, children are at risk for problems in mental health, school, employment, and other areas throughout their lives. Peer mediation programs are one way schools can nurture the constructive social abilities needed to avert some of these problems. Two other promising components of violence prevention programs—adult mediation and classroom discussions of social issues—are discussed in the rest of this chapter.

Adults Responses to Conflicts During the Classroom Day

As mentioned earlier, the peer mediators in the Massachusetts school were available to mediate mainly during playground and breakfast time, although they occasionally mediated at classroom times. This varies from school to school. Some mediation programs have the peer mediators available throughout the day.

1. A young boy becomes frustrated over a game he is playing with others and gets up to leave.

2. John acknowledges and accepts these feelings and the boy returns to talk over the problem with others.

3. John listens carefully as the young boy describes what happened. ◆

A classroom teacher trained in mediation can quickly assist in problem solving when disputes arise, as in this kindergarten. Here the teacher simply needs to acknowledge feelings and restate the problem, and the children work out the solution on their own.

When conflicts arise in the classroom, they are sometimes delayed until a mediation session can be arranged at a later time that day. If the mediation program does not include this component for peer mediators, then an adult mediator responds to classroom conflicts. In any classroom, however, there are many disputes that do not require the formal intervention of a mediator. These need only a quick response from the classroom teacher. In this next section we will look at examples of these two kinds of adult responses to classroom conflicts.

Quick adult-child mediations

Many conflicts happen during the classroom day. Like preschoolers, elementary-age children often disagree over ownership of materials, social misunderstandings, and sharing of space. In addition, they sometimes have difficulties with the demands of academic work or routines. A classroom teacher trained in mediation can quickly assist in problem-solving when disputes arise over such issues. In many situations, the adult simply needs to acknowledge feelings and to restate the problem. At this point, children can often work out solutions on their own, as illustrated by the next story.

A conflict erupts over school play preparations

Mr. J., a first-grade teacher, was busy helping children finish up their projects as children rushed to gather their things and prepare for the bus ride home. It was a chaotic time of day. Two girls were finishing up costumes for a play and they began to argue over who got to wear a crown. Liza told Suki, "I should get to wear it 'cuz I'm the **real** important fairy."

"But I want to have a crown too!" Suki protested.

Mr. J. heard them arguing and noticed that their voices were getting louder and louder. He moved toward their table and leaned close to them so he could be heard without raising his voice against the din of busy children. "You both sound upset. It sounds like you have a problem. I heard you both say you want to wear crowns in the play. What do you think you can do so you both can wear crowns even though you're different fairies? Um? See what you can figure out."

Mr. J. left. There was silence for just a few seconds, then Liza began to describe the differences between the two fairies: "My fairy is the one that does the magic."

Suki suggested, "So maybe she should have extra sparkles on her crown." Liza agreed and suggested that Suki's crown could have colored feathers.

"Yeah!" they both exclaimed and began to clean up.

◆

This "shorthand" type of mediation is highly successful when the adult has learned the skills of mediation and can get to the heart of the matter quickly and impartially. As the adult accepts and names the children's escalating feelings, the children realize that they are having a conflict and that they need to begin to problem-solve together. Once children have experienced mediation a number of times, just hearing the conflict identified as a "problem" usually cues them to begin to think of ideas for solving it. As the adult quickly restates the problem, this clarifies what is happening and helps the children begin to work on solutions. In time, children will observe and participate in both peer and adult mediations, learning new ways to communicate. Successful conflict resolution then becomes easier and easier.

The role of adult mediators on the elementary school staff

Many elementary schools have created a special position so that there is at least one adult mediator on staff. Sometimes the special needs coordinator's job is expanded to include this role. In some schools, the mediator is called a "behavior interventionist" and has a variety of responsibilities related to children's behavior issues. Some schools receive state funding from alternative sources, such as the Massachusetts Healthy Futures grant. Though funding for mediation programs may be connected to a school's special education department, it is important that all children receive mediation support, not just those considered to have "behavior problems." Conflict is inevitable and essential to the expression of individual thoughts and feelings. The school mediator supports every child and every teacher in the school system, giving the peer mediators training and mentoring, and providing mediation when classroom teachers are unable to take the time to mediate themselves.

Frequently, children are challenged by social interactions during class time. To develop positive communication and social skills during these moments, children are very much in need of adult support. When the classroom teacher cannot take the time to talk things out with children, having another adult to call on is essential. This adult is available to leave the classroom with the child or children for mediation. Many elementary school mediation programs include peer mediators, a resident adult mediator, and a violence prevention curriculum, including classroom discussions, collaborative rule-making, role-plays, etc. This comprehensive approach, in which healthy social development is supported throughout the school day, has been found to be highly effective (see p. 359). The adult mediator plays an important supportive role when the classroom teacher is unable to take the time to facilitate mediation.

When the classroom teacher is unable to mediate

A teacher who is conducting large-group instructional activities or involved in work with individual children may not have the time to work with children having a conflict. Because of these responsibilities, or perhaps knowing that the children in the conflict have not had much experience with problem solving and need lengthy attention, the teacher may need to ask for help from the school's adult mediator.

The next story reports on a first-grade teacher who found herself with such a time dilemma. Jamal and Dan were chasing each other around a chair after she had instructed everyone to sit on the rug for math time. She did not feel she could take the time at the beginning of a math session to find out what was going on for Jamal and Dan; she also guessed that a long mediation might be needed because they were new to the school and new to mediation dialogues. Thus she used the intercom to call Mrs. B., the school mediator, to the classroom.

Chasing in the classroom: Young children struggle to communicate

When Mrs. B. entered the room, all the children, except Dan and Jamal, were sitting in a group, ready for math time. The teacher told Mrs. B. that Dan and Jamal needed "to get their energy out" and that they needed a reminder about safety. Mrs. B. asked the two boys to come with her to the library.

"What's going on?" Mrs. B. asked as they sat down together at a library table.

Dan spoke slowly, enunciating each word carefully, "Me and Jamal are not supposed to sit next to each other."

"I was trying to try it out," Jamal explained as he fidgeted in his chair.

"Let's let him talk now," Mrs. B. gently reminded Jamal.

Dan continued, very slowly, "Miss L. doesn't want us to sit together and he's trying to sit by me and I don't want to."

(Band music started up loudly from the gymnasium. Jamal winced and covered his ears. Realizing the music was bothering Jamal, Mrs. B. left for a few minutes, trying without success to find another room for the mediation. She returned and resumed the discussion.)

"So what I'm hearing, Dan, is that Jamal was trying to sit next to you today?" Mrs. B. asked.

"Yeah, and I don't want to," Dan told her.

"And you didn't want to sit next to Jamal. Okay. How does that make you feel today...that he's wanting to sit next to you?" Mrs. B. asked Dan.

"Like he doesn't want to listen," Dan told her.

"He's not listening to you today," Mrs. B. restated.

"No, I mean to the teacher," Dan clarified.

"Oh, okay, so you feel if the two of you sit together, you won't be able to listen to the teacher," Mrs. B. restated.

"Yeah," Dan said.

"'Cuz Jamal doesn't want to listen to the teacher," Mrs. B. continued.

"Yeah," Dan said.

"I listen to her," Jamal protested, wiggling in his chair.

"Okay, Jamal, that's just the way Dan is feeling right now though, okay?" Mrs. B. reassured Jamal. "How are you feeling about this, Jamal?"

"I don't know," Jamal said, looking around the room.

Mrs. B. asked, "What happened today, Jamal?"

Asking "what" helped Jamal to focus on specifics. He told her, "We were like running around the chair."

"Why were you running around the chair today?" Mrs. B. asked.

"I don't know," Jamal answered.

Mrs. B. asked a question more focused on the details, "Did it have something to do with trying to get Dan to sit next to you?"

"Yeah," Jamal answered.

"So what was happening?" Mrs. B. asked again.

With Mrs. B.'s patience and willingness to adjust to

Jamal's needs, Jamal finally gave a very clear description of the problem. "I wanted to sit next to him and he wouldn't let me."

At this point in the discussion the problem was clear to Mrs. B. Two young boys, in the midst of a new friendship, were struggling to communicate. The teacher had mistakenly thought that the boys were "needing to get their energy out," an understandable assumption, given that the two boys were running around a chair. However, what Jamal and Dan actually needed was assistance in communicating appropriately. Dan's speech was very slow and deliberate, while Jamal often tried to communicate his requests using physical actions rather than words. The two boys really enjoyed each other but their communication styles were very different.

"So were you chasing him around the chair or were you both running around the chair?" Mrs. B. asked Dan.

"We were both running around the chair," Dan told her.

"Did you tell Dan that you wanted to sit next to him?" Mrs. B. asked Jamal.

"No," Jamal told her. His eyes roamed around the room as he spoke.

"How did Dan know that you wanted to sit next to him?" Mrs. B. asked.

"I don't know...'cuz I was chasing him?" Jamal responded.

Dan added, "I know why...that he wanted to sit next to me. Because I was moving and he was going where I was going. And when I got up, he got up and chased me."

"Yeah," Jamal confirmed.

Dan continued, "to make him feel like now he didn't want to sit next to me."

The boys had made a very important connection here between their physical actions and what they wanted to have happen. This was a very big step towards realizing that there might have been another way to handle the situation. Just knowing the "No running" rule had not been enough to change Jamal and Dan's impulse to run; however, knowing how to communicate more clearly might have made a difference. Mrs. B. continued to support the children in this unfolding awareness—she now restated what had been said.

> "So when you got up to go sit down [at math], Jamal was following you," Mrs. B. restated.
>
> "Yeah," Dan confirmed.
>
> "And then he started to chase you?" Mrs. B. continued.
>
> "Yeah," Dan responded.
>
> "And you were trying to get Jamal to feel like not wanting to sit next to you?"
>
> "Yeah," Dan answered.
>
> "What were you doing to let Jamal know that you were not wanting him to sit next to you?" Mrs. B. asked.
>
> "Well...I was trying...to go around the chair—and then he couldn't talk to me and then he wouldn't want to sit next to me."
>
> Mrs. B. restated for him, "Okay, so you were feeling that if you ran around the chair that Jamal wouldn't want to sit next to you? If you were running away from Jamal. Am I understanding you, Dan?"
>
> Jamal suggested another strategy, "You could tell me that you didn't want me to sit next to you."
>
> "Ahhh, what do you think about Jamal's idea, Dan? Did you try that?" Mrs. B. asked.
>
> Dan put his hands up onto his head and expressed sudden realization, "No."
>
> "Ahh, Jamal, that was a great idea. So what could you have done differently? What's Jamal's idea?"
>
> "That...that I would tell him that...that I didn't want to sit next to him," Dan told her.

Jamal, Dan, and Mrs. B. began now to discuss other issues involved in their problem. Working together had been an issue in the past and the teacher had asked, for now, that they not pair up for tasks. They also discussed the issue of classroom safety and not running in the room. As they finished with these issues, Mrs. B. brought them back to the problem of chasing when you really need to be talking, hoping that they would have a new strategy for next time.

Mrs. B. summarized, "So you were running to tell Dan something."

"I was running just to try to get him to sit next to me," Jamal stated calmly.

"Okay, all right, so you were running to catch Dan so you two could sit next to each other. So the two of you now know that there could have been a different way to handle that, right?" Mrs. B. asked. Both boys nodded yes.

Mrs. B. also noted to both the boys that they'd had a week with no conflicts, giving them recognition for that. She then moved onto the issue of safety, as their teacher had requested, before summing up their discussion and making sure of the agreement. Dan and Jamal briefly told Mrs. B. about the things that they could do if they got their math work done. She listened attentively.

"Great, all right. Are you ready to get back to class, 'cuz Mrs. K. doesn't want you missing this math assignment," Mrs. B. said. The boys nodded. "It sounds like you have some good ideas of how to make this work. Right?" They nodded again. "Now can you walk back to class?"

The boys got up slowly and reached for each other's hands. Hand in hand, looking around carefully, they went quietly back to class.

This discussion with Dan and Jamal had taken up precious time in the busy elementary school day. Was this time well spent? Teachers have to continually make decisions about what is important in a child's day. In this situation, the first grade teacher had to decide: Should Dan and Jamal simply be told to stop running and sit down for the math session? Or should Dan and Jamal's situation be fully discussed with a neutral adult who has time to really hear what is happening for them? It is easy to agree with her decision in hindsight. The two boys learned a lot about communicating verbally, identifying strategies that they could draw on the next time they wanted to work together. Rather than punish Dan and Jamal, which might have stifled their emerging friendship as well as denied them a communication opportunity, the adults assisted them at a time when they were highly motivated to learn to communicate more effectively. Not all classroom incidents need this kind of attention. But Dan

> "If a teacher believes that boys who are not doing well are simply uninterested, incapable, or delinquent, and signals this, it helps to make it so.... Teachers, rather than exploring the emotional reasons behind a boy's misconduct, may instead apply behavioral control techniques that are intended somehow to better 'civilize' boys."
>
> —*William Pollack, (1998, p. 17)*

and Jamal were new to the school, and the adults were just learning about their developmental needs. The teacher's decision to request mediation resulted in time well spent for both children, as well as additional information for the adults about each of the boys' needs.

The next story illustrates a different role for the school mediator. In this incident, Mrs. B. mediated between a teacher and a child who had "talked back" in class.

A teacher-child conflict: Serena has an outburst in the classroom

Serena, a fifth-grade student, and her classroom teacher, Miss G., sat down with Mrs. B. to talk about Serena's outburst in class. The outburst had happened after Miss G. suggested to Serena that she not go outside for recess because she needed to do her unfinished math work. The three decided to do the mediation during lunch. Serena set her tray on the cafeteria table and sat between Mrs. B. and Miss G.

Mrs. B., looking carefully at Serena's frowning face, asked, "How are you?"

"Frustrated," Serena said quickly, looking down at her hands.

"You look frustrated," Mrs. B. acknowledged.

"I haven't been out in three days, including today," Serena told her.

"What's happening at home? Are you getting out at home?" Mrs. B. asked.

"Not much 'cuz I have chores to do," Serena explained.

"So you're feeling like you're not getting enough outside time here?" Mrs. B. asked.

"Yes," Serena said curtly.

"How are you doing talking to Miss G. about that?" Mrs. B. asked.

"Bad."

"You don't think it's coming out in a respectful way?" Mrs. B. restated.

"Um...kind of, kind of not," Serena told her.

"Okay, well, let's check in with Miss G.," Mrs. B. said and turned to Miss G.

Miss G. began, "What just happened in the classroom was..."

"I wasn't yelling at you..." Serena interrupted.

Mrs. B. reached out and gently touched Serena's arm, "Let's let her talk."

"Ready?" Miss G. asked, looking at Serena.

Mrs. B. was unsure about this as well and asked gently, "Are you ready, Serena, or do you want to wait? I mean I'm wondering if you are ready right now. Do you think you're feeling ready?"

Serena responded somewhat tightly, "Sure."

"Okay," Mrs. B. said.

Containing her frustration, Miss G. quietly began again, carefully naming *actions* that were unacceptable: "What just happened in the classroom isn't okay. The tone of voice, the demanding, and the speaking out and making all of the noises when people were trying to study. There were a lot of kids in the room today. And then continuing to make noises when I asked you to stop. Continuing that and then the outbursts. Do you remember what you were saying?" Miss G. paused but Serena was silent. "You said, 'This will not happen again. I will not stay in!'"

Serena told her urgently, "It won't! I'll bring it home and then I'll do it and then I'll come back..."

Miss G. gently said, "Can I finish?" Serena nodded yes. "The tone of voice, the demanding, and the defiance within that...they're not okay. It can't happen that way. My concern with that, especially when it happens in front of other students, is how that looks and how it encourages other people to feel."

"Oh! It's...it's happening all the time!!" Serena said with frustration.

"What's happening all the time?" Miss G. asked.

Serena looked very frustrated but didn't answer.

"What's happening all the time?" Mrs. B. asked as well.

Serena, quietly, "Nothing."

Mrs. B. acknowledged what she knew so far, "So you're getting really frustrated during...was it before recess or...?" Mrs. B. looked to Miss G.

"It's the recess time," Miss G. told her.

"And she was in for recess because her work wasn't done," Mrs. B. restated.

"Right," Miss G. confirmed.

"I'll do it at home!!" Serena exclaimed.

Miss G. further explained her reminder about unfinished work, called the "Oops paper." Serena whispered intensely, "I'll do it at home!" Mrs. B. responded by placing her hand on Serena's arm.

Miss G. continued to explain that because sending messages home had not worked, she had decided to suggest that Serena stay in at recess to complete her work. She also noted that the unfinished work was always in math.

"Okay, but what about...is Miss L. [the math tutor] seeing her at all?" Mrs. B. asked.

"No," Miss G. answered.

Serena added sadly, "Nobody is."

Mrs. B. reached out and touched Serena's arm gently, "Nobody is. Okay, then that's an adult issue."

"Right," Miss G. agreed.

"And that's gotta be changed right away," Mrs. B. said.

Miss G. continued to describe her concern that Serena got frustrated when there was a lot of math. Mrs. B. asked Serena if she was getting frustrated with math, but Serena was unresponsive. She played with her food, seeming to have dropped out of the conversation. Mrs. B. asked Serena if it would be okay to put her food away for a while until they had finished talking. Serena agreed. Mrs. B. tried to re-focus the discussion

"Can you tell me about this? What is happening in math for you?"

"I don't understand it," Serena told her tensely.

"You don't understand it...so you're getting frustrated. And is that why the work is not getting done?" Mrs. B. restated.

"Some of the time," Serena said.

"And what about the other times?" Mrs. B. asked.

"That's it," Serena told her.

"That's it…so you feel like the work's not getting done because you're not understanding it. Now what Miss G. wondered is, if you understand it, but there's a lot of it, is that frustrating you or not?" Mrs. B. restated again.

"Not so much that there's a lot of it, but that it's going to take a long time," Serena clarified.

"Oh, okay," Mrs. B. said.

"It's the process of figuring it out," Miss. G. said, going on to describe some of the difficulties Serena had had that day with one of her math problems. "She's like, 'Aah! I can't go through all those numbers!' And I said, 'Yes, you can, you know what to do'…"

Mrs. B. looked at Serena, who was squirming with agitation. "Serena, are you listening?"

"Yes, and I don't want to hear it!" Serena told her emphatically.

Mrs. B. reached out to Serena again, "Okay."

"She knows what to do but it's a long process until the patterns start to develop," Miss G. explained.

Serena answered with frustration, "Yes, but I can see all the other kids running outside having fun!!" She threw her hands in the air in exasperation.

In a mediation between teacher and child, listening to both people in a balanced and fair manner is a challenge. As Mrs. B. continued to restate each person's concerns from the two different perspectives, her neutrality helped give Serena and Miss G. the control, responsibility, and respect that they both needed in order to find a way to solve this problem. This discussion would have been even more effective if Mrs. B. had responded to Miss G.'s third-person comments ("She knows what to do…") with a suggestion like "Since you and Serena are involved in this problem together, speaking to her directly will probably be most useful."

"Okay, so…I can see that there are a couple of things going on, Serena," Mrs. B. told her. "It sounds like the math is very frustrating and staying in for recess is very frustrating." Serena tapped the table rapidly with her hands. "Very frustrating. Is that right?"

"Yessss!" Serena said emphatically.

Mrs. B. then said to Miss G., "But what I'm concerned about, too, is it sounds like she's needing more help during math and she's not getting it."

"Um...possibly, possibly," Miss G. paused, then added, "A piece of that is the attention and the focus...there's that mental block. Getting up during the class in the middle of it, with me saying 'Serena you need to sit down,' right in the middle of a discussion that's about that particular problem that she's doing. But the block...it's an automatic [thing]. It's 'I'm not going to understand and so I'm going to do all these other things.' That's the piece I'm more concerned about."

"Right. Do you feel that that's happening, Serena?" Mrs. B. asked.

Serena answered with a quiet voice, "I don't know and I don't care."

"Okay...so it doesn't look to me as though you're ready to fully look at that part right now."

"Well, actually...[very quietly] oh God," Serena shook her head in frustration.

Mrs. B. asked her gently, "What? Would you like to go back to this at another time when you're in a better place?"

"No...'cuz it'll still be on my shoulders," Serena answered.

"Because it'll be on your shoulders. So this is really frustrating for you Serena," Mrs. B. acknowledged.

There was a long pause as Mrs. B. and Mrs G. gave Serena time to respond. She looked silently at her hands.

"There's a ninety-eight percent chance that the work that she has left to do could be done in forty-five minutes to an hour. I really believe that," Miss G. said.

"At home?" Mrs. B. asked.

"I said I'd do it! I said three times that I'd do it at home!" Serena exclaimed.

"Okay, so that was your plan? To get it done at home?" Mrs. B. clarified.

"Yes!"

Mrs. B. turned to Miss G., "But you've said she's made that plan at home and it's not happening."

"No we didn't!" Serena exclaimed.

"Yes, we did. We've made that plan more than once," Miss G. told them.

"Oh, God! Well then, I don't remember it," Serena said more quietly.

"Okay, but the problem still is that it's not getting done," Miss G. restated.

"I'll do it at home!" Serena answered with a frustrated whisper.

"Okay!" Miss G. answered with enthusiasm.

Mrs. B. began to sum up: "Okay, so we'll start a new plan today?"

"Well let's try it, yeah!" Miss G. said positively.

Mrs. B. turned to Serena, "So you're saying you're going to make up all this work tonight at home. It should take you about an hour. And you feel like you understand enough to do that at home without an adult."

"Yes! I get home…I do my chores…I do my work…I put out the dogs…and then I'll fix up the yard 'cuz it's Katie's birthday today," Serena told her.

"It's your sister's birthday today," Mrs. B. repeated.

"Hmm, she's fourteen," Miss G. added.

"So you think that even with your sister's birthday happening that you're going to be able to get this piece of homework done and into Miss G. tomorrow—which is Friday?" Mrs. B. asked.

"Yes," Serena told her calmly

"Okay, so I'm going to check in and make sure that plan happened. So that'll solve today!" Mrs. B. told them both with a smile.

"Great," Miss G. said.

Miss G. reminded Serena that she hadn't yet looked into the work due for that week and that there might be an "Oops paper" coming on Monday. Serena told her that all her work was done and then remembered that there was one sheet that was unfinished. They discussed this getting done over the weekend.

"I have one sheet left and I'd like to bring it home," Serena said.

"Okay! And that's your plan?" Mrs. B. confirmed.

"Yes!" Serena said emphatically.

"Great! So we're there!" Mrs. B. exclaimed.

"Yes," Serena agreed.

Mrs. B. turned to Miss G., "Okay. So today's work goes home. And tomorrow if that happens, she'll go out for recess."

"Yes. And then we'll check through all the 'oops papers' for this week," Miss G. added.

"Okay. Good! Okay, Serena?" Mrs. B. said, checking in with Serena one last time.

"Yup," Serena said quietly.

"You still seem pretty upset to me," Mrs. B. acknowledged.

"Nope," Serena said tensely.

"Do you just need some time to yourself to get it together, or do you need some help?"

Serena told her, with some quaver in her voice, "No, I'm fine."

Mrs. B. paused to give Serena more time, then turned to Miss G., "Okay. Thank you for taking your lunch time to figure this out with us, Miss G."

Miss G. reached out and touched Serena gently on the arm, "Serena, thanks to you too."

"You're welcome," Serena said looking at her for the first time.

Mrs. B. told Miss G., "I can take a couple of extra minutes with Serena" and put Serena's lunch back in front of her.

Mrs. B. and Serena sat for a few minutes as Serena ate. Serena became much more talkative, telling Mrs. B. about her music class. She looked relieved and relaxed. After a few minutes, as Mrs. B. got up to leave, she cautioned Serena not to rush through her lunch and reminded her where she was scheduled to go next. "If you want to talk more later we can," Mrs. B. said.

"Okay," Serena answered lightly.

This conflict between Miss G. and Serena was filled with tension and frustration for both. Mediation was created for exactly such challenges. Having a resident adult mediator available throughout the day is particularly effective in schools, like this one, where in the midst of implementation only a few of the teachers are trained in mediation. In settings where there is a mixture of behavior approaches being used, mediation can open up new channels of communication between a teacher with a traditional approach and a child. It is to Miss G.'s credit that she asked for mediation when she was feeling so frustrated with Serena. Although not trained herself, she obviously considered mediation to be a dignified, non-threatening, and potentially effective way to respond. In many elementary schools, a child speaking to a teacher as Serena had done would have resulted in a punishment. Such punishments are intended to let children know that their behavior is not acceptable. It is clear, however, that Serena already knew that she had spoken inappropriately ("bad" was her description). A punitive response would have emphasized her "badness" without allowing her to hear the specifics of Miss G.'s frustration and without giving Miss G. any insights into the problems Serena was experiencing. Serena's self-esteem *and* her relationship with Miss G. would have suffered as a result. Instead, this open discussion made it possible for Serena to come to a better understanding of her teacher's point of view. She also vented her own frustrations and received support in working *collaboratively* with Miss G. to find a solution that worked for both of them. This collaboration created the healing necessary for Serena and Miss G. to move forward positively in their relationship rather than become adversaries.

During the mediation it was evident to all three that Serena needed a lot more help due to her lack of confidence with math. This was a major academic and emotional revelation; resolution of this would very likely help Serena to feel less frustrated overall. The completion of the assignment was never in question, but *how* that work would get done was negotiated, with the resulting solution coming from Serena. This was an empowering moment for a child feeling out of control of a number of aspects of her life. In the end, Serena did complete the homework assignment and she did begin tutoring again. The mediation resulted in important academic progress as well as a moment of deepening connection and understanding between Serena and Miss G.

◆

Classroom Meetings That Support the Development of Communication Strategies

Chapter 6 discussed how to use class group times for solving classroom problems and improving positive communication skills. In the elementary grades, meeting in this way is also very productive. Older children also have classroom problems to solve and they are capable of exploring communication strategies through the use of more extended discussions and role plays. As I observed some of these meetings, I was struck by the enthusiasm of the students, particularly if the planned activity included a role play.

Topics discussed at these elementary level sessions include classroom problems such as noise, line-up problems, playground play, and cleanup. As in the preschool meetings, the teacher describes the problem and asks children to come up with solutions. Teachers find this to be a very effective way to encourage

In this school, students from kindergarten through sixth grade are engaged in skill-building activities that involve adult modeling, role play, and discussion. Such group activities, conducted on a regular basis, are highly effective at teaching problem-solving skills.

Better relationships on the playground are often the result of classroom discussions of communication strategies.

children to take responsibility for classroom issues and to interact more constructively with one another.

Many preschool and elementary schools also use a violence prevention curriculum called Second Step (Committee for Children, 1992a, 1992b). The curriculum teaches skills in empathy, impulse control, and anger management through the use of structured photo cards, puppet plays, and role-play formats. A foundation of the Second Step curriculum is its emphasis on interpreting body language. Strategies for expressing feelings in positive, non-hurtful ways are another important component of this approach. Many of the activities begin with discussions of large photos of children expressing a variety of feelings.

The next story reports how Mr. P., a first grade teacher, used his classroom problem-solving time to engage children in a discussion that began with a large photo of two children. The focus of the activity was to encourage children to make "I" statements; as an example, he provided a statement in the form "I feel _____ when you _____." (A somewhat different format for "I" statements is given on pp. 143–44.) After this introduction, the children practiced making "I" statements themselves.

I feel mad when my glue stick gets taken: A Second Step class discussion

Mr. P.: Today we're going to talk about when you have a problem, like if someone cuts in line in front of you and other problems you have. I'm going to show you a picture. Today is all about how you can tell someone how you're feeling, using the words that you need to tell someone how you're feeling. So here's a picture. The girl's name is Lucille and Lucille is glueing paper for an art project and her glue bottle ran out of glue so she's using Randy's *(pointing to Randy)* and Randy's mad. He feels like yelling at Lucille. He feels like yelling, "You took my glue! You make me so mad!" When you look at his face, can you tell from looking at him that he's mad? *(Some children say yes and some say no.)* Can anyone see a clue that let's you know that he's mad?

Troy: He's like this...*(makes fists and a face)* with his fists.

Mr. P.: Look at the way he's holding his hands.

Suzie: He's going like this *(makes a face)*.

Mr. P.: He's going like that, kind of clenching his teeth.

Brent: He's like *(makes a face and tenses his body)*.

Mr. P.: He's got his body and face scrunched up a little bit. *(Two more children share similar descriptions of the picture.)*

Mr. P.: Now do you remember why Randy is mad at Lucille?

Ruth: She took the glue stick.

Mr. P.: She took the glue stick. Did she ask first?

Several children: No.

Mr. P.: If she had asked first, how would Randy feel?

Kamud: A little bit better.

Mr. P.: Probably. Now how do you feel when somebody takes something and doesn't ask first?

Several children: Mad. Bad.

Mr. P.:	Do you think that Lucille meant to keep it or just use it?
Troy:	Borrow it.
Mr. P:	She was just planning to borrow it? Probably 'cuz in school when you need something, you don't usually need to keep it. Do you think Lucille meant to make Randy mad or hurt his feelings?
Ruth:	No.
Mr. P:	And why don't you think so?
Ruth:	'Cuz I don't think she would mean to be so mean and just take something like that.
Mr. P.:	So you don't think she was doing it to be mean to Randy. What do you think, Carl?
Carl:	She likes him, but maybe he wasn't looking… maybe she asked him, but he wasn't looking when she asked him.
Mr. P.:	He didn't have a chance to see, he wasn't looking. Oh, so maybe he didn't hear her ask. Well, Randy, right now he's feeling like yelling, but he's not yelling. But he's feeling like yelling, "You took my glue! You make me so mad!" So what do you think would happen if Randy actually yelled at Lucille? What do you think would happen, Adrian?
Adrian:	It would make her sad.
Mr. P.:	It would certainly make her sad. Lilian?
Lilian:	He'd get in trouble.
Mr. P.:	Who would get in trouble?
Lilian:	Randy.
Mr. P.:	He might get in trouble for yelling in class. Jemani, what do you think would happen?
Jemani:	Well maybe if he yells, he'd get into a fight.
Mr. P.:	So once he started yelling, they might get into a fight. What do you think Carl?
Carl:	Yeah, and then the whole class might fight.
Mr. P.:	So the whole class might join into the fight because the two of them were arguing over that glue stick. Well, letting people know how you feel helps solve problems. Letting them know

using words. Yelling, fighting, and name-calling don't help to solve problems. Telling someone how you feel by starting with the word "you" can make the other person feel mad. Just like when you say, "You are a thief," it's like you're pointing your finger. And that isn't a good way to solve the problem. Or if you say, **"You** make me feel so mad." So from now on when you want to tell someone how you feel, I want you to try using an "I" message instead. Instead of saying "you," you can say "I feel angry when you take a glue stick."

Jemani: But that's saying "you"—like blaming.

It is interesting here that a child heard the blaming in the phrase "when you." "I" messages that eliminate *you* altogether are most effective at avoiding blaming (see chapter 4, p. 144). Mr. P., perhaps thinking that this might be too much information, emphasized the "I feel…" part of the message for that day. When making up their own messages, most of the children did not follow the "when you" form but instead made up messages that focused on actions and did not involve another person (e.g., "I feel afraid when the tree falls over me"). During a previous observation in a fifth-grade classroom, I noticed that "I" messages were being taught with a careful emphasis on avoiding the use of "when you" (e.g., "I feel angry because name-calling hurts my feelings"). Mr. P. answered Jemani's concern about using "you" in this way with an explanation.

Mr. P.: Well it's a little different saying "I feel angry when you take a glue stick" than if you say "You are a thief." You're saying how you feel instead. You're saying, "I feel…" So let's practice doing that with some "I" messages. *(Next, Mr. P. asks each child if they want to complete an "I feel …" message.)* I'll say a sentence and you finish it. I feel happy when…Jemani, you start and I'll go right around the circle. *(All but one child completes a message. Here are a few of their messages.)*

Jemani: I feel happy when I get my glue stick back.

Mr. P.: I feel sad when…

Troy: Um, um…when I get hurt.

Mr. P.: I feel surprised when…

Lilian: I feel surprised when I fall.

Mr. P.: I feel afraid when…

Desi: When a tree falls over me.

Mr. P.: When a tree falls over you!

Adrian: I've got one.

Mr. P.: Okay, start it from the beginning. I feel…

Adrian: I feel happy when…um…I pet my dog.

Mr. P.: I feel proud when…

Suzie: When I get a medal or something.

Mr. P.: When you get a medal or something. *(To next child)* Do you want me to start it for you? I feel embarrassed when…*(Other children say "Ooo.")*

Mark: When my pants fall down. (Everyone laughs.)

Mr. P.: *(Mr. P. continues with "I feel proud, shy, and mad and then moves right on to the role plays. When he tells the children role plays are next, their faces brighten and some call out "yeah!" with excitement. This is clearly their favorite part.)* I'm going to tell you a situation that could happen at school or at home and you're gonna go with your partner to a place in the room. If it's something like you took somebody's glue stick without asking, you can actually get a glue stick and try it. And then you're gonna come back with your "I" statement so you can show the rest of the class how you would use words and how you would say "I feel…"

Some children: Mad.

Mr. P.: But all of them aren't mad. Some of them are different feelings. Carl, what's your question?

Carl: So all we're gonna do is say it?

Mr. P.: You're gonna say it, but first you're gonna show it. Say if you're arguing over a glue stick, if Micah's your partner, and he took your glue stick, just like Randy and Lucille, you would say, "I feel...," say it to Micah, "mad when my glue stick gets taken."

Mr. P.:   *(Mr. P. chooses names from an envelope and gives each pair of children a situation. After some time for practice and clarifications from Mr. P., everyone comes back and forms a circle with their chairs. Some of their role plays are presented next, with Carl and Suzie's first.)* Which one will you do?

Carl: Cutting in line.

Mr. P.:   Boy, cutting in line was a problem for us at the beginning of the year. *(The two children pretend to be in line and Carl then cuts in front of Suzie.)*

Suzie: I feel bad when you cut in line. *(Carl goes back behind her.)*

Mr. P.:   "I feel bad when you cut in." Do you think he knew he was cutting?

Suzie: Yes.

Mr. P.:   When he found out how you felt, he went back to the end of the line. Okay, a little applause please. *(Everyone claps).* Thank you, Carl and Suzie. Our next actors are Adrian and Tina. *(Tina holds a marker with no top and pretends to use it, and then gives it back to Adrian.)*

Adrian: I feel mad when the markers are dry.

Tina: Sorry.

Mr. P.:   Okay, a little applause, audience! *(Everyone claps.)* Next actors up. Which one are you doing?

Rachael: The one that somebody took something and they didn't tell the truth. "I know you took my train. I know you did. I feel bad when you take my train."

Brent: Did not! Ha! *(They start back to their seats.)*

Mr. P.:   Oh, the one that wasn't true and you ended up telling how you felt.

Rachael: Yeah, and it was funny when I said "I feel bad" and he said "Did not!"

Mr. P.:	So Brent, right to the end, you weren't telling the truth, were you?
Brent:	*(Smiling)* No.
Mr. P.:	Before we stop today's session, I just want to write two words on the board that will help you remember. "I feel…" and "You…" whatever. The dots show that there's something that comes after each. And I'd like it if someone could explain the difference in how you feel when someone says,"I feel mad when you don't share with me" instead of "You make me mad." How does it make you feel differently when you say "I feel"?
Carl:	"You…" is like…you're telling the person what they already know and "I feel…" tells them what your feelings are.
Mr. P.:	The "I feel…" tells them what's inside you.
Carl:	What their feelings are.
Mr. P.:	What their feelings are. Jemani?
Jemani:	When you say "You…" it's like saying…*(She makes an angry, scolding face and points her finger and speaks in a harsh tone.)* "You did something really, really wrong, something really, really wrong!"
Mr. P.:	The way you said that with your face too, it's like you're accusing them of something. That could make the other person feel angry, couldn't it? *(Jemani nods. Mr. P. brings the discussion to a close.)*

As an observer of this exploration of how to express feelings, I thought how some of the children had shared, quite specifically, their awareness of the importance of subtleties. ("'You'…is like…you're telling the person what they already know and 'I feel' tells them what your feelings are.") Mr. P. had followed this so sensitively with "The 'I feel' tells them what's inside you." As Jemani gave her animated rendering of the accusing harshness of "you" statements, the meeting came to a close. As equals, adults and children together had explored a delicate

During a mediation training session, students participate in a teamwork exercise as they cooperate to create a "human machine" together.

and profoundly important area of human communication. Those closing moments provided me with a hopeful vision of what is possible in the classroom.

 *Knowing the attributes that are important to healthy social development, we can now plan curriculums that support constructive social growth. It is imperative that we take time amid the many demands of the elementary school day to support awareness of feelings, empathy, positive peer relationships, negotiation skills, acceptance of diverse people, and other attributes of social competence. Every classroom is a community, a rich and diverse place in which children can acquire a complete set of tools for navigating life while also making that community a more joyful and accepting place to be. We know that if we take the time to teach and support conflict mediation skills, children will use these skills at school and at home, developing a more positive attitude toward conflicts and conflict resolution.*

Afterword

In looking back at all that we've considered over the length of this book, the opportunity for social growth from infancy to elementary age seems vast, building from one encounter, one conflict, and one solution to the next. As I recall the stories, I think of young toddler Stan clinging to his Mom and saying "Frightened," I hear 3-year-old Tom offering limited choices to his younger brother Jack, and I see the group of tender faces watching as we buried the dead toad. I feel delight as I think of Raven and Anita problem-solving independently, I laugh remembering Benny's loud "raspberry" (dinosaur talk for "Get off!"), and I am moved by what is possible as I think of the group of five elementary-aged boys, at first teary and frustrated, sorting out how ball games could be played so that everyone would "get along." So many children have come so far, have grown so much, and will continue to learn and to teach others.

We began with the story of David's plea, "You tell them that kids can think of their own ideas *themselves!*" And so we will end with a story of children deciding what to do about a problem themselves. This incident happened at a preschool in an urban area in the U.K. It concerns two 4-year-olds, Sarah and Amjad. Through many conflicts, adults had problem-solved with Sarah and Amjad, using the six steps. In the beginning, the conflicts included very intense feelings and long struggles to find solutions. For Amjad, a Pakistani child who was also acquiring English as he learned to problem-solve, communicating about problems in words was especially demanding. Nonetheless, the children's skills improved day by day, week by week, conflict by conflict. On this day, after about 4 months of mediation experiences, their teacher, Cathy, watched with delight from an adjacent area as the two children negotiated. Cathy retells the story in this way:

Sarah and Amjad: "Could I have a go...?"

Children were busy throughout the room, playing in many different ways. Sarah was riding on the rocking horse. Amjad watched her from the block area. Eventually he approached Sarah, and said to her, "I want to have a go now."

> Sarah answered, "No, I'm on the horse."
> Amjad asked, "Could I have a go in a minute?"
> Sarah said, "In four minutes."
> Amjad asked, "What does four minutes look like?"
> Sarah held up five fingers and Amjad copied her. Holding up five fingers, he said, "Okay, four minutes." Amjad went back to playing with the big building bricks. About 2 minutes later, he went back to Sarah and said, "It's my turn now—it's four minutes." He held up five fingers. Sarah happily said okay and got off the horse. Amjad got on and began to rock.

The essential problem-solving skills are all here. First, neither child got upset as they now had skills to solve problems before frustration set in. Second, there was a simple exchange of what was wanted and then the negotiation began: Amjad asked for what he wanted, Sarah suggested a solution, Amjad asked for specifics ("What does four minutes look like?"), and Sarah gave the abstract solution the concrete clarity it needed. An agreement was made based on something they both could understand—five fingers!

From this story, as with all the others, I too am learning. And I understand now, with certainty, that the human desire to connect—to know one another and ourselves in new ways with new expressions—is strong. If we are mindful, this desire will always remain with us. We can nurture ourselves and one another with each new skill acquired and every fresh opportunity to use that skill.

As I've participated in the growth of my children and the children of others, I've sought to be a more perfect parent, a more perfect teacher. I sometimes succumb to regrets for things I did not know when they were young, for feelings and words I could not form. And when I emerge from these regretful thoughts, I see that the chance to connect is not past. And so I ask you, dear reader, to take the time to talk and listen to the children in your lives, young or old. Open your hearts to feelings and mediate the conflicts in your home or in your classroom in the very best way you can. It is our collective *effort,* rather than perfection, that will create change. It is this loving partnership with children—our shared longing for harmony, learning, and fun—that is ours to cherish. ◆

Appendix:
Easing Home-to-School Transitions

[Parent Letter: Home visit]

Dear Parent,

We are very excited about your child's arrival on the first day of school. We want to make sure this transition to school goes very smoothly for your child. We would like to make a home visit on_____. This visit is an informal occasion that we hope will give your child time to get to know his or her new teachers in the safety and comfort of your home. It also is a good time to ask any additional questions that you may have about our program.

Children react in different ways to this visit; some become very excited, some are very shy and quiet, some even run and hide! Whatever happens is okay with us. Just seeing us in your home will communicate our interest in your child and may help your child feel more comfortable at school.

During this visit, we may try to discuss with your child the choice of a "symbol" or special picture that he or she would like to have used at school as an identification mark. Symbols are often pictures of favorite objects or activities. This symbol will be drawn by the teachers next to his or her name on artwork and where personal belongings are stored. "Picture reading" of symbols supports growth toward reading and will also help other children recognize your child's materials.

We look forward to seeing you soon!

Sincerely,

The teachers at _____ Early Childhood Center

[This is a reproducible page.]

[Parent Letter: About Separation]

Dear Parent,

The start of school is an emotional time, full of anticipation of new friends, hopes for playful learning, and fears about your child's adjustment. Whether your child is returning to preschool or coming for the first time, he or she may experience separation anxiety. This a feeling of fear and discomfort about being separated from familiar people. Separation anxiety is a normal reaction that most people feel at one time or another. Adults experience it when they leave home and things are not the same. Unfamiliar stores, new and different ways of speaking, and foods that seem "foreign" can all can make us feel uncomfortable and anxious—no wonder McDonald's is the same from coast to coast!

Even E. T. (a movie character from outer space) suffered from separation anxiety. Despite the efforts of his newfound friends, E. T. still yearned to go home. E. T. however, had an advantage over most preschoolers. Although he was as frantic and upset as a 3-year-old, he had unusual electronic skills to cope with his homesickness (E. T. phoned home with a coat hanger, an umbrella, and an old record player). But young children have no such communication skills and their efforts at expressing their distress can be confusing and painful to watch and interpret.

Each child expresses these feelings about leaving parents in a slightly different way. Some children may protest right away, crying loudly at school or complaining at home. Some may complain of aches, pains, or illnesses. Others may have difficulty weeks after school has begun, when the initial excitement has worn off. Some children may show anger toward the new adults or children in their life.

It may help to remember that separating from home and becoming attached to new surroundings are vital parts of becoming independent. Children need our understanding and support as they make these steps. Enclosed is a list of suggestions that you can use to support your child during this transition. We hope you will find these strategies helpful and useful.

Sincerely,

The teachers at _____ Early Childhood Center

[This is a reproducible page.]

Making a Separation Plan

Leaving parents at the beginning of the school day can be diffi-cult for any child, no matter how loved and secure the child feels. Here are some ideas you can use to make this transition smoother for you and your child:

▲ **Help your child anticipate what will happen each day of school.** If your child is returning for a second or third year in the program, let him or her know that there will be new chil-dren as well as some old friends in the group. Create a "separa-tion ritual or plan" to follow with your child each day as you drop him or her off. Keep your plan simple (for example, a sto-ry together followed by a wave at the window or a few minutes together at the breakfast table). The teachers will be glad to help you decide on a ritual, if necessary.

▲ **Be consistent about following your plan.** If your child is having a particularly difficult time, adding "one more story" at the last minute will not ease these feelings; in fact, your child's sadness or anxiety may become stronger.

▲ **If difficulties continue, reassess your plan with the teachers.** Ask the teachers for suggestions and support—they have been through this many times with other children. Ask them what they do to support your child after you have left, making sure that your child's feelings are being fully acknowl-edged. Ask them what activities happen right after you leave so you can go over this with your child at home. (If you are still worried about your child after you leave, you can always call the school from your work place to see how your child is do-ing.)

▲ **Acknowledge your child's feelings yourself, both as you leave (if there are strong emotions) and at home when you dis-cuss it.** "Acknowledge feelings" means to make simple state-ments that label the feelings. For example, say "It's really hard when we have to say goodbye at school. You feel really sad when I leave" or "It makes you mad when I leave you at day care." As you talk to your child, use a soft, calm voice and touch your child gently, to communicate that you understand. Pause and wait for your child's response. It is important to show you

▲

Making a Separation Plan (cont.)

accept your child's feelings, even if his or her outbursts are upsetting to you. This acceptance will let your child know it is okay to have strong feelings about your leaving. With your encouragement your child will fully express feelings of sadness or anger—this usually helps children "let go" of the feelings and begin to adjust to the new friends and environment.

▲ **If your child is not upset, avoid pressuring him or her to be sad that you are going.** Instead know that your child cares very deeply about you and that you can take pride in your child's independence.

▲ **Know that your child cannot begin to cope with your leaving until you actually leave.** After your last goodbye, it is important that you leave without further ado. Children become confident that they are okay only after they have experienced their own ability to carry on without you in the new setting.

▲ **Above all, show confidence in your child's ability to adjust by saying goodbye as planned.** Do not sneak away while your child is distracted. This will make your child distrustful of the whole separation process.

Following these simple suggestions will ease this daily transition for most parents and children. If you need more help with separation problems, please feel free to talk with the teachers. We will help in any way we can.

References

The American Heritage Dictionary (2nd college Edition). (1985). Boston: Houghton Mifflin.

Austin, L. Beyond Barbie and Batman [Handout]. (Available from Mountain Brook Children's Center, South Deerfield, MA 01373.)

Bernat, V. (1993, March). Teaching peace. *Young Children, 48,* 36–39.

Bronfenbrenner, U. (1979). *The ecology of human development: Experiments by nature and design.* Cambridge, MA: Harvard University Press.

Colorado School Mediation Project. (1995). *Coordinator's mediation training manual: Elementary school.* Boulder: Author. (Available from CSMP, 2885 Aurora, Suite 13, Boulder, CO 80303. Web site: www.csmp.org).

Colorado School Mediation Project. (2001, February 28). Common questions and answers [On-line]. Available: http://www.csmp.org/handouts/handouts.htm

Committee for Children. (1992a). *Second Step grades 4–5 kit* [Curriculum materials]. Seattle: Author. (Available from Committee for Children, 568 First Ave., Suite 600, Seattle, WA 98104-2804; 1-800-634-4449; Web site: www.cfchildren.org).

Committee for Children. (1992b). *Second Step grades 1–3 kit* [Curriculum materials]. Seattle: Author. (Available from Committee for Children, 568 First Ave., Suite 600, Seattle, WA 98104-2804; 1-800-634-4449; Web site: www.cfchildren.org).

Conflict Resolution/Peer Mediation Project, University of Florida, Gainesville. (2000, March 15). Effectiveness [On-line]. Available: http://cecp.air.org/preventionstrategies/conflict.htm

Crary, E. (1993). *Without spanking or spoiling: A practical approach to toddler and preschool guidance* (2nd ed.). Seattle, WA: Parenting Press.

Crary, E. (1996). *My name is not Dummy* (2nd ed.). Seattle, WA: Parenting Press.

Eisenberg, A. R., & Garvey, C. (1981). Children's use of verbal strategies in resolving conflicts. *Discourse Processes, 4,* 149–70.

Eisenberg-Berg, N., Haake, R. J., & Bartlett, K. (1981.) The effects of possession and ownership on the sharing and proprietary behaviors of preschool children. *Merrill-Palmer Quarterly, 27* (1), 61–68.

Evans, B. (1992/1996a). Helping children resolve disputes and conflicts. In N. A. Brickman (Ed.), *Supporting young learners 2: Ideas for child care providers and teachers* (pp. 27–34). Ypsilanti, MI: High/Scope Press.

Evans, B. (1992/1996b). Watch your language. In N. A. Brickman (Ed.), *Supporting young learners 2: Ideas for child care providers and teachers* (pp. 35–36). Ypsilanti, MI: High/Scope Press.

Evans, B. (1995/1996a). From superheroes to problem solving. In N. A. Brickman (Ed.), *Supporting young learners 2: Ideas for child care providers and teachers* (pp. 47–52). Ypsilanti, MI: High/Scope Press.

Evans, B. (1995/1996b). Superstrategies for superheroes. In N. A. Brickman (Ed.), *Supporting young learners 2: Ideas for child care providers and teachers* (pp. 53–56). Ypsilanti, MI: High/Scope Press.

Evans, B. (1996/1996a). Language that sets limits. In N. A. Brickman (Ed.), *Supporting young learners 2: Ideas for child care providers and teachers* (pp. 43–46). Ypsilanti, MI: High/Scope Press.

Evans, B. (1996/1996b). Punishment: What does it teach? In N. A. Brickman (Ed.), *Supporting young learners 2: Ideas for child care providers and teachers* (pp. 37–42). Ypsilanti, MI: High/Scope Press.

Faber, A., & Mazlish, E. (1999). *How to talk so kids will listen & listen so kids will talk* (20th ed.). New York: Avon Books.

Gartrell, D. (1994). *A guidance approach to discipline.* Albany, NY: Delmar Publishers.

Gartrell, D. (1995, July). Misbehavior or mistaken behavior. *Young Children, 50,* 27–34.

Genishi, C., & DiPaolo, M. (1982). Learning through argument in a preschool. In L. C. Wilkinson (Ed.), *Communicating in the classroom* (pp. 49–68). San Diego, CA: Academic Press.

Goleman, D. (1995). *Emotional intelligence: Why it can matter more than IQ.* New York: Bantam Books.

Graves, M., & Strubank, R. (1988/1991). Helping children manage themselves. In N. A. Brickman & L. S. Taylor (Eds.), *Supporting young learners: Ideas for preschool and day care providers* (pp. 35–41). Ypsilanti, MI: High/Scope Press.

Greenspan, S. I. (with Benderly, B. L.). (1997). *The growth of the mind: And the endangered origins of intelligence.* Reading, MA: Perseus Publishing.

Greenwald, D. (1987, July). *Conflict resolution in the schools: Final evaluation report.* Boulder, Colorado: The Colorado School Mediation Project (Available from CSMP, 2885 Aurora, Suite 13, Boulder, CO 80303. Web site: www.csmp.org).

Grossman, D. C., Neckerman, H. J., Koepsell, T. D., Liu, P.-Y. Asher, K. N., Beland, K., Frey, K., & Rivara, F. P. (1997). The effectiveness of a violence prevention curriculum among children in elementary school. *Journal of the American Medical Association, 277,* 1605–11.

Hay, D. F. (1984.) Social conflict in early childhood. In G. Whitehurst (Ed.), *Annals of Child Development:* Vol. 1 (pp. 1–44). Greenwich, CT: JAI Press Inc.

Hay, D. F., & Ross, H. S. (1982). The social nature of early conflict. *Child Development, 53,* 105–13.

Healy, J. M. (1994). *Your child's growing mind.* New York: Doubleday.

High/Scope Educational Research Foundation. (1998). *High/Scope Program Quality Assessment (PQA)—Preschool Version.* Ypsilanti, MI: High/Scope Press.

High/Scope Educational Research Foundation. (1998). *Supporting young children in resolving conflicts* [videotape]. Ypsilanti, MI: High/Scope Press.

Hohmann, M., & Weikart, D. P. (2002). *Educating young children: Active learning practices for preschool and child care programs* (2nd ed.). Ypsilanti, MI: High/Scope Press.

Johnson, D. W., & Johnson, R., (1997). *Reducing school violence through conflict resolution.* Alexandria, VA: ASCD.

Johnson, D. W., Johnson, R., Dudley, B., Ward, M., & Magnuson, D. (1995, Winter). The impact of peer mediation training on the management of school and home conflicts. *American Educational Research Journal, 32*(4), 829–44.

Kaiser, B., & Rasminsky, J. S. (1999). *Meeting the challenge: Effective strategies for challenging behaviors in early childhood environments.* Ottawa, ONT: Canadian Child Care Federation.

Kamii, C. (1984, April). Obedience is not enough. *Young Children 39,* 11–14.

Kohn, A. (1993). *Punished by rewards: The trouble with gold stars, incentive plans, A's, praise, and other bribes.* Boston: Houghton Mifflin.

Laursen, B., & Hartup, W. W. (1989). The dynamics of preschool children's conflicts. *Merrill-Palmer Quarterly, 35* (3), 281–97.

Levin, D. (1996). *Teaching young children in violent times: Building a peaceable classroom.* Cambridge, MA: Educators for Social Responsibility (ESR). (Available from 1-800-370-2515, www.esrnational.org).

McClellan, D., & Katz, L. G. (1993). Young children's social development: A checklist (ERIC Digest) [On-line]. Urbana, IL: ERIC Clearinghouse on Elementary and Early Childhood Education. Available: http://www.ericeece.org/pubs/digests/1993/mcclel93.html (EDO-PS-93-6)

National Association for the Education of Young Children [NAEYC] (1998). *Accreditation criteria & procedures of the National Association for the Education of Young Children* (1998 ed.). Washington, DC: Author.

National Center for Policy Analysis. (May, 1997). Course helps students unlearn violence [On-line]. Available: www.ncpa.org/pi/edu/may97h.html

Paley, V. G. (1987). *Wally's stories: Conversations in the kindergarten* (Reprint ed.). Cambridge, MA: Harvard University Press.

Paley, V. G., & Jackson, P. W. (1986). *Boys and girls: Superheroes in the doll corner* (Reprint ed.). Chicago: University of Chicago Press.

Piaget, J. (1965). *The Moral Judgement of the Child* (M. Gabian, Trans.). New York: Free Press.

Piaget, J., & Inhelder, B. (with introduction by Kagen, J.). (1966/2000). *The psychology of the child* (H. Weaver, Trans.). New York: Basic Books.

Pirtle, S. (1998a). *Discovery time for cooperation and conflict resolution.* Nyack, NY: Creative Response to Conflict, Inc.

Pirtle, S. (1998b). *Linking up!* [CD and Teacher's Guide]. Cambridge, MA: Educators for Social Responsibility (ESR). (Available from 1-800-370-2515, www.esrnational.org.)

Pollack, W. (1998). *Real boys: Rescuing our sons from the myths of boyhood.* New York: Henry Holt and Co.

Powell, A. (1990/1991). Be responsive. In N. A. Brickman & L. S. Taylor (Eds.), *Supporting young learners: Ideas for preschool and day care providers* (pp. 26–34). Ypsilanti, MI: High/Scope Press.

Shantz, C. U. (1987). Conflicts between children. *Child Development, 58,* 283–305.

Shantz, C. U., & Shantz, D. W. (1985). Conflicts between children: Social-cognitive and sociometric correlates. In M. W. Berkowitz (Ed.), *Peer conflict and psychological growth: New Directions for Child Development* (pp. 3–21). San Francisco: Jossey-Bass.

Slaby, R. G., Roedell, W. C., Arezzo, D., & Hendrix, K. (1995). *Early violence prevention: Tools for teachers of young children.* Washington, DC: NAEYC.

Tompkins, M. (1991/1996). In praise of praising less. In N. A. Brickman (Ed.), *Supporting young learners 2: Ideas for child care providers and teachers* (pp. 15–22). Ypsilanti, MI: High/Scope Press.

Wadsworth, B. J. (1978). *Piaget for the classroom teacher.* New York: Longman.

Story Index

To help readers use the child stories in this book for further study or training, each story is listed below, with the following information, in abbreviated form: **age range** (infant, toddler, preschool, elementary), **page number,** and **content** by the following categories: strong feelings (child or adult); conflict issues—objects, being friends, hurtful actions, taking turns, time, group safety, homework, resistance to problem solving; child and/or adult solution; no adult involvement.

General Index

About the Author

Betsy Evans has been working in the early childhood field since 1974. She began her teaching career as a family day dare provider and later founded the Giving Tree School, a non-profit educational organization in Gill, Massachusetts. She served as Lead Teacher/Director at Giving Tree for 23 years and continues to work as Program Consultant for the school. In 1989 she became a Field Consultant for High/Scope Educational Research Foundation and in that role, has conducted training workshops for early childhood educators across the U.S. and the U.K. She developed High/Scope's problem-solving approach to conflict over the past 10 years, writing articles and a training manual, and acting as script author and co-producer of the video, *Supporting Children in Resolving Conflicts*. She holds a bachelor's degree in Elementary Education and a master's in Early Childhood Education. She has three sons and lives with her husband in rural western Massachusetts.

Related High/Scope® Resources

Conflict Resolution

Supporting Children in Resolving Conflicts

This essential video will teach you six problem-solving steps you can use to help children in conflict situations. The problem-solving process is demonstrated with real scenes of successful conflict resolution from a New York City Head Start Center and from the High/Scope® Demonstration Preschool. Video guide included.

BK-P1130 rental $10, purchase $49.95
Video guide included. Color video, 24 minutes, 1998.

WALL CHART: Steps in Resolving Conflicts

A handy reference tool! Hang this poster in your classroom to help you remember the six steps to resolving conflicts successfully as you work with children. (See accompanying video.)

BK-P1134 $5.95
2-color glossy, 22" x 34". 1998. 1-57379-075-3.

High/Scope's LATEST Preschool Manual & Study Guide

Educating Young Children: Active Learning Practices for Preschool and Child Care Programs, 2nd Ed.

Written for early childhood practitioners and students, this manual presents essential strategies adults can use to make active learning a reality in their programs. Describes key components of the adult's role: planning the physical setting and establishing a consistent daily routine; creating a positive social climate; and using High/Scope's 58 key experiences to understand and support young children. Other topics include conflict resolution, family involvement, daily team planning, creating interest areas, choosing appropriate materials, the plan-do-review process, small- and large-group times. Offers numerous anecdotes, photographs, illustrations, real-life scenarios, and practical suggestions for adults. Reflects High/Scope's current research findings and 35 years of experience.

BK-P1178 $42.95
M. Hohmann & D. P. Weikart. Soft cover, lavishly illustrated, 560 pages, 2002. 1-57379-104-0.

Now available in Spanish. BK-L1016 $42.95 (1995 Edition)

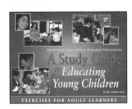

A Study Guide to Educating Young Children: Exercises for Adult Learners, 2nd Ed.

The study guide you've been waiting for—a must-have workbook for High/Scope's latest preschool manual! Designed for early childhood college courses, inservice training, and independent study. Will increase your confidence and competence in using the High/Scope® Preschool Curriculum. Contains active learning exercises exploring the content of the manual in depth. Chapter topics parallel *EYC's*. Abundant, interactive exercises include hands-on exploration of materials, child studies, analysis of photos and scenarios in *EYC*, recollection and reflection about curriculum topics, trying out support strategies, and making implementation plans.

BK-P1179 $15.95
M. Hohmann. Soft cover, 275 pages, 2002. 1-57379-163-6.

To order these or any other High/Scope® products, contact High/Scope® Press: phone (800)40-PRESS fax (800)442-4FAX
To see a full listing of High/Scope® preschool products, visit our Web site: www.highscope.org

Related High/Scope® Resources

Practical Strategies for Teachers and Child Care Providers

Supporting Young Learners 1: Ideas for Preschool and Day Care Providers

Provides practical answers to the day-to-day questions that arise in early childhood programs. The selections, which originally appeared in *Extensions,* are updated and deal with these and other timely issues in developmentally appropriate education.

BK-P1083 $29.95
N. Brickman and L. Taylor, Eds. Soft cover, 314 pages, 1991.
0-929816-34-X.

Supporting Young Learners 2: Ideas for Child Care Providers and Teachers

Like its popular predecessor, this book is packed with practical strategies and tips for making an active learning program the best it can be. Contains over 50 *Extensions* articles that have been updated to reflect the latest thinking on the High/Scope® Curriculum. A must-have for early childhood professionals!

BK-P1105 $29.95
N. Brickman, Ed. Soft cover, photos, 328 pages, 1996.
1-57379-006-0.

Supporting Young Learners 3: Ideas for Child Care Providers and Teachers

High/Scope's third compilation of updated *Extensions* articles brings you sound answers to important issues you face each day. The practical advice this book offers is based on the High/Scope approach to working with young children from birth through elementary school age. Valuable tips for preschool teachers, Head Start staff, kindergarten teachers, child care staff, program directors, elementary school teachers, and family day care providers.

BK-P1169 $29.95
N. Brickman, Ed. Soft cover, photos, 432 pages, 2001.
1-57379-101-6.

Making the Most of Plan-Do-Review: The Teacher's Idea Book 5

Children in High/Scope settings learn how to plan their activities, accomplish their goals, solve unexpected problems, make necessary changes to their original plans, and reflect on the outcomes of their actions. These are valuable skills they will use throughout life. High/Scope's daily plan-do-review process makes it all happen. This book provides a blueprint for successful implementation. Includes support strategies, practical tips and suggestions, tried-and-true games and experiences for children, answers to frequently asked questions, real-life examples, sample notes to parents, a parent workshop plan, and planning and recall sheets to use with children.

BK-P1152 $25.95
N. Vogel. Soft cover, photos, 250 pages, 2001.
1-57379-086-9.